U.S. Army Small-Unit Action in Iraq, 2004–2007

TIP
OF THE
SPEAR

GENERAL EDITOR
JON T. HOFFMAN

Global War on Terrorism Series

TIP OF THE SPEAR

U.S. Army Small-Unit Action in Iraq, 2004–2007

Jon T. Hoffman
General Editor

Center of Military History
United States Army
Washington, D.C., 2009

Library of Congress Cataloging-in-Publication Data

Tip of the spear : U.S. Army small-unit action in Iraq,
2004–2007 / Jon T. Hoffman, general editor.
    p. cm. — (Global war on terrorism series) 1. Iraq War,
2003—Campaigns. 2. Counterinsurgency—Iraq. 3. United States. Army—
History—21st century. I. Hoffman, Jon T., 1955– II. Title. III. Series.

DS79.764.U6T56 2009
956.7044'342—dc22

2009027069

CMH Pub 70–113–1

First Printing

CONTENTS

MAPS

No.

ILLUSTRATIONS

Illustrations courtesy of the following: pp. 20, 2d Battalion, 12th Cavalry; 23, 27, 31, 34, Aaron J. Munz; 29, 62, Maj. Rick Ryczkowski; 38, 47, 49, 50, Spec. Jarob Walsh; 66, 80 (*bottom*), 49th Military History Detachment; 74, 77, 79, Maj. Kevin S. Badger; 80 (*top*), Google Earth; 89, 93, 95, 97, 98, 101, Spec. Mark C. Sauve; 108, 114, 115, 121, 124, 126, 1st Battalion, 67th Armor; 131, 133, 137, 139, 141, Capt. Ben R. Simms; 148, 155, 160, 163, 170, Operational Detachment Alpha 563; 172, Maj. Brent A. Clemmer; 177, CWO4 Daniel McClinton; 184, Capt. Thomas J. Loux; 185, Cpl. Nathan Hoskins. Other illustrations from Department of the Army files.

FOREWORD

The lightning campaign that toppled the Saddam Hussein regime in Iraq in the spring of 2003 seemed to herald the arrival of a new way of war, as Germany's blitzkrieg had done at the beginning of World War II. But the initial victory soon devolved into a persistent counterinsurgency conflict reminiscent of the long U.S. effort to pacify the Philippines after the rapid defeat of Spain in 1898. In Iraq, American soldiers and their Coalition partners had merely traded one fairly weak and generally conventional opponent for a more deadly, diverse, and determined foe relying on the tactics of the guerrilla and the terrorist.

This volume focuses on that second and longer campaign. But rather than a narrative of the overall course of the conflict, it provides a soldier's-eye view of the war by focusing on detailed accounts of selected engagements. Each illustrates the everyday challenges that America's soldiers faced in a difficult struggle against an inventive and often elusive enemy. Weapons, doctrine, and procedures developed to fight a conventional campaign against a similar opposing force had to be adapted to fit a different type of conflict. The U.S. Army's combat and support forces brought both resourcefulness and resilience to this task while continuing to demonstrate the same courage shown by previous generations fighting the nation's battles.

These stories not only symbolize the tip of the spear formed by units in contact, but they also represent the contributions of all American men and women who have served their country in Operation IRAQI FREEDOM. Taken together, these accounts will provide our deploying leaders and soldiers a better understanding of the environment that they will encounter and prepare them for the work that must be done.

Washington, D.C.   Jeffrey J. Clarke
27 August 2009   Chief of Military History

Jon T. Hoffman is chief of the Contemporary Studies Branch of the Histories Division at the Center of Military History. A retired Marine Corps Reserve officer, he has an M.A. in military history from Ohio State University and is the author of *Chesty: The Story of Lieutenant General Lewis B. Puller* (2001) and *Once a Legend: "Red Mike" Edson of the Marine Raiders* (1994).

Richard E. Killblane is a 1979 graduate of the U.S. Military Academy and has an M.A. in history from the University of San Diego. He served as an Army infantry and Special Forces officer and is a veteran of Operation Just Cause in Panama. Currently the Transportation Corps historian, he is the author of *Circle the Wagons: The History of U.S. Army Convoy Security* (2005) and *The Filthy Thirteen: From the Dustbowl to Hitler's Eagle's Nest: The True Story of the 101st Airborne's Most Legendary Squad of Combat Paratroopers* (2003).

John R. Maass has a Ph.D. in early U.S. history from Ohio State University. A former officer in the Army Reserve, he is currently a historian in the Histories Division's Contemporary Studies Branch at the Center.

Jon B. Mikolashek has a Ph.D. in U.S. history from Florida State University. He is currently a historian in the Histories Division's Contemporary Studies Branch at the Center.

Mark J. Reardon, a retired armor officer, is a senior historian at the Center specializing in World War II and the War on Terror. He received a B.A. in history from Loyola College in Baltimore and an M.S. in international relations from Troy State University. He is the author of *Victory at Morlain* (2002) and coauthor of *American Iliad: The 18th Infantry Regiment in World War II* (2004) and *From Transformation to Combat: The First Stryker Brigade at War* (2007).

Mark D. Sherry is a historian at the Center specializing in institutional history. He received both his M.A. and Ph.D. in history from Georgetown University. He is the author of the Center's *China Defensive* (1996) and *The Army Command Post and Defense Reshaping, 1987–1997* (2008).

Ben R. Simms is an assistant professor of military science at George Mason University in Fairfax, Virginia. An armor officer, he graduated from the U.S. Military Academy in 1998. Simms served in Kosovo from December 2000 to May 2001 and in Iraq from March 2003 to March 2004 and November 2005 to November 2006.

Curtis D. Taylor is the assistant operations officer of the 4th Brigade, 4th Infantry Division, at Fort Hood, Texas. An armor officer, he graduated from the U.S. Military Academy in 1994. He served in Korea from October 2000 to December 2001, in Afghanistan from November 2003 to May 2004, and in Iraq from November 2005 to November 2006.

Acknowledgments

Many individuals not mentioned in the narrative played an invaluable role in producing this publication. Mr. Jim Bretney shared his research on the Good Friday ambush with Richard Killblane. Brig. Gen. (Ret.) John S. Brown, U.S. Army, former chief of military history, and Dr. Richard W. Stewart, the chief historian, thoroughly reviewed the manuscript and provided valuable guidance in revising it. Others at the U.S. Army Center of Military History also read drafts and contributed useful suggestions: Dr. Jeffrey J. Clarke, chief of military history; Brig. Gen. (Ret.) Dr. John F. Shortal, assistant chief of military history; and Dr. Joel D. Meyerson, chief of the Histories Division. Under the direction of Keith R. Tidman, members of the Center's Publishing Division shepherded the manuscript into printed form: Beth MacKenzie, chief of the Production Branch; Diane Sedore Arms, chief of the Editorial Branch; S. L. Dowdy, cartographer; Michael R. Gill, visual information specialist; and especially Diane M. Donovan, who edited the volume.

The views expressed herein are the responsibility of the authors. They do not necessarily reflect the official policy or position of the Departments of the Army and Defense or the U.S. government.

TIP
OF THE
SPEAR

U.S. Army Small-Unit Action in Iraq, 2004–2007

INTRODUCTION

Official history typically paints a portrait of the higher level of war—decisions made by generals and operations carried out by brigades, divisions, and corps. Those broad canvases are composed of innumerable and largely unseen brushstrokes—the actions of small units and individual soldiers executing strategy and making direct contact with the enemy. This volume focuses on a representative sample of the latter category of engagements in Iraq during the period from the fall of Baghdad in April 2003 through the initial implementation of the Surge in 2007. The purpose is to shed additional light on the nature of the war as a whole. While the soldier-eye view is always a useful component of history, it is even more valuable in understanding this phase of the conflict, where large-scale battles were rare and squads, platoons, and companies often operated independently, with no other units on their left and right, minimal influence from higher headquarters, and no neat lines on the map demarcating the frontlines. In this environment, captains, sergeants, and privates carried even more weight than usual in determining success or failure in battle and ultimately in deciding the outcome of the war. These stories are a microcosm of the courage, determination, and professionalism demonstrated by hundreds of thousands of American soldiers fighting a long and difficult campaign against a tenacious foe.

The story started on 9 April 2003, when television viewers worldwide watched as U.S. forces helped Iraqi nationals topple a large statue of Saddam Hussein in Baghdad's Firdos Square. Any lingering doubts as to the popularity of the deposed dictator seemed to vanish as dancing and cheering citizens beat the prostrate bronze figure with the soles of their shoes in a traditional Arabic sign of disrespect. That cathartic event signaled the end of the campaign that had begun on 20 March. The "shock and awe" approach to modern warfare, advocated by Secretary of Defense Donald H. Rumsfeld, appeared validated. On 1 May, President George W. Bush addressed cheering sailors on the USS *Abraham Lincoln*, announcing the end of major combat operations in front of a banner declaring "Mission Accomplished." The U.S. Central Command headquarters began issuing orders for many American units to return home.

A residual force of about one hundred sixty thousand Coalition troops assumed the mission of implementing Phase IV of the invasion plan, which focused on stabilizing Iraq in the aftermath of regime change.[1] The major combat elements were the 82d and 101st Airborne Divisions, 4th Infantry Division, 1st Armored Division, 2d and 3d Armored Cavalry Regiments, and the I Marine Expeditionary Force (I MEF), along with British, Polish, Italian, Spanish, and other contingents. Lt. Gen. Ricardo S. Sanchez and his Combined Joint Task Force–7 (CJTF-7), a new headquarters created from V Corps staff, took charge of military operations in June. Sanchez worked alongside Ambassador L. Paul Bremer's Coalition Provisional Authority, an organization vested by presidential decree with executive, legislative, and judicial authority over Iraq until a new government could be elected by the Iraqi people. Bremer soon appointed the Iraqi Governing Council to draft a temporary constitution and prepare for national elections. The council's twenty-five members represented the ethnic and religious makeup of the country, but it gained little popular support.

Although most Iraqis welcomed the end of the dictatorship, many in the Sunni minority were unhappy at their loss of political influence and the possibility that the long-suppressed Shi'ite majority would now assume power. In May, Bremer announced his decisions to strip many Ba'ath Party members of their government jobs and to formally disband the Iraqi military (which had largely melted away during the course of the war and already largely ceased to exist of its own accord). Those actions placed hundreds of thousands out of work and added fuel to the lawlessness that had arisen during the vacuum of power following the collapse of the old regime. Still other Iraqis grew impatient with the occupation of their country by foreign troops, especially in the absence of any schedule for a turnover of civil authority to an Iraqi provisional government. As the weeks passed, a diverse collection of former regime elements, religious extremists, and Iraqi nationalists took up arms against Coalition forces. In addition, foreign fighters began to enter Iraq in hopes of killing Americans in furtherance of a global war against "the infidel." Many of the latter formed the core of what became known as al-Qaeda in Iraq, a Sunni group that dedicated as much effort to destroying Shi'ite "apostates" as it did to defeating the United States.

---

[1] For general background, see Donald P. Wright and Timothy R. Reese, *On Point II, Transition to the New Campaign: The United States Army in Operation IRAQI FREEDOM, May 2003–January 2005* (Fort Leavenworth, Kans.: Combat Studies Institute Press, 2008).

Attacks initially were small and uncoordinated but steadily grew in frequency during 2003. August marked the beginning of a campaign using vehicle-borne bombs to inflict devastating damage on facilities and personnel—typically civilian targets. The violence occurred largely in the Sunni Arab–dominated regions of western and central Iraq and the mixed zones in and around Baghdad. (*See Map 1.*)

While the Coalition focused at first on militarily defeating Sunni insurgents, the emergence of armed Shi'ite militias added a new layer of complexity. Some of these were branches of longstanding underground Shi'ite political parties, such as the Supreme Council for the Islamic Revolution in Iraq (SCIRI), which had historically opposed the Ba'athist regime. One major player, however, brought a relatively new force into play. Moqtada al-Sadr was the son of a revered grand ayatollah who had been assassinated by Saddam Hussein's agents in 1999. The young cleric's family name, his natural charisma, his fiery public opposition to the occupation, and his organization's charitable works generated a large following in the Shi'ite community, particularly among the less fortunate. His armed followers, often garbed in black, styled themselves as the Mahdi Army.

These militias grew in size and importance as they became a bulwark against Sunni attacks on the Shi'ite population. They also fought among themselves as their leaders jockeyed for power, adding to instability in the country. On 10 April 2003, members of a crowd at a mosque in Najaf assassinated Abdul Majid al-Khoei, a leading Shi'ite cleric and moderate who had just returned from exile in London. That August, a car bomb exploded outside the same mosque, killing more than eighty people, including Ayatollah Muhammad Bakir al-Hakim, leader of SCIRI. Both men were competitors with Sadr for postwar influence in Iraq, and he was implicated directly in the death of Khoei. Sadr proved to be the main source of trouble since he actively opposed the Coalition presence in Iraq, whereas most other Shi'ite parties focused on the struggle for power within the nascent Iraqi government. Militia violence occurred mostly in Shi'ite southern and central Iraq and along the demographic fault lines with the Sunni minority.

In addition to these homegrown Shi'ite militias, Iran would eventually sponsor its own armed bands, some of them composed of members still nominally part of the Mahdi militia. Dubbed special groups by Coalition forces, these units were better trained, equipped, and financed than other militia forces. They launched revenge attacks against Sunnis, targeted American soldiers, and generally sought to sow instability in Iraq.

The diverse and divided nature of this opposition, unlike the more typical monolithic insurgency, made it difficult to develop a useful intelligence picture of the enemy and take effective counteraction. In some cases, Coalition units resorted to rounding up large numbers of military-age males rather than precisely targeting key individuals and organizations. These tactics affronted family and tribal honor, thereby alienating even more of the population. The

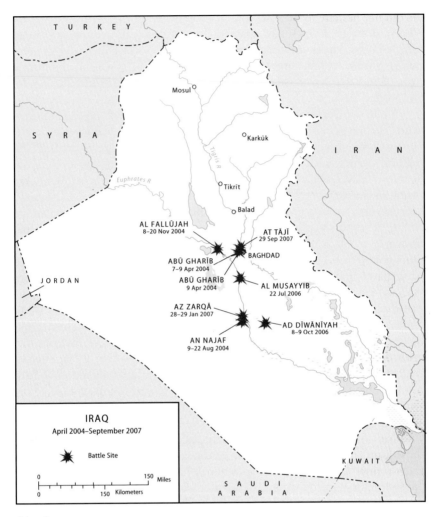

Map 1

capture of Saddam Hussein near Tikrit on 13 December 2003 thus had little effect on the spiraling violence, since he had little to do with fomenting and controlling it.

Another important but nonviolent element to be reckoned with in Iraq was a loose grouping of senior clerics headed by Grand Ayatollah Ali al-Sistani. While he and his colleagues had no desire to hold political power themselves, their pronouncements regarding correct religious thinking on a wide range of issues held great sway in Iraq, particularly among the Shi'ite population. Both Coalition and Iraqi leaders actively sought, or at least hoped for, Sistani's approval of important initiatives. A moderate voice in many respects, he did not hesitate to use his mantle of religious authority to influence decisions and events in order to further his view of Iraq's future.

Two unrelated chains of events stoked the simmering war to a boil in the spring of 2004. The first reared up on 28 March, when Ambassador Bremer ordered Sadr's incendiary newspaper, *Hawza*, shut down as a first step in a process designed to bring him to justice. Several days later, Coalition forces in Najaf took into custody one of Sadr's high-ranking deputies who stood accused in Ayatollah Khoei's murder. In response, the radical cleric's followers held massive protest rallies while his Mahdi militia seized public buildings and police stations in Najaf, Kufa, Kut, and Sadr City (a slum in the eastern part of the Iraqi capital named for Sadr's father). Fighting between U.S. forces and the Mahdi militia erupted in Baghdad and spread to other cities in southern Iraq as the Coalition launched a general offensive to restore government control throughout the region.

In purely military terms, Sadr's uprising failed and he declared a cease-fire in June; but he had catapulted himself and his organization to the forefront of the Iraqi opposition. He publicly declared that he would renounce force and focus his efforts in the political and social realms; but the Mahdi militia merely adopted a more furtive role. In turn, the Coalition decided not to arrest him, thereby avoiding a renewed clash at a time when it already had its hands full dealing with major unrest in Sunni areas. This course of action came at a cost, as one American brigade commander noted: "By allowing Sadr to survive, the Coalition had given him artificial credibility for standing up to a superpower and pointed the way to others who sought political power in the country: form a militia, battle for control of the streets, and seize power through the barrel of a gun."[2]

The heightened challenge from the Sunnis began, apparently by coincidence, on 31 March. That day, insurgents ambushed and killed four Americans, private security guards with Blackwater, in Fallujah, one of the largest cities in Sunni-dominated Anbar Province. The bodies, mutilated, hung from a bridge, and set on fire, prompted calls from the highest levels of the U.S. government for a robust military response. On 4 April, I MEF launched an offensive in Fallujah. The operation galvanized the disparate Sunni insurgent groups into loose cooperation for the first time, and the fighting spread to other cities such as Ramadi, the Anbar provincial capital. Sunnis in the Abu Ghraib suburb northwest of Baghdad carried out attacks there loosely designed to cut the main supply route to Fallujah and relieve some of the U.S. pressure on their brethren in Anbar. Those smaller battles in Abu Ghraib are the subject of chapter 1, "Hell in a Very Small Marketplace," and chapter 2, "Good Friday Ambush."

When the *al-Jazeera* network reported that American artillery and air strikes were inflicting casualties on civilians, the Iraqi Governing Council

[2] Peter A. Mansoor, *Baghdad at Sunrise: A Brigade Commander's War in Iraq* (New Haven, Conn.: Yale University Press, 2008), p. 333.

asked Ambassador Bremer to halt military operations. Other Sunni-dominated Arab nations also brought political pressure to bear on the United States, leading the Coalition to declare a unilateral cease-fire in Fallujah on 9 April. Soon after, I MEF turned over security in the city to a makeshift Iraqi force designated the Fallujah Brigade, which proved ineffective and short lived.[3] The apparent ability of the insurgents to retain control of the city in the aftermath of a major American offensive left them with the impression that they could prevail in a military and political test of wills with the United States. In late April, reports publicly surfaced of detainee abuse at the American-run prison in Abu Ghraib. Widely circulated photos and descriptions of illegal and unethical actions tarnished Coalition forces and further inflamed Iraqi opposition.

The fighting in south-central Iraq, Baghdad, and Anbar erupted as the U.S. military wrapped up one of its largest movements of forces since World War II. Changing a policy used in major wars throughout the twentieth century, the United States decided to rely on unit rotation rather than individual replacements in this conflict. The 1st Cavalry Division, 1st Infantry Division, and 1st Marine Division, along with brigades from the 2d and 25th Infantry Divisions, replaced the 82d and 101st Airborne and 4th Infantry Divisions. The unexpected outburst of widespread combat resulted in the outgoing 1st Armored Division remaining behind rather than returning to Germany as scheduled. The incoming units, although new to Iraq in some cases, possessed several advantages over their predecessors. They had done some predeployment training for counterinsurgency, prepared most of their artillery units to serve as provisional infantry, and substituted up-armored Humvees (more suitable for patrolling) for many of their heavy armored vehicles.

The Coalition's military command structure also underwent significant changes during this period. Multi-National Force–Iraq (MNF-I) replaced CJTF-7 as the senior military headquarters in Iraq on 15 May 2004. It would focus on strategic issues while its newly created subordinate, Multi-National Corps–Iraq (MNC-I), would oversee the operational fight. At a higher level, the Coalition Provisional Authority and Iraqi Governing Council turned over political sovereignty to the Interim Iraqi Government on 30 June. This appointed body, headed by Prime Minister Ayad Allawi, a secular-minded Shi'ite, would oversee the development of a constitution and elections for a national government.

On 1 July, General George W. Casey Jr. assumed command of MNF-I and tasked his staff to develop a revised campaign plan addressing the worsening operational and political environment.[4] Concerned that Coalition forces

---

[3] John D. Banusiewicz, "1st Marine Expeditionary Force Creating 'Fallujah Brigade,'" Armed Forces Press Service, 30 April 2004, copy in Historians files, U.S. Army Center of Military History (CMH), Washington, D.C.

[4] Wright and Reese, *On Point II*, p. 177.

were outstaying their welcome in Iraq's major cities and inflaming opposition by their mere presence, Casey decided to redeploy combat units from urban operating bases and consolidate them on large installations located in less populated areas. The change would facilitate the goals of upgrading force protection and reducing American casualties. In addition, a third new Coalition headquarters, designated Multi-National Security Transition Command–Iraq, came into being in late June 2004 to oversee the training and equipping of the Iraqi Army and police force.

Despite an emerging policy of slow disengagement, the Coalition could not ignore the festering sores of Fallujah and the Mahdi militia. The latter posed one of the biggest challenges to the nascent Iraqi government, inasmuch as it had widespread support among the Shi'ite population that would form the majority voting bloc in future elections. Sadr's fighters and organizers retained considerable influence in Karbala and Najaf, both cities important due to their religious symbolism. Moreover, his organization derived practical benefit from skimming cash from businesses involved in the lucrative pilgrimages to these holy sites. That ill-gotten gain purchased arms and ammunition and supported charitable works, further cementing Sadr's popularity.

The dispute with Sadr and his militia jumped to the forefront again in late summer 2004. On 31 July, Coalition forces arrested one of his top deputies in Karbala, sparking widespread demonstrations by supporters. On 2 August, a Marine patrol ventured into the neighborhood in Najaf where Sadr lived, leading to a battle when his followers interpreted this as an attempt to arrest their leader.[5] The violence quickly spun out of control as Mahdi militiamen attacked government facilities and police stations in the city. A portion of that battle is described in chapter 3, "Fighting in the Valley of Peace." Sistani, who had been out of the country for medical treatment, returned to Najaf to negotiate a cease-fire that prevented damage to one of Shi'ite Islam's holiest shrines and restored government control in the city. After suffering heavy losses in a second standup campaign with Coalition forces, the Mahdi militia would rely more and more on pinprick guerrilla action involving indirect fire, small-scale ambushes, and what came to be known as the improvised explosive device (IED). The latter encompassed any type of explosive, but most often mortar or artillery shells, rigged to detonate when Coalition vehicles or soldiers came near.

With Sadr temporarily neutralized, MNF-I turned its main attention to the Sunni insurgency. In a search-and-clear campaign that lasted most of the summer, the 1st Infantry Division regained control of Samarra, the capital of Salahuddin Province and the heart of the so-called Sunni Triangle north of Baghdad. General Casey then prepared for the critical offensive in Fallujah by

---

[5] Scott Baldauf and Dan Murphy, "Uneasy Truce Evaporates in Najaf," *Christian Science Monitor*, 6 August 2004, copy in Historians files, CMH.

reinforcing I MEF with Army heavy units and obtaining necessary political backing from both Iraqi and U.S. leaders. The marines shaped the battlefield with a psychological operations campaign that caused most of the population to evacuate the city. With the possible loss of innocent lives minimized, American firepower could now play its full role. The joint Marine-Army offensive, codenamed AL-FAJR (New Dawn), opened with extensive preparatory fires before ground troops moved into the city on 8 November 2004. Army engineers helped pave the way for the main assault and participated in the weeks of intense combat that followed, an effort chronicled in chapter 4, "Engineers at War." When the campaign was over, the city lay in ruins and Sunni insurgents had learned the same lesson as their Shi'ite counterparts—fighting the Americans head-on was a suicidal proposition.

Having won a respite from large-scale warfare, the Coalition and the fledgling Iraqi security forces oversaw a peaceful election on 30 January 2005 that established a Transitional National Assembly. These representatives formed a new interim government and took on the task of drafting a permanent constitution. While this first democratic election was an important milestone, most Sunnis had boycotted it and thus had little representation in the political process that followed. Finding themselves largely marginalized in determining the future of their country, many more Sunnis decided to participate in the 15 October referendum that ratified the constitution, as well as the 15 December elections for a 275-member parliament. In April 2006, that legislative body selected Nouri al-Maliki, a Shi'ite, as the prime minister. While the Shi'ites dominated the government due to their greater numbers and greater willingness to vote, they remained divided. In the Shi'ite areas, Hakim's SCIRI took control of most provincial government posts and local police forces, but Sadr's movement found favor in many of the poorer neighborhoods of the larger cities. Animosity between the two factions would heighten in 2006 due to a dispute over creating a semiautonomous Shi'ite region, as authorized under the Iraqi constitution. Sadr, a proponent of a strong central government, opposed the idea.

Even as the war raged in Iraq, the U.S. Army undertook a different campaign to restructure its combat and support forces, both active and reserve components alike. Dubbed Modularity, the reorganization pushed various combat and support capabilities from the corps and division down into the brigade combat team to make the latter a largely self-sufficient outfit that could deploy and fight on its own. That would enhance the ability of the Army to move forces rapidly around the globe in response to a crisis, thus increasing its utility in the post–Cold War environment.[6] Gains in combat power from the addition of reconnaissance, artillery, and supporting elements also would allow a reduction of one maneuver battalion in each brigade (from

---

[6] William H. Donnelly, *Transforming an Army at War: Designing the Modular Force, 1991–2005* (Washington, D.C.: U.S. Army Center of Military History, 2007), p. iii.

three to two), thus saving enough manpower to create additional brigades. Those extra units provided an immediate benefit by reducing some of the strain of frequent deployments to Iraq and Afghanistan. The reorganization also brought the introduction of a medium-weight brigade built around the Stryker wheeled armored vehicle, which was more easily deployed than the Abrams tanks and Bradley fighting vehicles of traditional Army heavy units. The first Stryker brigade went to Iraq in December 2003. The first completely modular brigades, from the 3d Infantry and the 101st Airborne Divisions, appeared in the war in 2005. The 4th Infantry Division became the first entirely modular organization of that level in Iraq when it deployed in 2006.

Meanwhile, battlefield necessity brought about many other changes in Army organization, equipment, and doctrine. The nature of the enemy, almost entirely dispersed and foot mobile, placed a premium on action by small units. To achieve the synergy of combined arms in this arena, brigades routinely cross-attached armor, mechanized infantry, and other types of units between battalions. The resulting battalion task forces in many cases carried the process even further and cross-attached such elements at the company level and below. This mixing of capabilities had not been practiced to this degree in the U.S. Army since armor divisions did it with regularity in the latter stages of World War II. Changes in doctrine and materiel soon followed as the Army adjusted to the new demands of the insurgency.

During 2005, al-Qaeda in Iraq began to play an increasingly prominent role in the conflict. On 14 September, Jordanian-born Abu Musab al-Zarqawi, head of the organization, declared war against the Shi'ites. The next day, twelve coordinated explosions rocked Baghdad, killing one hundred sixty-seven and wounding six hundred. Two weeks later, three suicide car bombs inflicted over two hundred casualties in the Shi'ite town of Balad. To combat this scourge, more Shi'ites rallied to the various militias. Some factions in the Shi'ite-dominated interim government also armed and funded illegal groups to conduct revenge attacks against Sunnis. These groups sometimes wore police uniforms, drove police vehicles, and carried police identification cards as they engaged in a campaign of assassination and intimidation. Sunnis came to regard many elements of the Iraqi security forces, most notably the national police, as their deadly foes. While the various strains of the insurgency continued to fight the Coalition, they also directed as much or more effort to the internecine sectarian conflict between Sunnis and Shi'ites.

Intermingled with these two wars was an increase in lawlessness that was both a product of the poor security environment and the inability of the fledgling government to provide basic services to its citizens. Understaffed and ill trained, the Iraqi bureaucracy provided vast opportunity for corruption and abuse of authority at almost every level. Some administrators stole from the treasury or shook down those who sought government services, while some police and army officers skimmed money from their unit coffers and extorted local merchants for protection money. Militias did the same, sometimes fighting each other to control sources of profit, including the smuggling of oil and black-market sales of gasoline. Criminal elements robbed and kidnapped with impunity. In this descent toward anarchy, Coalition troops sometimes found themselves involved in battles that had little to do with fighting terrorism or establishing democracy in Iraq. One such engagement is covered in chapter 5, "Unanticipated Battle."

This upward spiral of violence exploded to new heights on 22 February 2006, when al-Qaeda blew up the golden dome of the al-Askari Mosque in Samarra. The shrine was reputed to be the site where the Mahdi (the Guided One, often referred to as the Hidden Imam) disappeared in 878 A.D. In addition, his father and grandfather were buried there. That made it one of Shi'ite Islam's holiest sites. Although the bombing killed no one, it ignited a firestorm of revenge. Shi'ites killed Sunnis in the streets and attacked dozens of Sunni mosques across the country. Attempts by political and religious leaders to calm the situation with words accomplished little. The prevailing code of family and tribal honor in Iraq further escalated the violence as each death required that relatives and neighbors kill someone else to avenge the loss.

Fighting hard to maintain order throughout 2006, Coalition forces achieved some progress. In June, they tracked down and killed Zarqawi, eliminating the most radical proponent of sectarian conflict. Ironically, the Jordanian terrorist had already sown the seeds that would weaken his own movement. In violently imposing a draconian version of Islamic law in the areas he controlled, the leader of al-Qaeda in Iraq had alienated the majority of the Sunni population. Equally important, he had undercut the authority of the tribal sheiks. Local leaders began to see U.S. forces as the lesser evil that would help them cut out this cancer in their midst. By the end of the year, according to one report, fourteen tribes had joined the growing Anbar Awakening movement.[7] Less-extreme opponents were also beginning to realize that American leaders were firmly committed in Iraq and would not give up the fight in the near term solely as a result of increasing fiscal costs or a lengthening list of casualties.

These positive developments, coupled with the installation of an elected constitutional government and a large increase in Iraqi security forces over the past year, led senior American military commanders to contemplate a sharp reduction of U.S. troop strength in Iraq over the course of 2007. Prime Minister Maliki likewise proclaimed his desire that Iraqis take responsibility for providing their own security.[8] Aided by Coalition forces, his administration launched Operation Together Forward I in early July 2006. The objective was to restore peaceful conditions and government authority throughout

---

[7] Linda Robinson, *Tell Me How This Ends: General David Petraeus and the Search for a Way Out of Iraq* (New York: Public Affairs, 2008), pp. 104–05.

[8] U.S. Department of State, Bureau of Near Eastern Affairs, Iraq Weekly Status Report, 21 June 2006, Historians files, CMH.

the capital. The effort featured widespread searches of homes, more patrols and checkpoints, a curfew, restrictions on carrying weapons, and targeted raids against insurgent cells. As U.S. troops cleared each neighborhood of suspected terrorists and militia fighters, Iraqi Army and police moved in to take responsibility for its security. But Maliki's forces still proved too few and too ineffective to assume the security responsibilities in many areas, and often insurgents and criminals returned to their old haunts once the Americans moved on to a different section of the city. The Iraqi security forces were still too weak to serve as a capable partner and ally.

Despite the lack of real progress in Baghdad, the Coalition continued with its plan to hand over authority for security operations in each province as American and allied leaders determined that Iraqi officials and forces were ready to exercise control. The process started on 13 July 2006, when British troops transferred Muthanna Province to the Iraqis. Italian forces turned over Dhi Qar Province on 21 September. On 20 December, Najaf Province, which included the holy cities of Najaf and Karbala, passed to Iraqi control. Even though the Shi'ite south was relatively quiet compared to the central and western reaches of the country, local militia forces were still troublesome and Iraqi security forces still had difficulty maintaining order. As a result, U.S. forces had to intervene to assist the Iraqi Army and police on a number of occasions. Two of those fights are covered in chapter 6, "The Battle for Salem Street," and chapter 7, "Shrouded in the Fog of War."

Contrary to the hopes of many, the process of slow disengagement from Iraqi cities and the handover of provinces to Iraqi control had no discernible impact on the overall level of violence. If anything, the reduction of a Coalition presence in Baghdad and other hotspots only served to give the competing factions more opportunity to strike out at each other. A United Nations report tabulated 34,452 violent civilian deaths in Iraq during 2006, a roughly twofold increase over the previous year.[9] With violence rising, many lamented that the cause had become hopeless, nothing could stop the nation's self-destructive civil war, and more rapid withdrawal was the only option to stem Coalition losses.

Any plans to draw down American forces in Iraq ended abruptly when President Bush made a televised address to the nation on 10 January 2007. In the opening moments of his speech, he summarized the state of the war:

> The [Iraqi] elections of 2005 were a stunning achievement. We thought that these elections would bring the Iraqis together—and that as we trained Iraqi security forces, we could accomplish our mission with fewer American troops.

[9] Sabrina Tavernise, "Iraqi Death Toll Exceeds 30,000," *New York Times*, 17 January 2007, copy in Historians files, CMH.

> . . . But in 2006, the opposite happened. The violence in
> Iraq, particularly in Baghdad, overwhelmed the political
> gains the Iraqis had made.[10]

Bush further observed: "Eighty percent of Iraq's sectarian violence occurs within 30 miles of the capital. This violence is splitting Baghdad into sectarian enclaves, and shaking the confidence of all Iraqis."[11] The solution, according to the president, was to place the highest priority on securing the Iraqi capital. If that could be done, the vicious cycle would be broken and the competing factions might be able to reach accommodation. After admitting previous security plans had been hamstrung by too few troops, Bush announced that he had approved additional deployments. Thus was born the Surge, an effort to secure Baghdad once and for all with thirty thousand additional U.S. troops.

He also appointed new senior American commanders in Iraq—General Raymond T. Odierno at MNC-I and General David H. Petraeus at MNF-I. Only time would tell if the president's decisions would produce a turnabout in Iraq. For many soldiers, however, the day-to-day demands of their hazardous duty remained much the same. Chapter 8, "Hellfire and Brimstone," recounts a typical Apache gunship mission—attempting to keep the main supply routes safe for Coalition forces on the ground—which exploded into combat with no warning. Success would ultimately depend on the accomplishment of such seemingly routine tasks, whether undertaken by Surge forces in Baghdad or Coalition and Iraqi troops in the surrounding countryside.

---

[10] CNN, "Bush: We Need to Change Our Strategy in Iraq," 11 January 2007, copy in Historians files, CMH.

[11] Ibid.

CHAPTER ONE

Hell
IN A VERY SMALL
Marketplace

MARK J. REARDON

A tank battalion's defense of a platoon outpost develops into a two-day running battle with small groups of insurgents throughout a sprawling Baghdad suburb.

Abu Ghraib—April 2004

Three U.S. Army high mobility multipurpose wheeled vehicles (HMMWVs, or Humvees) drove at moderate speed down a dusty thoroughfare in the city of Abu Ghraib on the morning of 3 April 2004. The twelve men in the patrol wore the shoulder patch of the 1st Cavalry Division and belonged to Capt. Scott T. Allen's Company B, 2d Battalion, 12th Cavalry. From the top of each vehicle, a helmeted machine-gunner peered warily over turret armor at parked cars, piles of trash, and potholes, all potential hiding places for an improvised explosive device (IED). In spite of the precautions taken by the soldiers, at 0925 a roadside blast engulfed one of the Humvees, damaging it and wounding three of its occupants, one seriously. The patrol ground to a halt, gave first aid to the casualties, and transferred them to one of the remaining vehicles, which then headed for Logistics Base Seitz, the closest Coalition installation with a medical staff and helicopter landing pad. Meanwhile, the battalion command post dispatched a quick reaction force and vehicle recovery team to the scene. The American reinforcements caught a group of insurgents closing in on the same objective and unleashed a withering barrage of automatic-weapons and small-arms fire. The startled Iraqis fled, leaving behind one of their number killed. Intelligence sources later learned the reaction force had prevented the enemy from achieving their goal of capturing one or more Americans.[1]

This small action proved to be the opening gambit in a larger effort by a group of roughly two hundred Sunni insurgents led by a radical cleric named

---

[1] After Action Review (AAR), 2d Bn, 12th Cav, n.d., sub: The Holy Week Battle for Abu Ghraib, p. 2, Historians files, U.S. Army Center of Military History (CMH), Washington, D.C.

Sheik Adil al-Hadithi. He had ordered the attack in the hopes of bolstering his standing among anti-Coalition elements in northwestern Baghdad.[2] The ensuing battles would unfold in Abu Ghraib, a sprawling suburb of more than a million people located between Baghdad proper to the east and Anbar Province to the west. This zone was the domain of Lt. Col. John T. Ryan's 2d Battalion, 12th Cavalry, 1st Cavalry Division. His command had assumed responsibility for the area just a few weeks prior and had gained familiarity with it during numerous patrols.[3] In addition to residential areas, the city featured a large open-air market, a dairy plant, numerous Hussein-era military installations and barracks, scenic parks and palm groves, and a racetrack. The population consisted of a mix of Shi'ite and Sunnis, with the latter predominating and including a significant portion of Islamic fundamentalists. Saddam Hussein had given many of his trusted followers homes in the city, so many residents were former Ba'ath officials, Republican Guards, Fedayeen irregulars, and defense workers.

In the postinvasion period, American units occupied a former presidential palace and other installations in and around Abu Ghraib. Just to the south of town sat Baghdad International Airport, the main aerial hub for Coalition forces. Arrayed around it like spokes on a wheel was the Camp Victory Complex. On the eastern side, in one of Saddam's most opulent private retreats, was Camp Victory, home to Combined Joint Task Force–7. To the northeast was Camp Victory North, occupied by elements of the 1st Cavalry Division. To the northwest was Logistics Base Seitz, and close by was Forward Operating Base (FOB) Thunder (taking the nickname of the 2d Battalion, 12th Cavalry, that occupied it). (*See Map 2.*) Ten miles to the west, on the opposite end of the city, lay the soon-to-be infamous confinement facility of the same name. The Americans also manned a combat outpost, known as Raider Base, overlooking the marketplace in the center of town. Two major highways ran through the area—Routes Cardinals and Huskies (the latter recently renamed from its previous designation of Sword). These served as main supply routes for both the Camp Victory Complex and for Marine forces to the west in Anbar Province.

Lt. Col. Jose R. Rael's 515th Corps Support Battalion made its home at Seitz. While New Mexico Army National Guardsmen manned the headquarters, the 515th included Army Reserve maintenance and quartermaster companies and an Illinois National Guard medium truck company. A journalist noted that the post "was established when relations between Americans and Iraqis were still good enough that soldiers wandered into the town of Abu Ghraib for supplies, they ate in Iraqi restaurants and talked to Iraqis on the streets." Some occupants

---

[2] AAR, 2d Bn, 12th Cav, n.d., p. 3.

[3] Spec John S. Wollaston, "From Bulldogs to Blackjacks: Ceremonies Mark the Beginning of the End for Bulldogs' Baghdad Mission," *The Old Ironsides Report,* 19 February 2004, pp. 1–2, copy in Historians files, CMH.

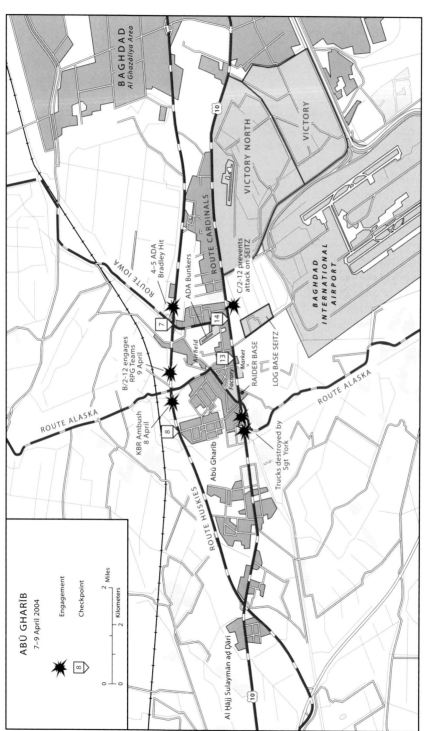

ABŪ GHARĪB
7–9 April 2004

Engagement
Checkpoint

0   2   Miles
0   2   Kilometers

BAGHDAD
Al Ghazāliya Area

4–5 ADA
Bradley Hit

ROUTE IOWA

ADA Bunkers

ROUTE CARDINALS

10

C/2-12 prevents
attack on SEITZ

VICTORY NORTH

VICTORY

BAGHDAD
INTERNATIONAL
AIRPORT

B/2-12 engages
RPG Teams
9 April

7

14

Airfield

13

Factory

Market

RAIDER BASE

LOG BASE SEITZ

ROUTE ALASKA

KBR Ambush
8 April

ROUTE ALASKA

8

Abū Gharib

Trucks destroyed by
Sgt York

ROUTE HUSKIES

Al Hājj Sulaymān aḍ Ḍārī

10

MAP 2

now thought of it as a "mortar magnet and a buffer zone for the much larger Camp Victory."[4]

Despite frequent attacks on the compound, the 515th's executive officer, Maj. Rick Ryczkowski, proclaimed: "We supported anyone and everyone that came to us."[5] In addition to providing combat units with food, fuel, and ammunition, Seitz's helipad served as an intermediate stop for wounded personnel en route to advanced medical facilities in the Green Zone. The 515th's treatment team, consisting of two Wisconsin Army National Guard physician assistants and six medics, did such an outstanding job that Colonel Ryan's unit went to the aid of the 515th with the same zeal as if they were assisting their fellow 1st Cavalry Division troopers.[6]

Abu Ghraib did not represent the sole potential flashpoint within the Iraqi capital during the first week of April. In recent days, relations with Moqtada al-Sadr and his followers had deteriorated markedly when the Coalition Provisional Authority closed his newspaper and arrested one of his top deputies on suspicion of murder. The latter action sparked huge protest marches on the same day as the attack against the patrol from Company B. The next day, Sadr's Mahdi militia attacked a U.S. patrol in Sadr City, located in northeastern Baghdad. A quick reaction force found itself pinned down by heavy fire. After intense fighting, a company of Abrams tanks dispatched by the 1st Armored Division extricated both of the trapped units. Eight Americans and dozens of Shi'ite militiamen died during the daylong fight. The engagement highlighted Sadr's increasing willingness to use violence to achieve his political ambitions.[7]

The 1st Cavalry Division's 2d Brigade, responsible for northwest Baghdad, noted the dramatic upswing in violence. The brigade combat team commander, Col. Michael D. Formica, tasked Ryan's battalion with forming a reserve force consisting of a tank platoon and a mechanized infantry platoon. Ryan chose Company B for the mission. Captain Allen would command the force, which would be under Formica's direct control. Allen assembled six M1A2 Abrams tanks, which had been parceled out in pairs to each of his platoons, into a consolidated tank platoon and headquarters section. Capt. Hugh D. Perry's Company A, 1st Battalion, 5th Cavalry—a mechanized infantry company cross-attached to the 2d Battalion, 12th Cavalry, for the duration of the deployment—contributed a platoon of four M2A3 Bradley infantry fighting vehicles.

---

[4] Zélie Pollon, "The Baghdad Project," Blog Entry, 30 Dec 04, Historians files, CMH.

[5] Ltr, Maj Rick Ryczkowki, XO, 515th Corps Spt Bn, to author, 28 Sep 07, Historians files, CMH.

[6] AAR, 2d Bn, 12th Cav, n.d., p. 11.

[7] Jeffrey Gettlemen, "G.I.'s Padlock Baghdad Paper Accused of Lies," *New York Times*, 29 March 2004; "A Martyr Awaits," *Asia Times*, 7 April 2004; "U.S. Secretary of State Remembers Slain Cleric," *Radio Free Europe/Radio Liberty Newsline*, 5 April 2004; Melinda Liu, "Mean Streets," *Newsweek*, 27 April 2004; Maj John C. Moore, "Sadr City: The Armor Pure Assault in Urban Terrain," *Armor* CXV (March-April 2006): 18–24; CBS News, "Fighting Kills Dozens of Iraqis, Eight U.S. Soldiers," 6 April 2004, copy in Historians files, CMH.

Those Abrams and Bradleys would be sorely missed as Ryan's outfit continued patrolling Abu Ghraib. Prior to deploying to Iraq, all of the 1st Cavalry Division's mechanized and armor battalions had lost one of their maneuver companies as part of an Army-wide restructuring initiative. The 1st Cavalry Division also left much of its heavy armor at Fort Hood, Texas, in favor of lighter vehicles more appropriate for navigating crowded city streets and irrigated farmland. Although Allen's company deployed from Fort Hood with ten of its fourteen tanks, four of those remaining Abrams were on loan to the 91st Engineer Battalion. Capt. Aaron J. Munz's Company C had turned in all fourteen M1A2s before departing its home station and had drawn just four tanks from theater stocks after arriving in Kuwait. In exchange for Captain Perry's unit, Colonel Ryan had sent his own Company A, led by Capt. Kevin S. Badger, to the 1st Battalion, 5th Cavalry. Captain Perry's company fielded ten of its normal fourteen Bradleys.[8]

Insurgents from both major religious sects threatened Colonel Formica's area of operations. Sunnis were inflamed by the ongoing Marine offensive in Fallujah, while Shi'ites were responding to the recent crackdown on Sadr and his Mahdi militia. Coalition forces had prevented a number of Sunni insurgents bound for Fallujah, located twenty-five miles to the west, from entering that city. Instead of returning home, they began gravitating toward Abu Ghraib. On 5 April, Sadr supporters in the Hurriyah neighborhood northeast of Abu Ghraib confronted a patrol from Lt. Col. Christopher W. Martin's 91st Engineer Battalion. The faceoff ended only after an American tank destroyed a militia machine-gun position. At the conclusion of midday prayer in Abu Ghraib, both Shi'ite and Sunni clerics began broadcasting calls over mosque loudspeakers for *jihad* (holy war) against the Americans. Sheik Hadithi and his men were among those ready and willing to respond; but there was no centrally directed operation by an organized force, just bands and individuals answering the call to arms. Their primary weapons would be rifles, machine guns, rocket-propelled grenades (RPGs), IEDs, and a few mortars.[9]

Soon after the Abu Ghraib market opened for business on 6 April, the local governing council canceled its regular midmorning meeting with Colonel Ryan. At noon, groups of young men began hustling bystanders and merchants alike from the marketplace. By 1400, the commercial area appeared deserted. As the mosques repeated earlier exhortations to take up arms, Ryan convened an emergency session of the governing council.[10] The

---

[8] AAR, 4th Bn, 5th Air Defense Artillery (ADA), n.d., sub: A Brief History of 4th Bn, 5th ADA's Opns from 2 Mar to 31 Jul 04," p. 7, Historians files, CMH; Interv, Capt Steven W. Johnston, 54th Military History Detachment (MHD), with Capt Scott T. Allen, CO, Co B, 2d Bn, 12th Cav, 10 May 04, IFIT J-F0019, Global War on Terrorism (GWOT) Collection, CMH.

[9] AAR, 2d Bn, 12th Cav, n.d., p. 2.

[10] Ibid, p. 8.

Iraqis informed the American commander that local resistance fighters were preparing to attack before Coalition forces could cordon off Abu Ghraib in a fashion similar to Fallujah and Sadr City. The rest of the day passed without incident, with the exception of one mortar round exploding within Camp Victory North.

After analyzing the earlier brush with Sadr's militia, Colonel Formica's intelligence section determined that the Mahdi headquarters in nearby Hurriyah had received a large number of RPG launchers from local arms dealers with access to Saddam-era stockpiles. On the same afternoon Formica met with the Abu Ghraib council, he ordered Colonel Martin to conduct a raid within forty-eight hours for the purpose of seizing the RPGs. Unsure of the level of opposition his unit might encounter, Martin asked Colonel Formica for additional troops. After approving Martin's request, Formica directed Ryan to send a tank company to reinforce the engineers. Colonel Ryan chose Allen's Company B to carry out the mission. After meeting with Colonel Martin in his command post, Allen observed, "You could see things had started to escalate at that point because they were calling the mission a deliberate attack rather than a cordon and search."[11] In addition to Allen's unit, Formica told Ryan to detach Captain Munz's Company C to Martin's unit in support of the operation. While Munz did not have a direct role in the assault on the compound, his company would cover the engineer unit's withdrawal upon completion of the raid.

The departure of Companies B and C reduced the combat strength of the 2d Battalion, 12th Cavalry, to a pair of Bradley platoons from Captain Perry's unit, a platoon's worth of up-armored Humvees remaining from Companies B and C, and a truck-mounted Estonian infantry platoon. In partial compensation, Colonel Formica provided Ryan with eight M6 Bradley Linebackers (armed with air-defense missiles in place of the antitank missiles) from Capt. Curran D. Chidester's Battery A, 4th Battalion, 5th Air Defense Artillery, and a platoon of M7 Bradley fire support team (FIST) vehicles from the 3d Battalion, 82d Field Artillery.[12]

Determined to avoid the unfortunate experiences of the recent battle in Sadr City, Colonel Ryan instructed his subordinates to decline combat on the enemy's terms until the detached companies returned. That did not mean he would grant free rein to the insurgents in Abu Ghraib. At 0215 on 7 April, an infantry platoon from Captain Perry's mechanized company conducted a cordon and search operation. The action netted nine suspected insurgents, including two cell leaders.[13]

[11] AAR, 91st Engr Bn, n.d., sub: Task Force 91 Unit History, Jan 04–Present, p. 6, Historians files, CMH; Interv, Johnston with Allen, 10 May 04.

[12] AAR, 4th Bn, 5th ADA, n.d., p. 7; Interv, Johnston with Lt Col John T. Ryan, CO, 2d Bn, 12th Cav, 10 May 04, IFIT I-J-0022, GWOT Collection, CMH.

[13] AAR, 2d Bn, 12th Cav, n.d., p. 6.

The city remained quiet as dawn broke a few hours later. Company A's 1st Platoon, led by 1st Lt. Michael G. Mannix, manned Raider Base at the southwest corner of the marketplace. At 1242, he reported normal activity in the area. An hour later, however, insurgents fired RPGs at a mounted patrol consisting of two Bradleys led by Mannix's platoon sergeant. While the enemy antitank teams failed to score, the electronics in one Bradley failed, prompting the patrol's return. At 1524, Captain Perry's 2d Platoon reported six mortar rounds exploding near Logistics Base Seitz. Shortly after 1600, a single mortar round exploded within the walled compound of Raider Base. Metal shards hit one soldier, but his wounds were not serious.[14]

A short while later, a barrage slammed into Raider Base. The first mortar round landed in front of the southeastern guard tower. Seconds later, another detonated inside the compound, peppering an Iraqi Army vehicle with fragments. Three more shells exploded near an M113A3 armored personnel carrier parked at the front gate. The Americans fortunately suffered no casualties.[15] But this was merely the preparatory bombardment for a larger attack on the outpost. Within moments insurgents began firing small arms and RPGs as they closed in.

The Americans manned their defensive positions and returned fire. Spec. Jose M. Lazala, a member of Mannix's 1st Squad, killed four enemy fighters using an M203 40-mm. grenade launcher. Spec. Joshua McCowan, a Bradley gunner, eliminated several insurgent teams. Using the high-powered optics on their fighting vehicles, Lieutenant Mannix's platoon located two mortar crews. Sgt. Brandon C. Goodman employed his Bradley's 25-mm. cannon to silence one tube located twelve hundred yards to the northeast.[16] The second, hidden within the Bilady Dairy Factory just across the road from Raider Base, lobbed more rounds. Captain Perry requested artillery support to eliminate it; but division vetoed the mission, citing possible damage to nearby civilian housing.

That same afternoon, Battery A, 4th Battalion, 5th Air Defense Artillery, reported to the 2d Battalion, 12th Cavalry. Growing concerned about Raider Base, Colonel Ryan directed Captain Chidester to send a platoon to reinforce Perry's company. Chidester chose 2d Lt. Cameron W. Smith's 1st Platoon, which was equipped with four Bradley Linebackers and one infantry fighting vehicle. Perry, who was visiting Raider Base during the attack, directed Smith to establish mounted observation posts along Route Cardinals. The air defenders were to watch for insurgents attempting to emplace IEDs. At 2130, Smith asked Captain Perry for permission to return to Camp Victory North so his men could get some rest prior to their next patrol scheduled for 0500. The

[14] Ibid., p. 9; AAR, 1st Plt, Co A, 1st Bn, 5th Cav, 22 Apr 04, sub: The Battle of Abu Ghraib, p. 2, Historians files, CMH.
[15] AAR, 2d Bn, 12th Cav, n.d., p. 10.
[16] AAR, 1st Plt, Co A, 1st Bn, 5th Cav, 22 Apr 04, p. 2.

Captain Perry scans the Abu Ghraib market from Raider Base. Bilady Dairy Factory, in the background, served as a staging point for insurgent attacks throughout the battle.

company commander approved the request, and the air defense platoon began reassembling for the move back to base.

The battalion operations center, which received reports of an IED near Checkpoint 8 on Route Huskies, overrode Perry's instructions and ordered the Linebackers to confirm the information. Lieutenant Smith moved to the area, used 25-mm. cannon fire to destroy a suspicious object on the side of the road, and then resumed movement back to Camp Victory North at 2300. Moments later, as the Linebacker commanded by Sgt. Mark O. McKane drove out from under an overpass, an RPG struck the rear of its turret. The round penetrated the armor, ricocheted inside, and severely wounded the NCO in his left arm. The gunner, whose own face was bleeding from numerous small cuts, attended to his injured vehicle commander while the driver maneuvered out of range and rejoined the platoon.[17]

Personnel at the logistics base were monitoring the battalion command net and took the initiative to request a medical helicopter. Colonel Ryan's battle staff also dispatched the battalion reaction force to Smith's location. Rather than chance the loss of a helicopter at night in an enemy-infested area, Captain Perry directed the Linebacker platoon leader to link up with the reaction force and move to Seitz's helipad. The Abrams encountered no resistance during their movement to the site. Taking up position at the

---

[17] AAR, 4th Bn, 5th ADA, n.d., p. 8.

head and tail of the air defense platoon, the tanks shepherded the unit to the logistics base.[18]

While Lieutenant Smith's Bradleys engaged insurgents north of Abu Ghraib, Colonel Martin's battalion completed its preparations for the raid to seize the RPG cache in Hurriyah. At 0300 on 8 April, a column of 91st Engineer Battalion vehicles emerged from FOB Thunder. The column crossed Route Cardinals before continuing north toward a bridge spanning the creek dividing Hurriyah into northern and southern halves. Using a slightly different route, Captain Allen's Company B departed from Camp Victory North a few minutes later. Both units operated in blackout conditions in the hopes of achieving surprise. The lead platoon of Company B, 91st Engineer Battalion, had barely crossed the Gazaliya Bridge, however, when three daisy-chained IEDs exploded. The M1114 up-armored Humvees unscathed, the platoon shook it off and pressed onward. A patrol reconnoitering along the flank of the main body also encountered an IED. One Humvee had two tires flattened, but the soldiers repaired the damage and continued the mission.[19]

Rather than risk more IED strikes by remaining road bound, Colonel Martin directed a D9 bulldozer to open a cross-country bypass through piles of trash and other debris. Although the task appeared simple, the dozer operator reported it would take some time to complete the work. After determining he could not afford to remain stationary for a lengthy period, Martin instructed his unit to resume movement. But instead of continuing along the main road, the column detoured through a nearby neighborhood.[20] The American vehicles did not encounter any antitank teams as they crept past darkened houses, which proved a welcome surprise given the reports of large RPG shipments to Sadr's militia.

Meanwhile, Colonel Martin's three engineer companies, reinforced by Captain Allen's unit, took up positions around the militia compound in Hurriyah. Just before dawn, two OH–58D Kiowa Warrior helicopters arrived on station. After securing the buildings overlooking the compound, the Americans sent a tank crashing through the courtyard wall followed by soldiers from Company C, 91st Engineer Battalion. The engineers seized four computers, documents, and IED components without encountering resistance but found no stockpile of RPGs.[21] Colonel Martin concluded that the weapons had already been distributed to Mahdi fighters. As if to confirm his supposition, when the Kiowa Warriors departed to refuel, an RPG team and machine-gun crew opened fire. The raid force eliminated both in short order.[22]

---

[18] AAR, 2d Bn, 12th Cav, n.d., p. 11.

[19] AAR, 91st Engr Bn, n.d., p. 6.

[20] Interv, Johnston with Lt Col Christopher W. Martin, CO, 91st Engr Bn, 10 May 04, IFIT J-I-0024, GWOT Collection, CMH.

[21] AAR, 91st Engr Bn, sub: Holy Week Battle, 5–13 April 04, p. 4, Historians files, CMH.

[22] Ibid.; Interv, Johnston with Allen, 10 May 04.

Captain Munz's unit rolled out of Camp Victory North at 0400 to cover the engineer battalion's withdrawal route. His 1st Platoon was organized with a section of two M1A2s under Sfc. John P. Sczerby and a section of two M1114s led by S. Sgt. Charles R. Armstead. The 2d Platoon had three Bradley Linebackers and two up-armored Humvees led by 2d Lt. Matthew D. Hartzell and Sfc. Michael A. Klein. The 3d Platoon fielded two Abrams and two M1114s commanded by 1st Lt. Justin D. Harper and Sfc. Frederick S. Tripp. Munz's headquarters element consisted of two Linebackers, two up-armored Humvees, and an M113A3 medical evacuation vehicle.

Munz's company met no resistance as it occupied positions affording a good view of the main roads south and west of Hurriyah. His 2d Platoon settled down near the intersection of Route Huskies and the north-south secondary road leading to Hurriah. The 3d Platoon concentrated its surveillance on the latter, while the 1st Platoon observed Route Huskies along with an adjacent road, Route Force.

Minutes after Munz's 1st Platoon established its outpost, Sergeant Sczerby observed smoke rising from burning automobile tires arrayed across Huskies. He surmised that the object was to slow down Coalition convoys traversing an ambush site. The sergeant directed his vehicles into positions from which they could engage any enemy spotted in the vicinity. Several minutes later, an RPG team appeared to the rear of Sczerby's tank. An Iraqi raised his launcher into position from behind a low wall, but Sczerby's wingman fired a 120-mm. high-explosive round and both M1114s loosed a spray of bullets at the enemy. The insurgents died before they could fire a shot.

Disregarding the first team's fate, a second RPG crew attacked Lieutenant Hartzell's platoon. Arriving via an orange and white cab, they pulled up on a nearby side street. The driver fired a rocket at the nearest up-armored Humvee but missed. The Humvee turret gunner, Cpl. Paul N. Stebenne, responded with more accuracy and killed his assailant. Two Linebackers joined the fray, destroying the taxi with 25-mm. rounds. Twenty-five minutes later, a third RPG team engaged Hartzell's platoon with the same lack of success and a similar fate. At 0845, vehicles from the 91st Engineer Battalion started emerging from Hurriyah. Thirty minutes later, Company C made its way back to Camp Victory North where Munz's troops, along with Allen's Company B, were released back to their own battalion.[23]

Later that morning, Allen, Munz, and Perry attended a meeting at 2d Battalion, 12th Cavalry, headquarters convened by Ryan. The colonel laid out plans to deal with the upswing in activity in Abu Ghraib—his top priority would be locating and destroying the mortars firing on Raider Base. Captains Munz and Perry each received new instructions from Ryan. Companies B and C would conduct mounted patrols to locate the enemy

---

[23] AAR, 2d Bn, 12th Cav, n.d., p. 13.

Corporal Stebenne engages an insurgent RPG team on the morning of 8 April from the turret of his HMMWV. His unit, Company C, 2d Battalion, 12th Cavalry, was supporting the 91st Engineer Battalion raid on the Mahdi militia compound in al Hurriyah.

positions while Captain Allen also provided two tanks for a battalion reaction force.[24]

While Ryan issued those orders, Lieutenant Mannix passed control of Raider Base to 1st Lt. William P. Mercucci's 3d Platoon.[25] The situation grew tense as Mannix's troops departed the outpost. RPG teams hiding in the marketplace opened the fight by taking potshots at the trio of 1st Platoon Bradleys. Seconds later, a transmission from one of Mercucci's fighting vehicles blared over the radio speakers in the 2d Battalion, 12th Cavalry, tactical operations center: "Thunder Mike, this is Annihilator Blue 1, Raider base is under attack from RPGs and snipers."[26] The sound of an M240B machine gun in the background punctuated the report as the Bradley's gunner loosed a long burst. Ryan's emphasis on the enemy's indirect-fire weapons proved prophetic, as mortar rounds soon began to fall within the outpost. The Americans replied with their 25-mm. cannons.

The volume of insurgent fire directed at Raider Base increased while the battalion began organizing reinforcements to go to the aid of the outpost. Three soldiers went down. Sgt. Randy R. Clark was shot twice in the leg, but his body

---

[24] Interv, Johnston with Allen, 10 May 04.
[25] Ltr, M. George Mannix, Plt Ldr, 1st Plt, Co A, 1st Bn, 5th Cav, to author, 19 Sep 07, Historians files, CMH.
[26] AAR, 2d Bn, 12th Cav, n.d., p. 13.

armor saved him from graver wounds to his torso. Sgt. Anthony J. Bowdler was hit in the back by fragments from an RPG. S. Sgt. Joe A. Frye received wounds to his shooting hand but stayed in the fight.[27] American return fire broke up the insurgent assault before it could gain momentum, but Lieutenant Mercucci now had to get the severe casualties to a medical facility.

Captain Perry tasked his 1st Platoon with the mission of evacuating the wounded. The unit would be short S. Sgt. Michael N. Holland's Bradley, which remained behind due to problems with turret electronics. Lieutenant Mannix, accompanied by his platoon sergeant, Sfc. Curtis W. Wood, departed Seitz for Raider Base. The pair of Bradleys turned west onto Route Cardinals after clearing the main gate, then came under a hail of small-arms fire and RPGs near the Abu Ghraib market. Although Mannix's and Wood's vehicles were each hit several times, they suffered minor damage. Both sprayed machine-gun and 25-mm. cannon rounds at buildings, rooftops, and alleyways as they pushed through to Raider Base.[28]

Not waiting for the cavalry to come to the rescue, one of Mercucci's soldiers, Cpl. Daniel K. Petrik, had decided to evacuate the casualties using an M113A3 armored personnel carrier parked inside the outpost. Disregarding intense mortar and RPG fire, he began unloading crates of ammunition stored in the vehicle. Petrik then helped Sergeants Clark and Bowdler to the carrier while ignoring explosions all around the compound. Onlookers watched in awe.

The 1st Platoon Bradleys, one in front and the other behind, escorted Petrik's M113A3 through the marketplace gauntlet to deliver the wounded men to Logistics Base Seitz. Lieutenant Mannix felt the corporal's "personal courage was extraordinary and he undoubtedly risked his own life and limb repeatedly for the sake of his comrades." After Petrik and the Bradley crews carried the casualties to waiting medics, all three vehicles took up positions along Seitz's northwest berm in anticipation of an attack against the support base.[29]

The battalion reaction force, consisting of two Company B tanks commanded by S. Sgt. Curtis G. Wright and Sgt. Matthew T. York, constituted the first permanent reinforcements for Raider Base. The Abrams departed Camp Victory North bound for a former Iraqi Army bunker complex located southwest of the outpost. That site offered the tank crews a clear field of fire overlooking the roads leading to the market and the dairy factory. Wright and York were barely in position when an insurgent mortar crew targeted them. Both Abrams maneuvered behind a row of bunkers that shielded them from direct observation while still affording a good view of the area.

Captain Perry departed Camp Victory North soon after the reaction force. Accompanied by another up-armored Humvee, he decided to take a less-

---

[27] Ibid., p. 14.

[28] AAR, 1st Plt, Co A, 1st Bn, 5th Cav, 22 Apr 04, Encls: Award Recommendations, Pfc Michael D. Lawler, Spec Jose A. Beltran.

[29] Ltr, Mannix to author, 19 Sep 07.

traveled route to Raider Base. Making a wide detour to the west, both vehicles drove as fast as possible to present a difficult target to RPG teams. With the outpost in sight, Perry ordered his driver to pour on the speed. The vehicles entered the outpost trailing a cloud of dust.

Braking to a halt, Perry ordered his men to add their vehicle machine guns to the outpost's defenses. One gun team and two riflemen reinforced the southern perimeter, while the other crew augmented the western flank. Perry sent his company master gunner, S. Sgt. Kevin M. Schuller, to take charge of the Bradley facing the marketplace. Mercucci's second Bradley covered the main thoroughfare leading from the marketplace to Abu Ghraib's western-most outskirts.[30]

As the men scrambled to respond, Captain Perry clambered up the stairs of the building serving as Raider Base's headquarters. Lieutenant Mercucci, clutching a radio in each hand, joined him on the rooftop. A sandbagged guard tower offered some shelter from the bullets that continually cracked overhead. Instructing Mercucci to focus on holding off a ground attack, Perry started coordinating the long-range fight against the insurgent mortars pummeling the outpost.

Meanwhile, Captain Munz at Camp Victory North succeeded in assembling ad hoc crews for four tanks and two up-armored Humvees. He decided to leave behind two M1A2s, commanded by 1st Sgt. Charles Q. Taylor and Sergeant Armstead, as a reserve. He took his own Abrams, accompanied by Lieutenant Harper and trailed by the Humvees, and moved out at 1015. After exiting Baghdad International Airport's east gate, the column turned left toward Abu Ghraib. As the American vehicles headed north, they encountered an ambush consisting of fifteen to twenty RPG teams emplaced on both sides of the road and adjacent rooftops. Munz could see and hear antitank rockets streaking by, but none scored a solid hit.[31] Intent on presenting a difficult target to the enemy, his driver mashed down the accelerator. Harper's Abrams followed suit while the up-armored Humvees fell behind, which helped them because the insurgents seemed to aim all their rockets at the tanks.

The lagging Humvees found themselves in a good position for another reason. Sergeant Sczerby and his wingman, S. Sgt. Frank Ballesteros Jr., could see the insurgents who revealed their positions to fire at the Abrams. The two gunners, Sgts. Aaron B. O'Connor and Tyrrell J. Decoteau, fired repeated bursts at the distracted RPG teams and inflicted a number of casualties before the Iraqis could seek cover or disperse. The ambush broken, Munz's column continued on to Route Cardinals. As the American vehicles turned west toward Checkpoint 14, however, mortar rounds began to impact around them. Convinced it was too risky for the Humvees to stay with the Abrams, Captain

---

[30] AAR, 2d Bn, 12th Cav, n.d., p. 16.

[31] Interv, Johnston with Capt Aaron J. Munz, CO, Co C, 2d Bn, 12th Cav, 10 May 04, IFIT-I-J-0021, GWOT Collection, CMH.

Munz ordered Sczerby and Ballesteros to return to Camp Victory North via a circuitous route.

Once the Humvees departed, Munz and Lieutenant Harper headed toward Checkpoint 23, located north of Abu Ghraib. Within minutes, Sergeant Sczerby radioed Munz that he could see stationary convoys on Route Huskies. Three Marine Corps light armored vehicles, six Humvees, and several heavy equipment transporters en route to Fallujah had halted in the westbound lanes. On the opposite side of the median heading east toward Baghdad was a line of Kellogg, Brown and Root contracted civilian cargo vehicles and their military escorts. Insurgents had ambushed the latter convoy, and several trucks were burning. Both convoys suffered casualties, with one marine in need of aerial medical evacuation and a contract driver nursing a serious leg wound.[32]

Disregarding mounting small-arms fire directed at Sczerby's M1114, Sgt. Casey J. Blanchette, the platoon's medic, sprinted over to the wounded civilian huddled under a truck. Sliding under the bullet-riddled vehicle, Blanchette noticed that the driver had a compound fracture of the leg. The medic performed first aid before lifting the man to his feet. The pair half-stumbled and half-ran back to the waiting Humvee.[33] With intense RPG fire preventing him from taking the wounded civilian to Logistics Base Seitz for medical treatment, Sergeant Sczerby radioed Captain Munz for help.

Responding to the request, Munz and Lieutenant Harper maneuvered onto a small hillock near the halted convoys. The slight advantage in elevation provided both tanks with a clear view of the surrounding area. They also became a magnet drawing all the attention of the insurgents, who unleashed a hail of rocket-propelled grenades and mortar rounds. The two Abrams gave back better than they got, replying with methodical, accurate fire. Munz's gunner, Sergeant Tripp, wiped out a mortar crew with a single round of 120-mm. high explosive. Harper's gunner, Sgt. Ethan R. Atkin, eliminated an RPG team in similar fashion. Alternating between cannon and machine gun, the tanks destroyed seven more small groups before the insurgents broke contact and retreated.[34]

Monitoring incoming situation reports over the battalion radio net, Captain Allen ordered his 3d Platoon leader, 1st Lt. Murugan Palani, to get the three Company B tanks remaining at Camp Victory North ready for combat. The trio of Abrams departed at 1200 with Allen in the lead, Palani next in the column, and S. Sgt. Keith L. Gates bringing up the rear. As the tanks neared the northeastern outskirts of Abu Ghraib, Allen spotted the ambush site on Route Huskies.[35] After talking to his fellow company commander, Captain Allen loaned Lieutenant Palani's tank to Munz to assist in escorting the two convoys to Camp Victory North. Allen

---

[32] Ibid.; AAR, 2d Bn, 12th Cav, n.d., p. 17.

[33] Ltr, Aaron J. Munz, CO, Co C, 2d Bn, 12th Cav, to author, 4 Oct 07, Historians files, CMH.

[34] AAR, 2d Bn, 12th Cav, n.d., p. 17; Interv, Johnston with Munz, 10 May 04.

[35] Interv, Johnston with Allen, 10 May 04.

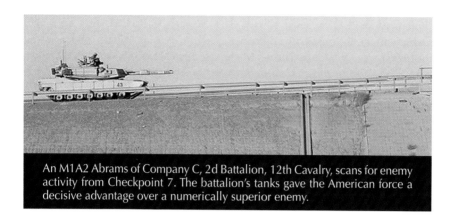

An M1A2 Abrams of Company C, 2d Battalion, 12th Cavalry, scans for enemy activity from Checkpoint 7. The battalion's tanks gave the American force a decisive advantage over a numerically superior enemy.

and Gates remained at Checkpoint 7 for the rest of the day to prevent the insurgents from making another attempt to block the main road.

As Munz headed back to Camp Victory North early that afternoon, combat flared up again at Raider Base. Sergeant Schuller, manning the Bradley protecting the eastern perimeter, killed five insurgents trying to sprint across the marketplace. The other M2A3 engaged a rooftop position near the dairy factory. Then Schuller loosed a TOW antitank missile at Iraqis firing from a building on the northern side of the marketplace.[36] That large explosion seemed to quiet the enemy for a bit, but firing picked up again when a pair of Kiowa Warrior helicopters appeared overhead.

Colonel Ryan had succeeded in obtaining the OH–58D section from the 1st Battalion, 25th Aviation Regiment, to assist in the defense of Raider Base. The mission of the aviators was to locate enemy mortar teams; but each time an aircraft dropped down to spot insurgent positions, it met heavy small-arms and machine-gun fire. One helicopter, flown by CWO2 Norman M. Armstrong and CWO2 William I. Reed, sustained hits in its fuel tank and had to head for Logistics Base Seitz. The OH–58D made a safe landing, but fuel spilling out of the damaged aircraft forced the 515th to shut down one of its main helipads for the remainder of the battle.[37]

As the insurgents focused on the aerial threat, they again made themselves vulnerable from another element of the American combined-arms team. Lieutenant Mannix's platoon sniper, Spec. Reynaldo Cabrera, had settled into firing position behind the earthen berm surrounding Seitz. Sergeant Holland could see an insurgent firing at the helicopters from a rooftop over one thousand yards distant. Although the range made a successful engagement problematic, Holland instructed Cabrera to take the shot. With Holland serving as observer,

---

[36] AAR, 2d Bn, 12th Cav, n.d., p. 16.
[37] Ibid., p. 18; Ltr, Maj Rick Ryczkowski, XO, 515th Corps Spt Bn, to author, 28 Sep 07, Historians files, CMH.

the sniper fired. The bullet missed, but it sent the Iraqi darting for cover. Cabrera made the necessary adjustments to his telescopic sights while waiting for his target to reappear. The insurgent stepped back into view a few minutes later, talking on a cellular phone to his comrades. Cabrera again squeezed the trigger of his rifle, and this time the Iraqi toppled off the roof as the echo of the shot faded away.[38]

A second team of Kiowa Warriors arrived on station soon afterward. These helicopters also received fire each time they flew over the marketplace. When Captain Perry warned the pilots about intense ground fire, he received the laconic response: "No kidding." Moments later, Ghostrider 04, piloted by CWO3 Cody K. Sharp and CWO2 Jason L. Ray, was hit when it dipped down to engage several enemy spotted in the open.[39]

Sharp suffered multiple gunshot wounds to the left arm and right hand and told his copilot that he could no longer fly the helicopter. Ray, himself hit in the right arm, took the controls with his left hand.[40] Neither man had time to inform the troops on the ground about their predicament. To the soldiers below, it looked like the Kiowa Warrior was making a low-level pass straight at Raider Base. As the olive-drab helicopter approached, incredulous onlookers watched it execute a hard left turn and touch down twenty-five meters south of the outpost.

Captain Perry yelled into the radio handset that "a helicopter has just been shot down right in front of me." Both pilots climbed out but could not find a way to scale the walled compound surrounding Raider Base. The soldiers of Company A tried to attract the aviators' attention by yelling, but their efforts went unheeded due to the gunfire. Perry sent both Bradleys out the front gate, accompanied by several soldiers led by Sergeant Frye, to retrieve the helicopter crew. The remainder of Raider Base's garrison sprayed fire at every building within several hundred yards. When the Bradleys approached the downed aircraft, a three-man RPG team sprinted into the open in an attempt to get closer to the armored vehicles. The lead vehicle felled the enemy with a volley of 25-mm. cannon and coaxial machine-gun fire. The pilots clambered on board, and the Bradleys moved back inside the compound. As medics treated both wounded men, Chief Warrant Officer Sharp informed Sergeant Frye: "There goes my golf game."[41]

Getting the casualties to a treatment facility presented a difficult problem. Captain Perry could not use the Bradley section at Raider Base to transport them to Seitz without depriving himself of needed firepower at a critical moment. Given what had happened to the scout helicopters, air evacuation did

---

[38] AAR, 1st Plt, Co A, 1st Bn, 5th Cav, Encl: Award Recommendation, S Sgt Michael H. Holland.

[39] AAR, 1st Bn, 25th Avn Rgt, n.d., sub: First Month of Combat Operations Through April, p. 17, Historians files, CMH.

[40] Ibid., p. 17.

[41] AAR, 2d Bn, 12th Cav, n.d., p. 19.

The Kiowa Warrior, flown by Chief Warrant Officers Sharp and Ray, shot down near Raider Base. Although insurgents inflicted most of the damage with RPGs after the helicopter's hard landing, American troops kept the aircraft from falling into enemy hands.

not appear to be a viable choice. The only remaining option was the logistics base sending someone to pick up the wounded pilots.

Sfc. Christopher H. Kowalewski, of Captain Perry's 2d Platoon, volunteered for the mission, which surprised no one. While many vehicle commanders moved cautiously in the face of a possible ambush or IED, he took a different view: "If there was an explosion I moved top speed to it because the chances that there were American soldiers hit were extremely high."[42] Kowalewski's crew included Spec. Christopher J. Wells, who had earned a well-deserved reputation during previous evacuation missions as a very competent medic. Sergeant Taylor, along with Sergeant Armstead, agreed to escort Kowalewski. Before the medical evacuation convoy departed Seitz, Taylor inserted Kowalewski's Bradley between both Abrams. With Taylor in the lead, the vehicles departed Seitz, switching to a line-abreast formation after turning west onto Route Cardinals.

As the trio of vehicles neared Checkpoint 13, an RPG team at the northeastern corner of the market opened fire. The rocket exploded against

---

[42] Ltr, 1st Sgt Christopher H. Kowalewski, former Plt Sgt, 2d Plt, Co A, 1st Bn, 5th Cav, to author, 26 Sep 07, Historians files, CMH.

Taylor's vehicle without causing any damage. Taylor destroyed the insurgent antitank crew with a single 120-mm. high-explosive round. When a second RPG team hiding behind a white sedan in a nearby alley opened fire, Taylor's gunner, Sgt. Chad M. Persinger, eliminated it with a burst of machine-gun fire. When the armored vehicles reached their destination, Kowalewski's Bradley darted into Raider Base. The tanks remained outside. While they waited for the M2A3 to reemerge, Taylor and Armstead made several forays through the market to flush out would-be ambushers. When Kowalewski signaled his readiness, all three armored vehicles headed back to Logistics Base Seitz. During the return trip, numerous rocket-propelled grenades struck the tanks; but the Bradley, shielded by the Abrams on either flank, escaped damage.

Another predicament cropped up following the evacuation of the pilots. Higher echelon commanders directed 2d Battalion of the 12th Cavalry to secure the downed aircraft until it could be recovered. When Colonel Ryan asked for Perry's thoughts, the company commander told him that Raider Base's small garrison was not strong enough to defend both the outpost and the helicopter. In response, Ryan committed his last reserve—the four Bradley fire support team vehicles from the 3d Battalion, 82d Field Artillery. After running the marketplace gauntlet, the platoon established a protective cordon around the downed Kiowa Warrior.[43]

At 1400, unit mechanics completed repairing a sixth Company B M1A2 Abrams at Camp Victory North. Sfc. Wendell J. Franklin, still recovering from wounds received during the 6 April IED attack, took this tank into the fight. Meanwhile, at Checkpoint 7 overlooking the earlier ambush site along Route Huskies, Captain Allen moved his own Abrams and Sergeant Gates' tank to a new position that allowed them to engage any insurgents moving along a major north-south road just west of Hurriyah. They were joined a short while later by Lieutenant Palani and Sergeant Franklin. The four armored vehicles proved an irresistible lure for RPG teams lurking nearby. The enemy gunners inflicted minor damage on Palani's Abrams and tried to destroy the damaged trucks left on highway. Allen's tank inflicted a number of enemy losses and Sergeant Gates' crew killed four insurgents.[44]

While the four Company B tanks held Checkpoint 7, at the bunker complex Sergeants Wright and York remained in constant contact with the enemy. York observed two trucks loaded with armed men moving west. His crew blasted both vehicles with coaxial and .50-caliber machine guns, killing or wounding thirty enemy fighters. That provoked a mortar barrage that forced Wright and York to reposition their vehicles a second time. Scanning nearby buildings, the tankers identified a pair of insurgent spotters and eliminated them with main-gun rounds. The tanks also fired at another house shielding an enemy mortar. Not long afterward, Sergeant York spotted two more vehicles

---

[43] AAR, 2d Bn, 12th Cav, n.d., pp. 19–20.
[44] Interv, Johnston with Allen, 10 May 04.

Looking west from the vicinity of Checkpoint 7, an overpass crossing Route Huskies just north of the central district of Abu Ghraib. Captain Allen, along with Lieutenant Palani and Sergeants Franklin and Gates, occupied positions near here on 8 April and inflicted numerous casualties on insurgents trying to engage the American tanks with RPGs.

filled with armed men approaching Abu Ghraib. His gunner destroyed both, resulting in twenty enemy casualties.

As dusk approached, all six Company B tanks returned to Logistics Base Seitz for fuel and ammunition. After Wright and York completed replenishment, they returned to the bunker complex without encountering enemy resistance. Colonel Ryan ordered Captain Allen to redeploy his remaining tanks along Route Huskies to deny enemy access to the dairy factory and to prevent movement along the major roads north of Raider Base. As Allen's force neared Route Huskies, a single rocket-propelled grenade narrowly missed Lieutenant Palani's Abrams. When the RPG team attempted to escape by car, Palani riddled it with a sustained burst from his coaxial machine gun. Moments later, his gunner killed four insurgents moving between nearby houses.[45]

While Allen's tanks took position along Route Huskies, eighteen rounds of 60-mm. white phosphorus struck Raider Base, followed immediately by five rounds of high explosive. Under cover of that mortar barrage, several RPG teams sneaked past the Bradleys guarding the downed Kiowa Warrior. The Iraqis scored two direct hits on the helicopter, blowing off its nose. A third

---

[45] AAR, 2d Bn, 12th Cav, n.d., p. 19.

rocket impacted the southeastern corner of the Raider Base compound.[46] Under cover of the smoke screen generated by the white phosphorous, other insurgents gathered near the market for an attack against Captain Perry's eastern perimeter.

The enemy had chosen a poor time to launch another push against Raider Base. Their efforts drew fire from the four Bradleys of Perry's 2d Platoon and Captain Munz's and Sergeant Armstead's tanks, which had just arrived in the marketplace. Munz engaged the dairy factory water tower, used by insurgents as an observation post, with his main gun. With a single 120-mm. multipurpose round he also eliminated one of the RPG teams that had fired on the downed helicopter.

Meanwhile, the Bradleys at Raider Base spotted the muzzle blast of a mortar firing from within the factory. Unable to engage the enemy position with 25-mm. cannon, Lieutenant Mercucci requested artillery support. A platoon of 155-mm. howitzers, augmented by two of the battalion's own 120-mm. mortars, answered the call. "Once the sun set and it had become obvious there was no one left in Abu Ghraib who was not shooting at us, [brigade] received approval for use of artillery and mortar fire. . . . There were friendly rounds impacting everywhere. They silenced the mortars and set the market ablaze."[47]

Heightened enemy activity had not been confined to the area surrounding Raider Base. From their position along the protective berm surrounding Seitz, the battalion scout platoon leader, 1st Lt. Brandon H. Burke, and Sergeant Kowalewski spotted armed men gathering near a walled compound. The group appeared to be preparing to launch an attack against the base's perimeter. In response to Kowalewski's call for support, Captain Munz and Sergeant Armstead returned to Seitz from the marketplace. Once the tanks were in position, Kowalewski engaged the insurgents with several bursts of 25-mm. while Armstead and Munz blasted the compound with 120-mm. high-explosive rounds. The insurgents lost thirty to forty personnel killed or wounded, and the threat from that quarter dissolved.[48]

The situation in Abu Ghraib quieted down after midnight. Captain Munz used the breather to relocate his entire company to Logistics Base Seitz in anticipation of a coordinated assault on the Bilady Dairy Factory, which seemed to be a hub of enemy activity. Colonel Ryan attached two platoons from Battery A, 4th Battalion, 5th Air Defense Artillery, to Company C for the attack. The combined air-defense platoons boasted four M6 Linebackers, an M2A3 Bradley, an M1A2 Abrams, and three M1114 HMMWVs. Munz's scheme of maneuver stressed simplicity and mass. He planned to send tanks, Bradleys, and Linebackers straight through the marketplace under cover of

[46] Ibid., pp. 20–21.
[47] AAR, 2d Bn, 12th Cav, n.d., p. 22.
[48] Ibid.

darkness. Using a route that avoided the market, the wheeled vehicles would link up with the heavier armor after the factory walls were breached.[49]

Company C's assault on the dairy factory proved successful. The armored vehicles encountered only a little small-arms fire as they traversed the marketplace. Captain Perry's 2d Platoon leader, 1st Lt. Christopher J. Carlson, employed his M2A3 as a battering ram to open a hole in the eastern wall of the factory compound. Dropping the vehicle's ramp, a fire team scrambled out to search nearby buildings. More tanks and Bradleys moved into the complex, the latter disgorging additional teams who joined in the clearing effort.

While Lieutenant Carlson's search teams found an improvised mortar tube on a rooftop oriented on Raider Base, they did not locate its crew. Once Captain Munz was satisfied that his command had established a full security perimeter, he ordered his executive officer and Sergeant Taylor to lead the wheeled vehicles into the factory. At the same time, the 2d Battalion, 12th Cavalry, dispatched a team under the supervision of the battalion's chief logistics officer to recover the downed OH–58D. Things remained quiet until 0400 when nine RPGs arced over the outer wall to explode within the factory compound. The Americans did not suffer any casualties or damage to their vehicles. The battalion command post responded by firing two 120-mm. mortar rounds at the suspected point of origin.

By 0500, four Company B tanks, commanded by Lieutenant Palani and Sergeants Franklin, Wright, and York, were deployed along a screen line south of Route Huskies. The insurgents, intent on reoccupying ambush positions along the main highway, launched a coordinated RPG attack at 1000 against the tanks. An RPG team succeeded in hitting a road wheel on the right side of York's Abrams. None of the other vehicles were struck. All of the tanks began searching for their tormentors. Anxious to avoid being hit a second time, Sergeant York shifted his tank several hundred yards to the west. Moments later, he observed seven enemy armed with RPGs and AK47s. York wiped out the group using his coaxial machine gun and turret-mounted .50-caliber. York encountered another seven-man RPG team while he repositioned his vehicle yet again. Although both sides were surprised, the Iraqis got off the first shot, hitting the M1A2 with an RPG round that pierced the armored skirt protecting the suspension and track. The sergeant responded seconds later with a single main-gun round that killed everyone in the enemy force.

In the midst of yet another shift in location, York saw a third RPG team moving across an open area. The insurgents likewise spotted the tank and attempted to hide behind a building. Sergeant York fired a main-gun round into the structure, killing the enemy. Three men began shooting at York as he leaned out of his commander's hatch in an effort to pinpoint a safe route for his vehicle. Dropping back down into the turret, York engaged each in turn, killing two. Eight insurgents, including two RPG gunners, fired at the tank from

⁴⁹ Interv, Johnston with Munz, 10 May 04.

Captain Munz stands in the central courtyard of Bilady Dairy Factory. Seizing this objective brought an end to the enemy's direct confrontation with the battalion in early April 2004.

a nearby alley. York responded with coaxial and .50-caliber machine-gun fire, wiping them out before they could reload their launchers.

York's fire and maneuver stirred up a hornets' nest. Sergeant Franklin saw a large number of enemy dart behind several houses. Unable to bring his own weapons to bear, Franklin pointed out their location to York, who used an M203 grenade launcher to force them from cover. The tactic succeeded as Lieutenant Palani, Sergeant Franklin, and Sergeant Wright observed insurgents fleeing to the east. A fusillade from all three tanks killed or wounded twenty.

The tank platoon's skirmishes along Huskies appeared to be the last embers in a dying fire. The dairy factory was secure, the enemy was no longer targeting Raider Base, and the insurgents seemed to be breaking contact rather than attacking. The major factors that had brought about the battle remained—Sunnis were still facing the marines in Fallujah and Sadr's followers were still contesting Coalition attempts to reduce his influence in Iraq. But it seemed possible that the fighters in Abu Ghraib had lost too many men, as well as their will to stand up against American armor and firepower. Around midmorning, Colonel Ryan decided it was a good time to regroup and prepare for subsequent operations, so he called for a conference with his company commanders at Seitz.

Captain Munz returned to the logistics base accompanied by Sergeant Armstead's tank. Captains Allen and Perry were already there when Munz arrived. Colonel Ryan later remembered: "While we were meeting, we saw some black smoke plumes rising in the west. I had no situational awareness . . . so I sent out a section to investigate."[50] The source of those dark clouds smudging the horizon would become one of the most reported events of the Iraq conflict. The insurgents had not been withdrawing or going to ground in their homes but merely shifting to a more lucrative objective—an American supply convoy then making its way along Route Huskies. The 2d Battalion, 12th Cavalry's efforts over the past couple days had cleared portions of Abu Ghraib but had not destroyed the enemy or established control over the entire sprawling city. The urban area's size and population were both simply too large for the force at Colonel Ryan's disposal. That inability to secure the entire zone of action would ultimately allow the Iraqi opposition in Abu Ghraib to achieve Sheikh Hadithi's goal of taking American prisoners, but the insurgents would do so against a unit much less able to defend itself.

[50] Interv, Johnston with Ryan, 10 May 04.

GOOD FRIDAY AMBUSH

RICHARD E. KILLBLANE

An escorted fuel convoy runs the gauntlet of an ambush that far surpasses in size and ferocity anything yet encountered in the war.

Abu Ghraib—9 April 2004

On the evening of 8 April, Iraqi fighters demolished several bridges and overpasses south of the Iraqi capital while increasing the use of improvised explosive devices (IEDs) and small ambushes. These actions effectively severed the main supply routes from Coalition bases in Kuwait to Baghdad and points north and west. The insurgents, almost certainly Mahdi militia, apparently hoped to cut off fuel supplies to American units, primarily the 1st Cavalry Division then battling their brethren in Sadr City. They likely also wanted to impede the movement of U.S. troops to southern Iraq, where the Mahdis had seized control of several cities, including the important religious center of Najaf. Moqtada al-Sadr himself was leading operations in the latter location. As a side benefit, the interruption of logistics would impact Marine units fighting in Fallujah and thus put added pressure on the Coalition. The 13th Corps Support Command responded by arranging to deliver fuel from Logistics Support Area Anaconda, forty-five miles north of Baghdad, to the 1st Cavalry Division until the southern routes were reopened.[1] That decision would lead to one of the largest and most deadly convoy battles in the postconventional phase of the Iraq War.

Lt. Col. George G. Akin's 7th Transportation Battalion provided security for many of the convoys operating out of Anaconda. A Regular Army unit from Fort Bragg, North Carolina, it consisted of two transportation companies and an ordnance company. Once it arrived in Iraq, the 7th gained additional troops, including the 724th Transportation Company, a reserve outfit from

---

[1] Interv, Richard Killblane, U.S. Army Transportation School Historian, with Brig Gen (P) James Chambers, former CG, 13th Corps Support Command, 16 Oct 06, Historians files, U.S. Army Transportation School (USATS), Fort Eustis, Va.

Vehicles belonging to the 724th Transportation Company, most modified to serve as gun trucks, assemble for a precombat inspection at Logistics Support Area Anaconda on 9 April. The company provided armed escort for fuel tankers driven by American civilian contractors.

Bartonville, Illinois. While the normal mission of such units was to haul things, in the current war civilian contractors were doing most of that work and the logistics soldiers redirected their efforts to armed escort. That allowed armor, infantry, and military police outfits to remain focused on their primary combat roles. To handle the new duties, the transportation units fielded a mix of high mobility multipurpose wheeled vehicles (HMMWVs, or Humvees) and trucks with ring- or pintle-mounted heavy weapons—usually an M249 squad automatic weapon (SAW), the venerable M2 Browning .50-caliber machine gun, or an MK19 automatic grenade launcher. The battalion's maintenance shop, reinforced by Navy welders and dubbed the Skunk Werks, had added armor plate to many of these vehicles to give them additional protection for the mission.[2]

On the afternoon of 8 April, Capt. Jeffrey F. Smith's 724th Transportation Company received a mission to escort contractor-driven fuel trucks the next morning from Anaconda to Forward Operating Base Webster, located near al-Asad Airbase, about one hundred miles west of Baghdad. By midnight, as a result of the destruction of bridges earlier that evening, the destination changed to Camp Victory at the Baghdad International Airport. (Map 3) That represented a significant departure from the 724th's routine, as no one in the company had ever driven there. Since Smith's soldiers were unfamiliar with the route, the company commander asked for a guide. The battalion operations section tasked the 2632d Transportation Company, which assigned Sfc. Mark A. Hawley to accompany the convoy. After being awakened at 0130, Hawley

---

[2] Juliana Gittler, "Skunk Werks Armor Shop Helps Soldiers Through Better Protection for U.S. Vehicles," *Stars and Stripes Mideast Edition*, 31 October 2004, copy in Historians files, CMH.

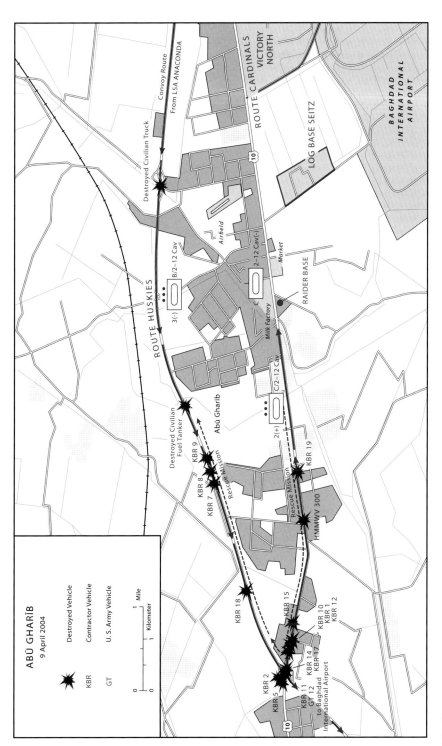

ABŪ GHARĪB
9 April 2004

Destroyed Vehicle
KBR   Contractor Vehicle
GT   U. S. Army Vehicle

0   1   Mile
0   1   Kilometer

Convoy Route
From LSA ANACONDA

ROUTE CARDINALS
VICTORY
NORTH

BAGHDAD
INTERNATIONAL
AIRPORT

Destroyed Civilian Truck

10

LOG BASE SEITZ

Airfield

B/2-12 Cav

ROUTE HUSKIES

3(-)

2-12 Cav(-)

Market

RAIDER BASE

Milk Factory

C/2-12 Cav

Destroyed Civilian
Fuel Tanker

Abū Gharīb

KBR 9

Rescue Mission

2(+)

KBR 8

KBR 7

KBR 19

Rescue Mission

HMMWV 300

KBR 18

KBR 15

KBR 10
KBR 1
KBR 12

KBR 2

KBR 14
GT 12   KBR 17

KBR 11
GT 12
to Baghdad
International Airport

KBR 5

10

MAP 3

learned he had orders to meet the 724th in the Anaconda staging area at 0700. The mission would be Sergeant Hawley's last trip before the 2362d, an Army National Guard unit based at San Bruno, California, departed Iraq for home.[3]

Captain Smith chose his 2d Platoon Leader, 1st Lt. Matthew R. Brown, to lead the convoy. Commissioned in military intelligence from the Reserve Officers Training Corps, the 27-year-old reserve officer was enjoying the challenge of active duty and considering a full-time career in the military. Since arriving in Iraq, Brown had formed a strong bond with his driver, Spec. Jeremy L. Church, a 25-year-old bartender and WalMart security guard from St. Louis, Missouri. The lieutenant brought Church to all the mission briefings, reasoning that if anything happened in the field his driver should be prepared to make decisions.[4]

Around 0130, Brown and his platoon sergeant, Sfc. Robert D. Groff, drew up a roster for the escort mission. The list included not only crews for the gun trucks, but also soldiers with small arms, known as shooters, to ride alongside the civilian contractors in the cabs of the fuel tankers. This represented the first time a convoy escort unit would employ the latter measure. The support command had resisted doing so in the past because it thought such a tactic would only encourage insurgents to target the civilian drivers. But attacks in recent days on several contractor convoys along the Baghdad-Fallujah highway led to the change. The 724th, in fact, had experienced its first enemy contact just two days earlier. The support command also provided military M915 five-ton tractors for this convoy in place of the contractor's usual Mercedes commercial haulers. The fuel itself would move in Army-provided green tanker trailers. Captain Smith also asked for air coverage along the route, and battalion headquarters forwarded the request up the chain of command.[5]

Brown and Groff's original plan called for splitting the fuel tankers into two separate convoys, each escorted in accordance with high-level policy requiring a ratio of one armed vehicle for every ten logistics trucks. In light of the recent ambushes, they now decided to combine the 19 contractor vehicles into a single convoy protected by 6 armed escorts: 2 M998 Humvees, 2 M931 five-ton tractors, 1 M923 five-ton cargo truck, and 1 M915 tractor. (*Table*) The latter

[3] Capt Jeffrey Smith, "Historical Narrative: 724th Transportation Company," n.d., Historians files, USATS; Sworn Statement, Sfc Mark A. Hawley, 14 Apr 04, 172d Corps Spt Grp Commander's Inquiry Regarding the 724th Transportation Company Hostile Engagement, Historians files, U.S. Army Center of Military History (CMH), Washington, D.C. (hereafter cited as Commander's Inquiry).

[4] Video, "Battlefield Diaries: Baghdad Convoy Attack," *Military Channel*, 2006; Interv, Killblane with Spec Jeremy L. Church, 14 Feb 07, Historians files, USATS.

[5] Interv, Killblane with Church, 14 Feb 07; Memo, Maj Mike W. Caraballo for Cdr, 172d Corps Spt Grp, 2 Aug 04, p. 2, Commander's Inquiry; S Sgt Paul L. Marsh and S Sgt Victor L. Febus, "On the Move with the 724th Transportation Company: Patriots in the Middle East," n.d., Historians files, USATS; Power Point Bfg, Col H. Gary Bunch, CO, 172d Corps Spt Cmd, to Kellogg, Brown & Root, 23 Feb 05, sub: Presentation of Collateral Investigation Results, p. 7, Historians files, CMH; Smith, "Historical Narrative."

Table—Fuel Convoy Composition, 9 April 2004

Vehicle Designation	Main Armament	Personnel (driver, passengers)
HMMWV 200	M249 SAW	Spec. Church, 1st Lt. Brown Sfc. Hawley, Sgt. Blankenship
HMMWV 26		Sfc. Adams, 1st Lt. Howard
Tanker 1		Nelson, Hamill
Tanker 2		Zimmerman
Tanker 3		Wood
Tanker 4		Tollison, S. Sgt. Hollingsworth
Tanker 5		Bradley
Gun Truck 160 (M915 five-ton)	M2 Browning Warlock Jammer	Spec. Row, Spec. McDermott
Tanker 6		Peterson, Pfc. Slaughter
Tanker 7		Hulett
Tanker 8		Johnson, Pfc. Maupin
Tanker 9		Parker
Tanker 10		Pfc. Goodrich
Gun Truck 102 (M931 five-ton)	M2 Browning	S. Sgt. Grage, Spec. Brown
Gun Truck 12 (M923 five-ton)	MK19	Spec. Bachman, Sgt. Watson
Tanker 11		Ross
Tanker 12		Sanchez, Sgt. Krause
Tanker 13		Stanley
Tanker 14		Stannard, Pfc. Walsh
Tanker 15		Bell
HMMWV 300	M249 SAW	Spec. Lamar, Sfc. Groff, Spec. Pelz
Tanker 16		Blackwood
Tanker 17		Brezovay
Bobtail 18		Fisher
Bobtail 19		Lester
Gun Truck 356 (M931 five-ton)	M2 Browning	Spec. Kirkpatrick, Spec. Bohm

Specialist Church and Lieutenant Brown of the 724th Transportation Company at an awards ceremony following their return from Iraq. Church received the Silver Star for bravery and initiative during the ambush that critically wounded Brown, his platoon leader.

carried a Warlock electronic jamming system to counter improvised explosive devices remotely detonated by radio signals.[6] The 644th Transportation Company, which would soon be operating in the area, added an armed M998 Humvee to the convoy to gain familiarity with the route, making a total of twenty-six vehicles and raising the escort ratio to one in three. But only a few of the gun vehicles were protected by any significant armor. Six of the twenty-three soldiers were shooters and would ride aboard contractor vehicles 4, 6, 8, 10, 12, and 14.[7] As an additional precaution, the 7th Transportation Battalion provided a double basic load of ammunition for all weapons. This package of security measures far exceeded those normally employed up to that point in the insurgency.[8] Despite those precautions, or perhaps in part due to the changes and the news of fighting breaking out across the country, many of the soldiers had a premonition of danger. For one gunner, though, all the extra ammunition provided "a warm and fuzzy feeling."[9]

---

[6] Clay Wilson, "Improvised Explosive Devices (IEDs) in Iraq: Effects and Countermeasures," *Congressional Research Service Report*, 10 February 2006, p. 4.

[7] Sworn Statement, Pfc Jeffrey Slaughter, 11 Apr 04, Commander's Inquiry.

[8] Bfg, Bunch, 23 Feb 05.

[9] Interv, Killblane with Church, 14 Feb 07; Video, "Battlefield Diaries."

The communications setup was bewildering at best. Three escort vehicles had military tactical radios with a range up to forty kilometers. Throughout the convoy, there was a mixed bag of short-range handheld radios, citizen's band radios, and movement tracking system devices. The latter provided text messaging via satellite as well as access to global positioning system data. Since the various systems could not communicate with each other, some vehicles had two or three pieces of communications equipment. Operation of the Warlock also could interfere with the signal of the tactical radios. This hodgepodge and the limitations of each type would make it difficult for the elements of the convoy to communicate effectively.[10]

The ninth of April was Good Friday and the first anniversary of the toppling of Saddam Hussein's statue and his regime in Baghdad. More important, on 11 April, the Shi'ites would celebrate a major religious holiday—Arbaeen, marking the end of forty days of mourning following the anniversary of the death of Hussein bin Ali, the grandson of the Prophet Mohammed. In the preceding days, hundreds of thousands of pilgrims would converge on the holy city of Karbala, where Ali had been martyred nearly fourteen centuries earlier. Al-Qaeda in Iraq had begun a campaign of terror attacks against Shi'ites during their holidays, and Sheik Hadithi, a Sunni cleric in Abu Ghraib, had called for large-scale operations to coincide with the week leading up to Arbaeen. While Lieutenant Brown was not aware of the latter specific threat, he realized the religious observance could heighten tensions and had already told his platoon to be prepared.[11]

At 0500, Brown arrived at the 7th Transportation Battalion's command post for an update on intelligence and operational developments. A nationwide system classified threat levels on major roads, with the color black indicating the greatest danger and signifying imminent or ongoing enemy contact. In such cases, the highway was to be avoided if at all possible. That morning Brown learned that the 49th Movement Control Battalion had coded the route to Baghdad International Airport as black.[12]

Thomas E. Hamill, the contractor convoy coordinator, reported for his initial briefing at 0600. The company's security adviser informed Hamill that all routes were closed, but he would check again to confirm.[13] Hamill next went to another office at Anaconda, where the contractor employees received their driving assignments for the day. Once that information was passed out, he gathered his nineteen vehicle operators to talk about the mission. Seventeen of them would be driving tankers. The remaining pair drove spare tractors (known

[10] Memo, Caraballo for Cdr, 172d Corps Spt Grp, 2 Aug 04, p. 3.
[11] Statement, Groff, 11 Apr 04; After Action Review (AAR), 2d Bn, 12th Cav, n.d., sub: The Holy Week Battle for Abu Ghraib, p. 4, Historians files, CMH; Sfc Doug Sample, "Helicopter Crew Killed," American Forces Press Service, 11 April 2004, copy in Historians files, CMH.
[12] Interv Sum, Maj Mike Caraballo with Spec Joseph Brown and Pfc Jeremy L. Church, 24 Apr 04; Sworn Statement, Sfc Robert D. Groff, 11 Apr 04, Commander's Inquiry.
[13] Thomas Hamill and Paul T. Brown, *Escape in Iraq; The Thomas Hamill Story* (Accokeek, Md.: Stoeger Publishing Co., 2004), p. 29; Video, "Battlefield Diaries."

as bobtails) that could take over a trailer in case one of the primary haulers broke down. After the meeting, the civilians climbed into their cabs, started their engines, and began their preoperation checks. About that time, Hamill learned that the route restrictions had been rescinded, though he sensed that the security adviser was still apprehensive.[14]

Lieutenant Brown received word of the reopening of the routes between Anaconda and Baghdad International Airport at 0900, though the convoy's departure time would still be delayed until 1100.[15] At 0954, due to a suspected IED along the route leading to the airport's south gate, the support command's chief of highway operations informed the 172d Corps Support Group operations chief that Brown's convoy would use the northern entrance. A minute later, the chief of highway operations contacted the 1st Cavalry Division for an update and learned that the route to the north gate had been the scene of intense fighting for the past two days. The chief dispatched an e-mail intended for the 49th Movement Control Battalion: "Sorry, it looks like [the route] is closed until further notice. I am trying to deconflict." The battalion, charged with disseminating route changes to units, never received the alert. Only later did the chief realize that he had sent the message to himself.[16]

Just before 1000, Lieutenant Brown assembled the 2d Platoon and the contract drivers for a brief.[17] Although most of it was standard stuff, there was one change to the rules of engagement. Given the uprising just launched by the Mahdi militia, anyone wearing the trademark colored head or armband and black clothing of a Sadrist fighter would be considered an insurgent and the soldiers were told to engage them without waiting to be fired upon first.[18] At the end, Sergeant Hawley reviewed the route to the airport's south gate. It was only then that the civilians learned they were going to Baghdad instead of Webster.[19] When the sergeant asked if anyone had questions, someone inquired: "Is that the route to the north gate?" Hawley replied in the negative. It was his turn to be surprised when Lieutenant Brown explained that they would be using the northern entrance. Hawley informed Brown that he could only vaguely remember his unit approaching the airport from that direction once.[20] Captain Smith, Lieutenant Brown, and Sergeant Hawley left the group to verify the route change. Upon receiving confirmation via radio,

---

[14] Hamill and Brown, *Escape in Iraq*, pp. 29–30.

[15] Statement, Groff, 11 Apr 04.

[16] Interv Sum, Caraballo with Lt Col James Carroll, 28 Apr 04, and E-mail, Lt Col James Carroll, 13th Corps Spt Cmd Ch of Opns, to Lt Col James Carroll, 9 Apr 04, both in Commander's Inquiry; T. Christian Miller, "U.S.: Iraq Convoy Was Sent out Despite Threat," *Los Angeles Times*, 3 September 2007, copy in Historians files, CMH.

[17] Written Statement, Spec Craig V. McDermott, 22 Apr 04, Commander's Inquiry.

[18] Interv Sum, Maj Mike Caraballo with 1st Lt Matthew R. Brown, 13 May 04, Commander's Inquiry.

[19] Hamill and Brown, *Escape in Iraq*, p. 31.

[20] Statement, Hawley, 14 Apr 04.

Hawley asked for and received from battalion headquarters the highway exit number for the road leading to the north gate. He then briefed the revised route to the assembled contract drivers and soldiers, drawing it out in the sand and gravel of the staging area. The trip, he explained, would take about two hours. While the 2d Platoon made its preparations, another convoy escorted by an Air Force gun truck company had departed on a similar mission but had soon turned back due to radio problems. That twist of fate would make Brown's unit the first that morning to roll down the route to Baghdad International Airport.

At 1015, the convoy exited the base's front gate heading west. Brown's vehicle led the way, with Hawley aboard to help navigate and Sgt. Terry Blankenship manning a pintle-mounted SAW. The 644th Transportation Company Humvee, carrying 1st Lt. Gregory Howard and Sfc. Darrell C. Adams, occupied the second position. Hamill followed in a tractor driven by Nelson Howell, with four more fuelers in trace. Next came the converted M915 tractor operated by Spec. Dustin L. Row and bearing a .50-caliber machine gun crewed by Spec. Craig V. McDermott. A typical Skunk Werks product, the doors had add-on steel plate and no glass so occupants could easily shoot out. There was another steel plate across the back of the cab and one mounted above the windshield to help protect the gunner standing up through the roof. After another five tankers, a pair of escorts occupied the middle of the convoy. S. Sgt. Donald C. Grage drove an armed five-ton carrying Spec. Jacob P. Brown and his M2 Browning, while Spec. Michael J. Bachman's gun truck bore Sgt. Bryan C. Watson and a ring-mounted MK19 grenade launcher. Five more fuelers preceded Sergeant Groff's Humvee, driven by Spec. Karon G. Lamar and mounting Spec. Patrick L. Pelz's M249 SAW. The final two tank trucks and the two spare tractors followed. Spec. Shawn E. Kirkpatrick's M931 five-ton truck provided rear security, with Spec. Matthew W. Bohm manning a .50-caliber machine gun.[21]

The plan was to maintain one hundred meters between vehicles, so that even a daisy-chained series of IEDs would likely hit only one. But that stretched the convoy out over two miles of road, resulting in spotty radio contact between Brown and Groff. Communications would be degraded even more when the tail vehicle's antennae hit an overpass and broke off.[22]

The first part of the trip through the city of Taji, eighteen miles north of Baghdad, passed without incident. Farther south, the long line of vehicles pulled onto Route Huskies, a six-lane freeway with a median strip and guardrails on either side and down the middle. It was known as IED Alley for the frequency of such incidents there (although a number of other roads around the country would earn the same name for a similar reason). Located on the outskirts of northwest Baghdad,

---

[21] Interv Sum, Caraballo with Spec Shawn E. Kirkpatrick, 13 May 04; Order of March Diagram, n.d., Commander's Inquiry.

[22] Marsh, "On the Move"; Video, "Battlefield Diaries"; Commander's Inquiry, p. 3.

the highway went west through the suburb of Abu Ghraib. The predominantly Sunni town had been the scene of fierce fighting over the past two days, as Mahdi militiamen attacked Americans to relieve pressure on their brethren in Sadr City and Sunnis did the same to assist their comrades in Fallujah.

As the convoy drove along Huskies, the soldiers and contractors saw fewer and fewer Iraqis in the area and the rare cars on the road began to pull off as the Americans approached. Soon, the leading elements of the convoy began dodging rocks, mounds of garbage, blocks of concrete, and tires—all placed in the road to slow them down. These were signs of a potential ambush, although they also might have been a result of the ongoing fighting in the area. Then Church and Brown saw a burned-out stake-bed truck just beyond the next overpass. It was painted white and an obvious remnant of an earlier contractor convoy. In the distance, the wind blew a thick black smudge across the highway. Brown announced: "Hey, Sergeant Hawley, I think we're in trouble here." The guide responded, "Yes, sir, I think we're going to get hit."[23] Church slowed down as he passed the hulk. The convoy followed, everyone's adrenalin pumping as they braced for trouble. It was around 1230, and the convoy was less than two kilometers from its destination. A turnoff from Huskies at that point went due south toward the airport but led right through the heart of Abu Ghraib. Instead, the planned route continued west for another eight kilometers on Huskies, at which point the convoy would take an exit ramp onto Route Cardinals. That four-lane road headed back east, roughly paralleling Huskies and skirting the south side of Abu Ghraib for six kilometers before the turnoff to the airport. While the most direct route would have been dangerous, the additional kilometers would prove to be a gauntlet through hell.

Less than a mile past the direct route to the airport, the lead Humvee passed three M1A2 Abrams from Company B, 2d Battalion, 12th Cavalry. The tanks were on the other side of the road firing south into Abu Ghraib. One of the armor soldiers waved at the trucks to go back. Brown either misinterpreted the signal or elected to press on, making what seemed a sound choice based on past experience. Prior ambushes consisted of one or a few IEDs or perhaps a handful of men inaccurately firing small arms. The best course of action was always to race through the short kill zone: speed (such as it was for a fully loaded tanker) enhanced security. In that typical situation, trying to stop and turn around a long, lumbering column of soft vehicles would be an invitation to disaster. But nothing about this day was turning out to be ordinary.[24]

A mile farther down the road, as the Americans emerged from another underpass, they could make out the source of the dark smoke, a contractor tanker on fire several hundred meters ahead. Then tanker 2 reported that it

[23] Video, "Battlefield Diaries;" Interv, Killblane with Church, 14 Feb 07; Lisa Burgess, "I'm Just Glad I Didn't Get Shot," *Stars and Stripes European Edition*, 14 June 2005, copy in Historians files, CMH.

[24] Video, "Battlefield Diaries"; Interv, Killblane with Church, 14 Feb 07.

An M1A2 Abrams from Company B, 2d Battalion, 12th Cavalry, engages insurgents near Route Huskies on the northeastern outskirts of Abu Ghraib. The presence of the tank was a signpost of trouble ahead for the fuel convoy.

had engine trouble. Whether that was a coincidence or a result of enemy fire no one ever knew, but within moments the soldiers and drivers at the front of the column heard the impact of gunshots striking their vehicles. Brown warned the convoy over the radio: "Small arms fire to the left." As the column drove deeper into the ambush site, rifle fire from both sides of the route increased in volume and everyone was on the net reporting it. Hamill reminded his drivers to step on the gas and keep going.[25] Sergeant Watson, near the center of the convoy, shot back with his MK19, but the drifting smoke made it hard to pick out targets.[26]

The driver of tanker 2, Tommy K. Zimmerman, radioed Hamill that his truck was continuing to lose power. The standard procedure was to have a gun truck secure the disabled vehicle until a bobtail could tow it to safety. Hamill contacted Brown: "I've got a truck that is breaking down. We need to get gun support there with him." One of the bobtails in the rear broke into the net and reported that it was taking gunfire—the entire column was now in the kill zone, one that far exceeded anything anyone had yet experienced. It was quickly becoming apparent to both leaders in the convoy that their situation was growing worse by the moment. Hamill refocused immediately on the safety of his men and told Brown: "We need to get this man picked up. Get the gun truck to pick him up. Let's leave the truck, just get the men."[27]

Just before the lieutenant reached the burning contractor tanker from a previous convoy, he saw a break in the guardrail for an off-ramp to the frontage road paralleling the freeway. He told his driver to take it and exclaimed into

[25] E-mail, Nelson Howell to Maj Mike Caraballo, 27 May 04, Commander's Inquiry.
[26] Marsh, "On the Move."
[27] Hamill and Brown, *Escape in Iraq*, p. 37.

the handset: "There's a truck on fire up ahead, we've gotta get off this road."[28] Church thought the blaze had been set to divert the convoy off the main highway and believed he could get around this new obstacle without turning off; but he obeyed the order. Meanwhile, tanker 2 was slowing down and others began to pass it, following the standard practice of speeding through a kill zone. In the resulting confusion, heightened by incoming fire and blowing smoke, the Humvee from the 644th Transportation Company and three of the first four tankers followed Brown. Tanker 2 and the remainder of the convoy continued down the main route.[29]

Rounds were pummeling Brown's Humvee, sounding like rain hitting a tin roof. Everyone, including the driver, returned fire out the sides of the vehicle while Sergeant Blankenship replied with long bursts from his SAW. Thirty meters in front of Church, a civilian sport utility vehicle accelerated onto the frontage road. Moments later, an IED exploded, killing the Iraqi driver.[30] Church was struck briefly by the irony of an enemy weapon claiming one of its own. With the convoy descending into chaos, everyone was shouting into their radios. Pfc. Jarob Walsh, riding shotgun on tanker 14, heard someone report: "The LT's truck just blew up and I don't know where to go or what to do!" Walsh looked at his driver, Raymond T. Stannard, and said: "It's about to get bad."[31]

Hamill picked up the movement-tracking system and began typing out a warning that would go out to other convoys. Before he could complete the message, however, a bullet struck his right forearm and the device tumbled onto the floorboard. Bleeding profusely from a large gash, he grasped the nearest thing at hand, a spare sock from his duffel, and used it to bind the wound. He then handed the radio microphone to his driver, Nelson Howell. The vehicle also sustained damage during the fusillade and began losing speed. Other trucks on the highway and the frontage road began to pass.[32]

Another few hundred meters beyond the turnoff to the frontage road, the highway curved slightly to the right. Houses filled the area on the southern side of the freeway and the fire seemed to intensify in proximity to the dwellings. To the men in the convoy, it seemed that hundreds of insurgents were firing rifles and rocket-propelled grenades (RPGs) and triggering IEDs. Although it was hard to tell for sure in the blur of intense combat, the enemy also may have employed heavy machine guns and mortars. The large tankers made easy targets, and all were soon leaking fuel, appearing to Hamill like "sprinkler systems wetting down the pavement." His driver, Howell, likened

---

[28] Marsh, "On the Move."

[29] AAR, 172d Corps Spt Grp, 9 Apr 04, sub: Good Friday Ambush—724th Transportation/ KBR–9 April 2004, Historians files, CMH.

[30] Interv, Killblane with Church, 14 Feb 07; E-mail, Howell to Caraballo, 27 May 04.

[31] E-mail, Pfc Jarob Walsh to Maj Mike Caraballo, 12 May 04, sub: 2d E-mail, Here Is My Story on the Ambush April 9th, Commander's Inquiry.

[32] Hamill and Brown, *Escape in Iraq*, p. 38.

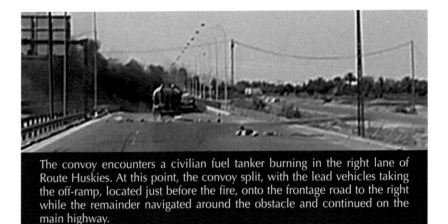

The convoy encounters a civilian fuel tanker burning in the right lane of Route Huskies. At this point, the convoy split, with the lead vehicles taking the off-ramp, located just before the fire, onto the frontage road to the right while the remainder navigated around the obstacle and continued on the main highway.

them to a "pasta strainer."[33] The asphalt grew more slippery with each passing vehicle, making the trucks slide "like hogs on ice."[34] Damage to engines and brake lines made it even more difficult to control the big rigs. Even the escort vehicles had trouble, especially when drivers were firing out the window with one hand and steering around obstacles with the other. Smoke from a growing number of fires also reduced visibility. All these factors posed a dilemma to each driver: slow down to avoid an accident or speed up to evade insurgent fire?

Tankers 6 through 10 were still arrayed in column behind Row and McDermott's gun truck. This group began to surge past now-crawling tanker 2 to draw even with the vehicles on the access road. Tanker 8, driven by Tony E. Johnson, with Pfc. Keith M. Maupin riding shotgun, took a number of hits. It lost power, dropped back in the column, burst into flames, then swerved to the right, plowed through the guardrail, bounded across a low ditch and the frontage road, and crashed into the wall surrounding a small compound. Johnson died in the crash or fire, while Maupin managed to escape the wreck, only to be captured by insurgents.[35]

Another tanker, probably 7, fishtailed on the slick pavement, careened onto its side, and came to rest in the median strip, where it exploded. The driver, Steve Hulett, managed to escape the cab but died later from multiple gunshot wounds. An RPG from the left side of the road slammed into a fueler, probably 9, when it stopped. Driver Jeffrey Parker might have been trying to help Hulett, but he also would die from a bullet wound.[36] When that vehicle burst into a ball of fire, it shot flaming liquid across the freeway and the frontage road. S. Sgt. Clearthur

[33] E-mail, Howell to Caraballo, 27 May 04.
[34] Hamill and Brown, *Escape in Iraq*, p. 40.
[35] Marsh, "On the Move"; Bfg, Bunch, 23 Feb 05, p. 16.
[36] Bfg, Bunch, 23 Feb 05, p. 16.

A tanker hit by enemy fire continues along Route Huskies with fuel pouring out of holes in its side. A gun truck is visible ahead through the smoke, while a crashed tanker burns to the right of the highway. The slippery asphalt became a skating rink for the lumbering trucks, adding to their woes in the midst of the deadly ambush.

Hollingsworth Jr., riding shotgun in tanker 4 on the frontage road, felt the blast "like a sledge hammer hitting me in the head."[37] Moments later, a round slammed into the doorframe near Hollingsworth, sending pieces of metal into his cheek and nose. His fueler, which had not suffered fatal damage, continued rolling.[38]

Farther along on the frontage road, Specialist Church was concentrating on avoiding obstacles the insurgents had put on the pavement. Like all the other drivers in the convoy, he was steering with one hand and firing his rifle out the window with the other. A bullet smashed through the windshield, striking Brown in the helmet. Shards of glass hit Church in the face, causing him to reflexively draw his head back. Just then, another IED exploded alongside the Humvee. The blast and debris entered the open windows and lashed Sergeant Hawley's face but whizzed past in front of Church, momentarily protected by his reaction to the bullet.[39]

Brown had not fared so well. Reaching up to his head in response to pain, his fingers explored his face and felt skin hanging over his left eye. The blunt

[37] Marsh, "On the Move"; Video, "Battlefield Diaries."
[38] Interv Sum, Caraballo with Rick Tollison, 28 May 04, and with S Sgt Clearthur Hollingsworth Jr., 26 Apr 04, both in Commander's Inquiry.
[39] Statement, Hawley, 14 Apr 04.

force of the round's impact had blown his helmet into the back seat, peeling his scalp from just above his left eye to below his left ear. His hand recoiled in momentary shock and he turned toward Church, wondering to himself, "Is everything else okay?" Church saw the weird look on the lieutenant's face, as if he wanted help but could not speak. Blood was running down from the wound. While still driving with one hand, the specialist popped open his first aid pouch, pulled out a field dressing, ripped open the wrapping with his teeth, and handed it to Brown, telling him to place it over his left eye.

Church resumed firing out the window while he encouraged his platoon leader to remain conscious. He told Brown to close his ballistic window to prevent further injury; but when the lieutenant failed to respond, Church reached over and did it. Just then, another IED detonated, blowing out the right front tire. The specialist pushed ahead on the three good tires, worried now about getting his lieutenant medical attention. After a few minutes, Brown blacked out. That was a "reality check" for the driver, who realized: "It's now up to me to get these guys through here." Knowing what he had to do, he relaxed and focused his thoughts on the mission at hand. Blankenship remained "rock solid," keeping up a steady fire throughout. Hawley was on the radio trying to call in the ambush and request air support, but he could not get reliable contact with anyone. The damaged Humvee now was reduced to about fifteen miles per hour.[40]

After that last IED, the surrounding area opened up with fewer buildings. Small-arms fire slackened. Church pulled out another battle dressing and again tore open the package with his teeth, then placed it over Brown's wound with his right hand. As the Humvee approached the next overpass, the frontage road paralleled the exit ramp and intersected with Route Cardinals. Hawley instructed the driver to turn left and onto the bridge, heading back east to the airport. The 644th Humvee and tankers 3 and 4 followed. At this point, the fire dwindled away and Church thought to himself: "It's finally over."[41] Hawley, on the other hand, knew there were several miles to go yet and ammunition was running low. He "was starting to think that we weren't going to make it."[42]

The middle of the column was still under heavy attack on Route Huskies. Specialist Row's M915 had its mirrors and windows blown out as rounds peppered it. McDermott blazed away with his .50-caliber Browning, piling spent cartridges all around his feet and killing at least two insurgents while Row fired his rifle out the window one-handed.[43] The driver didn't think he would make it and expected any moment to feel the sting of a bullet. He leaned more and more to his right to get what little protection he could from the body

[40] Award Citation for Silver Star for Spec Jeremy L. Church, n.d., Historians files, USATS; Marsh, "On the Move"; Video, "Battlefield Diaries"; Interv, Killblane with Church, 14 Feb 07; Statement, Hawley, 14 Apr 04; Burgess, "Just Glad."

[41] Award Citation for Church, n.d.; Marsh, "On the Move"; Video, "Battlefield Diaries."

[42] Statement, Hawley, 14 Apr 04.

[43] Statement, McDermott, 22 Apr 04.

of the cab. Just ahead of him, tanker 5, operated by William E. Bradley, had sustained many hits. As the rig took the exit to Route Cardinals and tried to negotiate the curving ramp, it slid off the narrow pavement and overturned in the ditch separating the ramp from the frontage road. The impact smashed the roof of the cab nearly flat, and the load burst into flames. Specialist Row, following behind in his M915, found the fuel-slicked ramp "like driving on ice."[44] He almost lost control of the gun truck and skidded to a stop, then drove onto the overpass and headed for the airport. Bill Peterson, driving tanker 6, had to turn on his wipers to clear the fuel off his windshield. His shooter, Pfc. Jeffrey Slaughter, kept up a heavy rate of fire with his SAW. Tankers 6 and 10, the only survivors of the second five, made it to the exit as well and negotiated the blowing smoke and slippery road to make it onto Cardinals. Jack Montague's 10 did not go far, however, before enemy fire destroyed it. His shooter, Pfc. Gregory R. Goodrich, escaped alive; but Montague apparently did not.

The remainder of the column was losing all semblance of order as damaged vehicles slowed and others sped around them in hopes of getting through the kill zone. Sergeant Grage's gun truck, one of two in the very middle of the convoy, came up on tanker 2, which was barely crawling forward. He moved in behind it and began pushing while his gunner, Specialist Brown, fought back with his .50-caliber machine gun.

As Grage attended to the stricken tanker, Specialist Bachman drove his gun truck onward to keep the rest of the column moving. Sergeant Watson fired off a box of MK19 rounds, used his M16 till it was empty, and then reloaded the grenade launcher. Bachman got hit in the neck but was able to keep driving. A bullet hit Watson, and the driver tried to help him tie off a field dressing as they kept moving. Distracted amid the swirling smoke, Bachman missed the exit to Cardinals and continued on the freeway. Tanker 11 blindly followed, running on flat tires and pockmarked by gunfire. Finally, Bachman realized that the rest of the convoy must have turned off and that he was alone except for tanker 11. When he saw the road ahead blocked with a pile of guardrails, he was loathe to go around and risk being forced toward an IED, so he drove right over and went airborne for a moment. Soon after, the two vehicles were free of the ambush and drove on for several miles unmolested. They eventually ended up on another main supply route heading southeast and came upon a military police unit not far from the west gate of Baghdad International Airport. The soldiers and the civilian were soon on a medical evacuation helicopter—their ordeal was over.[45]

Tanker 13 proved to be one of the lucky ones, making it onto the overpass and Cardinals with only minor damage. Riding shotgun on tanker 14, Specialist

---

[44] Hamill, *Escape in Iraq*, p. 41; Statement, Spec Dustin L. Row, n.d., Commander's Inquiry.

[45] AAR, "Good Friday Ambush–724th Transportation/KBR–9 April 2004"; Interv Sum, Caraballo with Spec Michael Bachman, 14 May 04, Commander's Inquiry; Miller, "Iraq Convoy."

Walsh was astonished as the fuelers around him on Route Huskies burned and exploded: "It really shook me up . . . it was just like something you would see in the movies."[46] But his driver, Stannard, who had been a machine gunner in the Marines, was impressed by Walsh's calmness as the soldier traded fire with the insurgents.[47] They drove past Maupin's flaming truck and the rig on its side in the median. As they neared another overturned fueler on the right, they saw a man lying prone, raising his head up to watch them. Walsh propped his rifle on the side mirror of his truck and took aim, thinking it was an insurgent intending to blow them up as they passed. Then he noticed the man was holding up something in his left hand. The soldier assumed it was a detonator, and his heart was pounding hard; but he still held his fire. Only as they came abreast did Walsh recognize that it was an American holding up his identification card. It was too late at that point—Stannard could not stop the heavy rig in time to help.[48] Gun trucks and bobtails were supposed to take care of stranded vehicles, in any case, and a stationary tanker would have been a sitting duck.

Soon after, as Walsh and Stannard approached the exit to Route Cardinals, they came up on a truck traveling about twenty miles per hour with its trailer on fire. They slowed down to help and saw it was Hamill and Howell. At that moment, Hamill's truck shook violently from the explosion of an RPG but managed to keep moving forward. Stannard passed him, negotiated the slippery freeway off-ramp, and turned onto the overpass. Then a rocket struck the truck and it rolled onto its passenger side and up against the bridge railing. Stannard tumbled down on Walsh, who used the butt of his rifle to break out the windshield so the driver could crawl out. Stannard tried to pull out the soldier by his helmet, but the seatbelt and a knee wedged in the wreckage held the shooter in place. The two men struggled, the civilian still attempting to rescue his companion and the soldier yelling for him to take cover before he got hit. Finally, Walsh worked free. As small-arms fire swept across the overpass, both low-crawled away from the wreckage in different directions.[49]

Hamill's tractor had slowed to ten miles an hour or less as it fishtailed while climbing the frontage road ramp to Route Cardinals. Another tanker, probably 15, passed them on the main freeway ramp and made the turn onto the overpass. Hamill and Howell followed, passing Stannard's overturned rig on the bridge. As they did so, the fueler that was racing ahead of them down Cardinals exploded and shot flames high into the air. Hamill's stricken vehicle was moving so slowly that Walsh, hobbling with a foot wound, was able to run up, jump on the passenger-side running board, and wrap his arm around the mirror. The trailer, with locked brakes and damaged tires, dragged behind the

[46] E-mail, Walsh to Caraballo, 12 May 04.
[47] Interv Sum, Caraballo with Raymond T. Stannard, 21 May 04, Commander's Inquiry.
[48] E-mail, Walsh to Caraballo, 12 May 04. In his later testimony, Walsh assumed that it was Tommy Hamill.
[49] Ibid.

cab "like an anchor"; only the slickness of the fuel-covered pavement allowed any forward progress at all. Walsh yelled over the din that they needed to drop the trailer, but Hamill thought it would be suicidal to get out of the cab to disconnect it.[50]

Specialist Walsh began firing at the insurgents from his exposed spot on the running board from the moment he leaped onto the cab. Unable to aim with one hand from his precarious perch, he clambered up onto the hood of the slow-moving rig and assumed a prone position. As the truck approached a blazing tanker sitting on the side of the highway, Hamill and Howell feared that their own leaking trailer would probably catch fire. Both men also realized their truck was about to quit anyway, so Howell braked to a halt. When it stopped, Walsh rolled off the hood onto the pavement and assumed a prone firing position.[51]

The ordeal continued for the vehicles still on Route Huskies. Sergeant Groff's Humvee was under fire and rocked by an IED blast. Moments later, Specialist Pelz felt like he was smacked hard in the back. He called out that he was hit, dropped down inside the protective box of his turret, and checked for blood but realized the bullet had hit the armored plate in his vest. Shaking it off, he stood back up and got his machine gun in action again.

At the first word that tanker 2 was experiencing difficulty, Steven Fisher in bobtail 18 had sped up and moved forward in the column to assist per standard procedure. He had just passed Groff's Humvee, twenty-first in the original line of march, when enemy fire disabled the tractor or its driver and it came to a halt on the right shoulder of Huskies short of the overpass. Specialist Lamar pulled over as Fisher climbed down from his cab. The civilian driver, his left side drenched in blood from a wound in his upper arm, seemed dazed and uncertain what to do, so Groff got out and pushed him into the back seat of the Humvee while Lamar and Pelz laid down covering fire. The escort vehicle got moving again, but Groff found it hard to see where they were going with the windshield smeared with fuel.[52]

Tanker 12, driven by Edward V. Sanchez, had been hit hard and fallen back in the column. The driver was shot in the buttocks, and the vehicle's radiator was failing. His shooter, Sgt. Elmer C. Krause, struggled to clear his jammed rifle. As Sanchez navigated in pain along the smoky freeway, he glimpsed a contract driver kneeling near his stricken vehicle, radio in hand, almost certainly the same man Stannard and Walsh had passed moments earlier. Jackie Lester, driving bobtail 19, was close behind. He saw no one on the ground along the smoky road but heard a voice on the radio screaming at

---

[50] Ibid.; Hamill and Brown, *Escape in Iraq*, pp. 41–42. Hamill's published account misidentifies the soldier, but it was Walsh.

[51] Ibid.

[52] Statement, Groff, 11 Apr 04. Statement, Spec Patrick Pelz, 26 Apr 04; Interv Sum, Caraballo with Jackie Lester, 13 May 04; both in Commander's Inquiry.

him: "Jack, you bastard, come back!" He had no idea where the man was or how to get to him and didn't know how to respond. "I couldn't handle that. I didn't want to answer. I didn't want to tell him, 'I can't help you.'" As the truck drove by, the last hope of the contractor disappeared in its wake.[53]

Up ahead, Sergeant Grage's gun truck was still pushing tanker 2. The slow-moving pair took a beating. The gun truck's radiator began to fail, rounds smashed the windows, and fuel from the trailer sprayed all over. The pair of tankers that had been near the end of the original column passed them and took the exit toward Cardinals. James Blackwood, driving 16, navigated through the hazards of spilled fuel and wrecked vehicles littering the ramp and overpass. Michael Brezovay in 17 was not so lucky. He let off the gas pedal to slow down going up the ramp; but he lost control making the turn, and his rig slammed into Stannard's overturned tanker. Brezovay's load burst into flames, and he jumped from the cab. He spotted Stannard nearby, and the two drivers joined up and crawled away from the tangled wreckage.[54]

Sanchez was the next one to drive past Grage and his gun truck pushing tanker 2. When Sanchez saw the exit to Cardinals, he thought it would lead to safety, but the enemy fire only intensified as his rig climbed the ramp and made the left turn onto the overpass. He heard what he thought was a heavy-caliber machine gun firing, and the vehicle shook each time a round hit it. His front tires were now shot out, and he slowed even more. As tanker 12 passed Stannard, the stranded driver saw his chance, leapt up, ran to the vehicle, and jumped on the driver-side running board. Brezovay did the same on the passenger side. Their rescue was short lived, as the fueler caught fire and ground to a halt on Cardinals. The two civilians bailed off the cab, but Sanchez briefly got his feet hung up in the steering wheel as he tried to climb out the window while bullets smacked around him. Krause was hit as he tried to follow, and the tractor was soon engulfed in flames. The three drivers crawled along the exposed pavement to get away from the burning hulk.[55]

Grage's gun truck got the dying rig most of the way up the ramp but lost all traction on the fuel-slicked incline and could go no farther. As Grage backed off from the stalled fueler, Lester's bobtail and the tail-end gun truck driven by Specialist Kirkpatrick came up alongside. All four vehicles were

---

[53] T. Christian Miller, "Iraq: Halliburton Convoy Unprepared for Last, Fatal Run," *Los Angeles Times*, 26 March 2005, copy in Historians files, USATS; Interv Sum, Caraballo with Edward V. Sanchez Jr., 28 May 04, Commander's Inquiry; Testimony, Edward V. Sanchez, Former KBR/Halliburton Employee, Before Senate Democratic Policy Committee, sub: An Oversight Hearing on Accountability of Contracting Abuses in Iraq, 18 Sep 06, Historians files, CMH.

[54] Interv Sum, Caraballo with Michael Brezovay, 20 May 04, Commander's Inquiry.

[55] Sanchez's congressional testimony was that Goodrich was his shooter and escaped from the cab with him, but all the witness statements much closer to the event show that it was Krause and that he did not make it out of the cab. Testimony, Sanchez, 18 Sep 06. Interv Sums, Caraballo with Sanchez, 28 May 04; with Brown and Church, 24 Apr 04; with Stannard, 21 May 04; with Brezovay, 20 May 04.

now stopped on the exit ramp. Both Kirkpatrick and Lester yelled at tanker 2's driver, Zimmerman, who seemed stunned as he methodically tried to gather his personal gear from his cab. The urgency of the moment grew more apparent when Kirkpatrick's gunner, Specialist Bohm, killed an insurgent toting an RPG launcher.[56] Finally, Zimmerman climbed into Lester's cab and the bobtail took off. The two gun trucks made the left turn onto the overpass soon after. Groff's Humvee took the exit around the same time.

Those were the last elements of the convoy to make it onto Route Cardinals. Of the twenty-six vehicles that had left Anaconda that morning, only fourteen had made it through the trial by fire along Huskies. That included all seven military escorts, which were smaller targets than the tankers and were protected by some level of armor and firepower. Eleven of the seventeen tankers and one of the two bobtails now littered the freeway, the exit ramp, and the overpass. Of the four men whose vehicles had never made it off Huskies, one was already dead and the others would not make it back alive to friendly hands. Four others already had died on or near the overpass. Seven men—Howell and Hamill from tanker 1, Goodrich from 10, Sanchez from 12, Stannard and Walsh from 14, and Brezovay from 17—were stranded in that area. The ordeal of the survivors, whether mobile or on foot, was far from over.

Specialist Church, driving the lead vehicle in the convoy, had been the first to head down Cardinals. Although he had thought the worst of the ambush was over once he made it onto the overpass, he discovered that was not the case. The fire resumed and if anything was more intense as he drove east on the four-lane divided highway. The entire area already had been stirred up by the fighting of the past few days. In addition, Cardinals was roughly parallel to Huskies and only several hundred meters or less away from it for much of its length. It was easy for insurgents to make their way from one road to the other and take a second crack at the American convoy.

The badly damaged Humvee made slow progress as the enemy attacked with small arms and RPGs. Sergeant Blankenship swung his SAW from side to side as he saw targets, taking out two fighters in white robes with rocket launchers and hosing down a building that seemed to be the source of a lot of fire. Church and Hawley engaged with their rifles out the windows. Danny Wood (tanker 3), Rick Tollison (tanker 4), and the 644th Humvee were right behind them.[57] An RPG had hit Wood's cab and he was desperate to get out of the kill zone, at one point purposely bumping a slow-moving Humvee to get it to accelerate. Tollison thought of Cardinals as "death alley" due to the level of incoming fire.[58] His wounded shooter, Sergeant Hollingsworth, managed to return fire despite the cuts to his face. It took about fifteen

---

[56] Interv Sum, Caraballo with Kirkpatrick, 13 May 04.

[57] Statement, McDermott, 22 Apr 04. This contains the only reference to the 644th Humvee during the course of the ambush.

[58] Interv Sum, Caraballo with Rick Tollison, 28 May 04, Commander's Inquiry.

minutes to cover a couple of miles, but then the soldiers saw an Abrams tank and a concertina barrier in the road ahead. They were approaching the Bilady Dairy Factory, located on the northwestern corner of the Abu Ghraib market and the scene of heavy fighting for the last couple of days. Capt. Aaron J. Munz's Company C, 2d Battalion, 12th Cavalry, had occupied the site during the night of 8 April.[59]

S. Sgt. Thomas J. Armstrong's Abrams and three Humvees from Sfc. Michael A. Klein's 2d Platoon were securing the checkpoint in front of the dairy. As Church drove toward them, the cavalry troopers aimed in on him, being cautious in the wake of recent reports of insurgents stealing five Humvees from the Anaconda base. After a few seconds, however, the soldiers could see that the vehicle's occupants were Americans. When the Humvee halted at the barrier, Sergeant Hawley jumped out and pulled back the concertina wire and motioned Church, Wood, Tollison, and the 644th Humvee forward. Guides led the tankers the few hundred meters into a safe area inside the dairy compound while Church's Humvee remained near the checkpoint for the time being. Aided by one of Munz's men, S. Sgt. Donavan D. Simpson, Church carried Lieutenant Brown to a vehicle for evacuation to an aid station.[60] Hawley made a report of the ambush and tried unsuccessfully to get air support while Blankenship kept his weapon trained out over the concertina and attempted to raise Sergeant Groff on the radio.

In the next few minutes, tankers 6 and 13 pulled into the compound. As they arrived, an insurgent mortar round landed and set fire to a pool of fuel.[61] While some of the cavalry and convoy soldiers put out the blaze, 1st Sgt. Charles Q. Taylor's medics—Pvt. Mark D. Meaney, Pfc. Ronald J. Kapture, Spec. Justin B. Onwordi, and Sgt. Casey J. Blanchette—started treating the wounded convoy soldiers and contract drivers.[62] The men of Company C thought the civilians looked shaken by their experience, while the contractors felt the soldiers had no idea what the convoy had been through. Danny Wood was amazed when one soldier asked him where his spill kit was so he could deal with the fuel leaking from his shot-up tanker.[63] Sergeant Klein, accompanied by Sergeants Mehall and Simpson's Humvees and Sfc. Christopher H. Kowalewski's M2A3 Bradley, sortied from the dairy to mount a rescue attempt for the remainder of

---

[59] E-mail, Lt Col John T. Ryan to Richard E. Killblane, 8 Jan 07, Historians files, USATS; Smith, "Historical Narrative."

[60] Sworn Statement, Sfc Michael A. Klein, Co C, 2d Bn, 12th Cav, 13 Apr 04, Historians files, CMH.

[61] Interv Sum, Caraballo with Tollison, 28 May 04; Interv Sum, Caraballo with Danny Wood, 28 May 04, Commander's Inquiry.

[62] "Rescue of the 724th Trans—9 April 2004," Extract from Task Force 2-12 Cav Draft History, Historians files, USATS; Award Citation for Church, n.d.; AAR, 2d Bn, 12th Cav, n.d.; Award Citation for Silver Star for 1st Sgt Charles Q. Taylor, n.d., Historians files, USATS; Marsh, "On the Move"; Video, "Battlefield Diaries."

[63] "Rescue of the 724th Trans"; AAR, 2d Bn, 12th Cav; Church Citation; Interv, Killblane with Church, 14 Feb 07; Interv Sum, Caraballo with Wood, 28 May 04; Marsh, "On the Move"; Video, "Battlefield Diaries."

the convoy. This would be the first external assistance the beleaguered group received. Specialist Church volunteered to go along.

The remaining few vehicles of the long column were just then starting down Cardinals or strung out along it. Specialist McDermott kept up a high rate of fire from his .50-caliber machine gun, killing one RPG gunner for sure and causing others to duck away as his gun truck passed. Bullets smacked into his ring mount and the ammunition can attached to his M2, but he was not hit. Specialist Row drove as fast as he could; but with the tires shot out and the highway slick with fuel, he was barely making ten miles per hour. He was firing his rifle as well and thought he hit one fighter before he ran out of magazines. When the gun truck reached safety at the dairy, Row, a trained combat lifesaver, went to work helping with the casualties. McDermott checked his ammunition supply. Out of the thousand rounds he had started with that morning (more than double what he normally would have had), he had less than a hundred left.

James Blackwood, driving tanker 16, saw a soldier and a couple of his fellow contractors on the ground as he drove away from the overpass; but the convoy pre-brief had stressed that the drivers were not to stop for anything, that the escort vehicles would handle breakdowns and other problems. He already had dropped his radio on the floor when he was shot in the hand. As he drove through the fire along Cardinals, he was hit again in the left leg, right arm, and back. He had served in Vietnam as a door gunner on a Huey helicopter and swore he "had never been under attack as on this day."[64] He managed to make it to safety at the dairy but had to be carried from his cab.

Lester and Zimmerman in the remaining bobtail did not make it through the heavy fire. An RPG hit the front of the vehicle, and the engine died. As the two men scrambled out of the cab to seek cover, two escort vehicles drove by. Lester was struck by the look of horror on the face of a gunner. The two contractors still had their handheld radio and heard one of the soldiers making a call for help on their behalf.

As Sergeant Grage's gun truck left the overpass, he drove across the median onto the opposite lanes to avoid the worst of the fuel-slicked pavement. Seeing a barrier ahead, he crossed back into the eastbound lanes and an IED exploded. Within minutes, a bullet pierced the door and struck him in the leg. Then another IED rocked his vehicle. Grage and his gunner, Specialist Brown, finally saw American tanks ahead at the cavalry checkpoint and pulled up alongside Church's Humvee at the concertina wire.

As Private Kirkpatrick's gun truck departed the overpass, he weaved around the destroyed tankers. Specialist Bohm, manning the M2 machine gun above him, had to shrink back from the intense heat of the burning fuel. An IED on Huskies already had shattered the windows in the truck and wounded Kirkpatrick in the legs, as well as giving him temporary hearing

---

[64] Interv Sum, Caraballo with James Blackwood, 20 May 04, Commander's Inquiry.

loss. Bohm had been shot in the foot. Now the gunner saw an American lying on the side of the road trying to flag them down. Bohm screamed down to Kirkpatrick to stop, but the driver neither saw the civilian in the midst of the swirling smoke and action nor heard the pleas of his fellow soldier. Bohm looked back as they drove on, probably registering the look of horror that Lester saw.[65]

The two soldiers kept firing as they headed east on Cardinals. When Kirkpatrick ran out of M16 rounds, he picked up the SAW in the cab and used that. Spotting the small cavalry rescue group led by Klein, Kirkpatrick jumped his truck over the highway median to head in their direction. As he did so and began braking, the vehicle hit spilled fuel, started to spin and then tip, finally slamming into a pile of dirt. The careening gun truck just missed Klein's Humvee.[66] The wild maneuver threw Bohm backward against his turret, and he collapsed in a heap. The driver managed to get going again and make it to the dairy, where cavalry soldiers pulled the injured gunner from his mount.

The handful of Americans stranded around the overpass had watched with dismay as a couple of escort vehicles had passed them. Groff's Humvee, the last vehicle still on the road, was their final hope. He already had Fisher, the wounded driver of bobtail 18, on board. Passing disabled tanker 1, the soldiers saw Specialist Walsh on the ground and civilian driver Howell getting out of his cab, so Specialist Lamar slowed down and pulled over. Walsh jumped up and sprinted toward the still-moving Humvee. Howell ran after Walsh. Hamill tried to follow; but weak from his wound and weighed down with body armor and Kevlar helmet, he could not keep up. The first two men dove in the passenger-side door. Hamill was only ten feet away when the Humvee accelerated and sped off. He yelled for it to come back. Inside the vehicle, Howell screamed that Hamill had been left behind; but no one seemed to grasp what he was saying.[67]

The Humvee's sudden departure left Hamill standing in the middle of the road. He remembered the advice proffered by his Vietnam veteran roommate in Kuwait: "If you are ever under fire, you get down on the ground as quick as you can and stay down." Hamill did just that. He tried to crawl toward a building to hide; but within minutes, he was captured by a gunman.[68]

Not far down the road, Groff's vehicle came upon more Americans crawling along to avoid enemy fire. Lamar stopped and four men piled in— Private Goodrich and drivers Brezovay, Sanchez, and Stannard. That made a total of ten men crammed into a Humvee designed for five at most. Bedlam reigned by this point. Goodrich was hardly inside when he was shot and cried out that he was hit in the chest. Fisher was begging for water. Sanchez yelled

[65] Interv Sum, Caraballo with Spec Matthew Bohm, 28 Apr 04, Commander's Inquiry; Interv Sum, Caraballo with Kirkpatrick, 13 May 04.

[66] Statement, Klein, 13 Apr 04.

[67] Interv Sum, Caraballo with Nelson Howell, 28 May 04, Commander's Inquiry.

[68] Hamill and Brown, *Escape in Iraq*, p. 43.

that he was a medic and asked for a first aid kit. Specialist Pelz, the gunner, was a combat lifesaver and began to help with the wounded. Others yelled for him to get back on his SAW, the vehicle's primary means of defense. Sanchez placed someone's fist into Goodrich's wound to stanch the flow of blood then bandaged Fisher's arm. Walsh jammed a rifle into Howell's hands and told him to start firing. Enemy fire continued to pepper the Humvee, and it finally died about halfway between the overpass and the dairy. For a moment everyone "sat in the back of the Humvee looking at each other."[69] Groff made repeated calls for help on every type of radio in the vehicle but received no answer. Then the soldiers handed weapons to the unwounded civilians who did not yet have one; Groff told them to conserve ammunition. The beleaguered group fired at anything that moved.[70]

While Groff's band fought for its life, Klein's small rescue force reached Lester's disabled bobtail. The soldiers were loading the two civilians into their vehicles when Kirkpatrick and Bohm's gun truck nearly sideswiped them. Klein led his group back to the dairy in trace of Kirkpatrick. They passed two Abrams tanks, commanded by 1st Sgt. Charles Q. Taylor and Sergeant Armstrong, heading in the opposite direction in search of survivors. At the same time, Groff finally made contact on one of the handheld radios used by the contract drivers. Sergeant Blankenship, the gunner in Church's Humvee, informed Groff that tanks were on the way.

As soon as Klein dropped off Lester and Zimmerman at the dairy, he turned his platoon around and went back up Cardinals. Specialist Church came along as a guide. After traveling half a mile, the small force received intense fire from gunmen concealed in houses along the right side of the road. With short, accurate bursts targeting all visible muzzle flashes, the experienced cavalry turret gunners eliminated or suppressed the enemy fighters. Klein continued for another mile before spotting Taylor's and Armstrong's tanks parked on either side of Groff's damaged Humvee.[71] Klein's vehicles pulled in front and behind, completing a protective box around the convoy survivors. Specialist Walsh thought the maneuver "was cool as hell!"[72] Church hurried to Groff to check on him and was surprised when he looked in the window and saw a mound of people inside.

Klein's men provided medical assistance and helped the wounded to the rescue vehicles. There was not enough space for all ten, so Klein arranged to link up with Sergeant Kowalewski's Bradley halfway toward the dairy. Church and Pelz agreed to remain behind to secure the sensitive items in the

[69] E-mail, Walsh to Caraballo, 12 May 04.

[70] Statement, Spec Karon Lamar, 11 Apr 04, Commander's Inquiry; Statement, Groff, 11 Apr 04; E-mail, Howell to Caraballo, 27 May 04; Interv Sum, Caraballo with Howell, 28 May 04; Statement, Pelz, 26 Apr 04; Testimony, Sanchez, 18 Sep 06; Interv Sum, Caraballo with Sanchez, 28 May 04;

[71] Statement, Klein, 13 Apr 04.

[72] E-mail, Walsh to Caraballo, 12 May 04.

disabled Humvee. As Klein's platoon departed, Sergeant Taylor's two tanks lumbered in the opposite direction, heading deeper into the ambush site to search for more survivors. As the 1st Cavalry vehicles receded from sight, Church heard a couple of insurgents approach, evidently assuming the shot-up Humvee was abandoned. The specialist popped out from cover and fired, killing both of them.[73] It was only a matter of minutes before Klein's trio of armed Humvees returned to whisk away Church and Pelz.

When the first black columns of smoke from burning tanker trucks had appeared in the sky, Captain Munz was in a meeting with his battalion commander at Logistics Base Seitz. He had departed immediately for the dairy, assuming there was trouble to be dealt with. He reached his company around the time Klein came in with the survivors from Groff's Humvee. The captain's tank, along with S. Sgt. Charles R. Armstead's M1A2, soon churned out the dairy's front gate and headed toward the ambush site. The pair halted at each disabled vehicle to check for survivors but did not find any. At the overpass, they saw fifty Iraqi men gathered in a nearby soccer field. Since none appeared to be armed, the tanks did not open fire; but the crowd scattered in all directions. Munz and Armstead returned to the dairy.[74]

Back at the dairy, Captain Munz asked Sergeant Groff for a status report on the convoy's personnel. Groff knew he was missing Sergeant Krause and Specialist Maupin, but Hamill had possessed the only roster of contractor personnel. Munz also dispatched his first sergeant with two tanks and a Bradley to recover any equipment or prevent it from falling into enemy hands. Sergeant Taylor's tank chased away Iraqis dancing on and around Groff's Humvee, then destroyed it with a main gun round. They found another tractor in flames, the heat so intense the first sergeant could feel it pushing through the small crack of his barely open hatch. His men attached tow cables to another tractor and towed it back to the dairy. They had cruised unmolested through the ambush site for almost an hour.[75] Iraqi fighters had learned over the past couple of days not to take on American tanks. Sergeant Klein's group did encounter a roadblock consisting of large metal spools on Cardinals as it returned from the ambush site. The insurgents fired several RPGs; but the Bradleys formed on either side of the Humvees, and all made it unscathed back to the dairy.[76]

The medics had their hands full treating the wounded from the convoy. Lieutenant Brown's injuries required the full attention of both Onwordi and Kapture. Specialist Onwordi controlled Brown's bleeding, inserted an intravenous tube and, when the lieutenant lost all signs of life, resuscitated him

---

[73] Interv, Killblane with Church, 14 Feb 07.

[74] Memorandum for Record, Capt Aaron J. Munz, CO, Company C, 2d Bn, 12th Cav,13 Apr 04, sub: The Battle for Abu Ghraib, Baghdad, Iraq 7–9 April 2003, Historians files, CMH.

[75] Marsh, "On the Move"; Award Citation, Taylor, n.d.; "Rescue of the 724th Trans."

[76] Statement, Klein, 13 Apr 04; "Rescue of the 724th Trans"; Award Citation, Taylor, n.d.

Lt. Col. Jose R. Rael (*right*), commanding officer of the 515th Corps Support Battalion, watches from Logistics Base Seitz as a column of smoke rises from burning 724th Transportation Company fuel tankers. This was the first indication to other American forces that something had gone terribly wrong along Route Huskies.

twice.[77] Although Steven Fisher and Gregory Goodrich died, Munz's medics were able to save all of the other wounded and evacuate them to Seitz. Some were put on medical flights to Baghdad.

Meanwhile, at 1230 Capt. Michael E. Ludwick, commander of a convoy travelling from Anaconda to Baghdad International Airport, contacted the 7th Transportation Battalion staff to let them know he thought the 724th had been ambushed. Ludwick could see towering columns of smoke rising along the route taken by the 724th convoy.[78] Ludwick related that he believed the entire convoy had been destroyed.

Colonel Akin was at the 172d Corps Support Group headquarters when he learned of the ambush. He did not want to accept the initial report but thought it prudent to return to battalion headquarters. His concerns were fueled by the fact that he could talk to every convoy except Lieutenant Brown's. Later that afternoon, Captain Smith walked into Akin's office to confirm that his unit had been caught in the ambush reported by Ludwick. At 1800, Sergeant Groff called Smith to inform that Private Goodrich was dead and that Specialist Maupin and Sergeant Krause were missing.

---

[77] "Rescue of the 724th Trans."
[78] Smith, "Historical Narrative."

Colonel Akin instructed Smith to begin collecting statements from the convoy survivors and to send forward the information required for next-of-kin notifications. Smith, who had prior enlisted service in the infantry and Special Forces, went back to his company, assembled his troops, and told them to take seats on the ground. The soldiers were in a state of shock because of the rumors. Smith then told them everything he knew at the time before requesting that anyone who did not want "to go outside the wire" raise his hand. No one did so.[79]

Since the end of the invasion a year earlier, no convoy in Iraq had encountered an ambush this large or intense. At the end of the day on 9 April, there were seven known dead: Sergeant Krause and Private Goodrich and civilian drivers Hulett, Johnson, Parker, Montague, and Fisher. Twelve soldiers and four contractor drivers were wounded.[80] Another four men were missing in action. The insurgents had captured Tommy Hamill and Specialist Maupin, but Hamill would escape after twenty-seven days of captivity. Driver William Bradley's remains turned up in January 2005. American troops located Maupin's body in late March 2008. One missing civilian, Timothy Bell, has never been found.[81]

Despite the best intentions of all involved to ready the convoy for danger and to get the fuel through to where combat forces needed it, the mission had failed. Leaders and planners had made a number of mistakes before the trucks had even departed their base. The process for accessing and acting on available intelligence was flawed, leading to poor route planning. Communications equipment and procedures were inadequate for maintaining contact with higher headquarters, supporting firepower or maneuver units in the area, and even between convoy vehicles. Standard tactics and techniques were geared solely to isolated, small attacks in spite of the recent onset of much larger clashes throughout Iraq. There had not been even an adequate system to maintain joint accountability over military and civilian personnel. The debacle that ensued on Good Friday brought about a searching examination of these systemic problems and led to major improvements in convoy operations.

While all those flaws had played a role in the outcome, Specialist Row summed up the impact of an attack that far exceeded previous experience: "It wasn't anyone's fault, it was just hell."[82]

[79] Interv, Killblane with Akin, 2 Nov 05, Historians files, USATS; Smith, "Historical Narrative."
[80] "Purple Heart Recipients for 724th Transportation Company," n.d., Historians files, CMH.
[81] Testimony, T. Scott Allen Jr. to Senate Democratic Policy Committee, 18 Sep 06, sub: An Oversight Hearing on Accountability for Contracting Abuses in Iraq, Historians files, CMH.
[82] Statement, Row, n.d.

CHAPTER THREE

FIGHTING
IN THE
VALLEY OF PEACE

MARK D. SHERRY

An armor-mechanized company team participates in operations to clear insurgents from a cemetery and holy shrine, leading to a battle in one of the strangest "urban" settings of the conflict.

Najaf—August 2004

On the morning of 9 August 2004, Capt. Kevin S. Badger's Company A, 2d Battalion, 12th Cavalry, prepared to enter the Wadi as-Salam (Valley of Peace) Cemetery on the left flank of an assault by Task Force 1-5 Cavalry (1st Battalion, 5th Cavalry). The mission was to root out Iraqi militiamen who were using the immense burial ground as a staging area for attacks on Coalition and government forces in the adjacent city of Najaf. If fighting in a cemetery struck any of the soldiers as otherworldly, they soon encountered something even more bizarre. As they moved up to their line of departure, they passed through a carnival complete with a large Ferris wheel. The juxtaposition of amusement and death would prove to be an omen for the strange battle the company would fight over the next three weeks.[1]

Badger's Company A had deployed to Iraq with the rest of the 1st Cavalry Division in January 2004. Col. Michael D. Formica, commanding the division's 2d Brigade Combat Team, had commenced predeployment training for his unit at Fort Hood beginning in the late summer of 2002. The brigade was just then completing unit-set fielding of the newest generation

---

[1] Intervs, Capt Steven Johnston, 54th Military History Detachment (MHD), with Capt Kevin S. Badger, Commanding Officer (CO), Co A, 2d Bn, 12th Cav, Task Force (TF) 1st Bn, 5th Cav, 2d Brigade Combat Team (BCT), 1st Cav Div, 7 Sep 04, pp. 8–9; with 1st Lt Steven D. Stauch, XO, Co A, 2d Bn, 12th Cav, TF 1st Bn, 5th Cav, 2d BCT, 1st Cav Div, 6 Sep 04, pp. 9–10; with 2d Lt Douglas J. Schaffer, 1st Plt, Co A, 2d Bn, 12th Cav, TF 1st Bn, 5th Cav, 2d BCT, 1st Cav Div, 6 Sep 04, pp. 12–13; with 1st Lt Christopher S. Dunn, 3d Plt, Co A, 2d Bn, 12th Cav, TF 1st Bn, 5th Cav, 2d BCT, 1st Cav Div, 6 Sep 04, pp. 9–10; all at Camp Banzai, Iraq; all in Global War on Terrorism (GWOT) Collection, U.S. Army Center of Military History (CMH), Washington, D.C.

An M2A3 Bradley moves down a lane in the cemetery. After initial experience in combat against dismounted enemy in the close confines of the burial ground, Company A paired an infantry fighting vehicle with each tank for mutual support.

of the Bradley fighting vehicle (the M2A3) and the Abrams tank (the M1A2 system enhancement package, or SEP). At the National Training Center in July 2003, the brigade worked at both high-intensity conventional warfare and tactical measures, such as cordon and search techniques, more germane to stability operations. When the brigade returned to Fort Hood, preparation focused on military operations in urban terrain since the command would deploy to Baghdad and its suburbs.[2]

Near the end of predeployment training, Formica reorganized the brigade's subordinate elements into combined-arms task forces. As part of this change, Lt. Col. Myles M. Miyamasu's 1st Battalion, 5th Cavalry (a mechanized infantry unit), and the 2d Battalion, 12th Cavalry (an armor unit), swapped their A Companies.[3] After joining the redesignated Task Force 1-5 Cavalry, Captain Badger's outfit then traded one tank platoon for a Bradley platoon. To further optimize the brigade for stability operations, some tank platoons (including one in Badger's company) traded their Abrams for high mobility multipurpose wheeled vehicles (HMMWVs, or Humvees), creating what Formica termed a motorized infantry brigade.[4]

   [2] Interv, Matt Matthews, Combat Studies Institute, with Col Michael Formica, CO, 2d BCT, 1st Cav Div, Fort Leavenworth, Kans., 21 Apr 06, pp. 4–5.

   [3] Ibid., p. 5.

   [4] Ibid., pp. 5–6; Interv, Mark Sherry, CMH, with Lt Col Myles Miyamasu, DAMO-FMF, Pentagon, 3 Oct 07, pp. 4–7, GWOT Collection, CMH.

Arriving in Iraq in early 2004, Task Force 1-5 Cavalry took over Camp Justice at Kadhimiya in northwestern Baghdad on the western bank of the Tigris River. The battalion's operations revolved around patrolling, cordon and search of surrounding neighborhoods, and route security for main thoroughfares running through the area of responsibility.[5] That low-level counterinsurgency routine lasted through the beginning of August, when events elsewhere in the country threatened to spin out of control.

About one hundred sixty kilometers south of Baghdad, Moqtada al-Sadr's Mahdi militia was stirring up trouble in Najaf. The city of over half a million was the capital of the province of the same name, but its real significance lay in its religious status. Najaf was home to the reputed burial site of Imam Ali, revered by Shi'ites as the first true successor to the Prophet Mohammed and therefore one of the holiest sites of that sect.[6] The city consequently had been a center of religious learning for centuries and was home to leading Shi'ite figures, in particular Grand Ayatollah Ali al-Sistani. Many faithful sought burial there, making the Valley of Peace Cemetery one of the largest in the world. Located on the northwest outskirts of the city, the L-shaped burial ground stretched a few kilometers in length and width. At the southern end of the sprawling maze of tombs, in the midst of the densely packed old city, was the Imam Ali Mosque, a gold-domed structure that served as the focal point of religious pilgrimages. (*See Map 4.*) A large parking garage, extending three stories underground and flanked north and south by a series of multistory hotels, stretched due west from the mosque.

Tensions had been escalating in Najaf since the fall of Baghdad the preceding year. On 10 April 2003, members of a crowd at the mosque assassinated Abdul Majid al-Khoei, a leading Shi'ite cleric and moderate who had just returned from exile in London. That August, a car bomb exploded outside the mosque, killing more than eighty people, including Ayatollah Muhammad Bakir al-Hakim, leader of the Supreme Council for the Islamic Revolution in Iraq. Both men were competitors with Sadr for postwar influence in Iraq. In April 2004, an Iraqi judge issued an arrest warrant for Sadr for reportedly ordering the killing of Khoei. At the same time, Mahdi militiamen launched an uprising throughout southern and central Iraq ahead of the scheduled 30 June 2004 handover of power from the Coalition Provisional Authority to Interim Prime Minister Ayad Allawi's government. One of their targets was a base for Spanish troops just outside Najaf. American forces assisted in restoring order, but followers of Sadr and Hakim battled on the streets the following month after Sadr's fighters took over the Imam Ali Mosque.

---

[5] Interv, Matthews with Formica, 21 Apr 06, pp. 4–7; Interv, Johnston with Lt Col Myles Miyamasu, CO, TF 1st Bn, 5th Cav, 2d BCT, 1st Cav Div, Camp Banzai, Iraq, 8 Sep 04, pp. 3–4, GWOT Collection, CMH.

[6] Albert Hourani, *A History of the Arab Peoples* (Cambridge, Mass.: Harvard University Press, 1991), pp. 55–56, 181–86. Ali was both cousin and son-in-law of Mohammed.

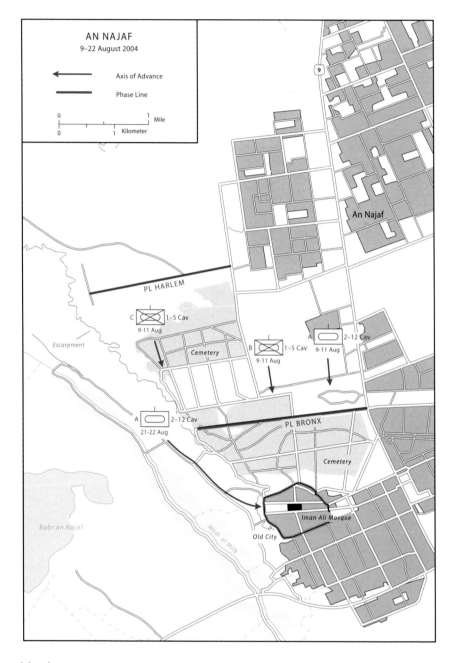

AN NAJAF
9–22 August 2004

⟵ Axis of Advance

▬▬ Phase Line

0 _____ 1 Mile
0 _____ 1 Kilometer

An Najaf

PL HARLEM

C ⊠ 1–5 Cav
9–11 Aug

Escarpment

Cemetery

B ⊠ 1–5 Cav
9–11 Aug

A ▭ 2–12 Cav
9–11 Aug

A ▭ 2–12 Cav
21–22 Aug

PL BRONX

Cemetery

Bahr an Najaf

Wadi al Milh

Iman Ali Mosque

Old City

MAP 4

At the end of July 2004, the Polish-led Multi-National Division–Central South assumed control over Najaf and Qadisiyah Provinces. The U.S. Central Command also shifted its reserve force, the 11th Marine Expeditionary Unit (MEU), to Forward Operating Base (FOB) Duke thirty kilometers north of Najaf.[7] Mahdi insurgents gave the Americans little opportunity to get settled in their area of responsibility, attacking a Marine patrol in Najaf on the evening of 2 August. Three days later, Sadr's militiamen struck against the main police station in the city, using the mosque and the cemetery as their base of operations. A Marine reaction force came to the aid of the policemen, and the insurgents shot down a Marine medical evacuation helicopter.

In response to the growing unrest, the provincial governor, Adnan al-Ziruffi, requested Coalition support for Iraqi Army and police forces in Najaf and the surrounding region. The MEU's ground combat element, Battalion Landing Team (BLT) 1/4, launched a raid into the cemetery. After clearing the eastern third of the burial ground and inflicting significant casualties on the insurgents, the marines withdrew on 6 August.[8] Realizing that more forces were needed to control the area, that same day Multi-National Corps–Iraq (MNC-I) directed the 1st Cavalry Division to send two battalion task forces to the city. The division ordered its 2d and 39th Brigades each to provide one of the required units. Colonel Formica turned to Task Force 1-5 Cavalry, calling Miyamasu at 1400 and giving him a verbal warning order to deploy his entire outfit "within the next twelve to twenty-four hours."[9] The task force began frantic efforts to pull its units in from scattered duties and prepare for movement. Adjacent units, including the 3d Battalion, 82d Field Artillery, assumed responsibility for Task Force 1-5 Cavalry's area of operations. The first elements of Miyamasu's force left by convoy eight hours after the initial alert.

MNC-I established special command arrangements for the upcoming operation, dubbed PACIFIC THRUST. The senior headquarters in Iraq approved a request from I Marine Expeditionary Force/Multi-National Force–West (I MEF/MNF-W) to temporarily assume authority for Najaf and Qadisiyah Provinces, as well as operational control of the 11th MEU, the two 1st Cavalry Division battalion task forces, and several battalions of the Iraqi security forces. Some of the latter units lost a large percentage of their manpower via desertion

---

[7] 11th Marine Expeditionary Unit (MEU) Cmd Chron, 1 Jul–31 Dec 04, Encl 1, pp. 11–12, 40, Archives and Special Collections, Library of the Marine Corps, Quantico Marine Corps Base, Va.; Staffs of I Marine Expeditionary Force (MEF) (Forward) and 11th MEU (Special Operations Capable [SOC]), "Battle for An Najaf, August 2004," *Marine Corps Gazette* 88 (December 2004): 11–12.

[8] Battalion Landing Team 1/4, Cmd Chron, Sec 2 Narr Sum, Archives and Special Collections, Library of the Marine Corps; I MEF (Forward) and 11th MEU (SOC), "Battle for An Najaf, August 2004," pp. 10–12; 11th MEU Cmd Chron, 1 Jul–31 Dec 04, Encl 1, pp. 11–13.

[9] Intervs, Matthews with Formica, 21 Apr 06, pp. 7–8; Johnston with Miyamasu, 8 Sep 04, pp. 4–6; Johnston with Stauch, 6 Sep 04, pp. 3–4.

after receiving orders to deploy to Najaf. To control the overall operation, I MEF formed a temporary headquarters, I MEF (Forward), commanded by Brig. Gen. Dennis J. Hejlik. The new command element took charge on 8 August. It would exercise tactical control of all ground forces in Najaf through the 11th MEU headquarters.

One of the major challenges in the upcoming battle would be the exclusionary zone that MNF-I had established around the Imam Ali Mosque and the old city.[10] While rules of engagement typically circumscribed military activity that would adversely impact any religious site, the international stature of this particular mosque made American and Iraqi authorities extraordinarily anxious to avoid any damage to it. The boundary of the exclusionary zone followed the perimeter road around the old city and was roughly a kilometer in diameter. It had two parts. A no-fire area encompassed the entire zone from roughly twelve o'clock around to nine o'clock and projected to the northwest about two or three hundred meters from the mosque. The remainder of the northwestern quadrant out to the boundary was a restrictive fire area. Any type of fire inside the no-fire area, including tank main-gun rounds that could ricochet there, required the prior approval of MNF-I. The I MEF commanding general could approve some fires into the restrictive-fire area, but no effects could spill over into the no-fire area.[11]

Captain Badger had received the warning order for the movement south just minutes after Formica called Miyamasu on 6 August. The Company A commander told his subordinate leaders to "be prepared to move out not later than 2200 . . . with all our equipment, combat loaded, ready to go fight a battle." He sent his company executive officer, 1st Lt. Steven D. Stauch, in the battalion advance party that flew down to Duke by helicopter at 2300 to prepare for the arrival of the main body.[12] Task Force 1-5 Cavalry divided its forces into three convoys, with Badger taking responsibility for the largest one, which had fifty-one vehicles and over a hundred people. There was no time for a route reconnaissance or written order. It took a while for the company commander to organize the long line of vehicles—many from other parts of the task force—and ensure that everyone had the correct radio frequencies and understood the control measures, so the column did not depart until about 0530 the next morning. While still inside the city limits of Baghdad, the convoy halted on Route Tampa to clear an improvised explosive device (IED). Thereafter, the column moved slowly and deliberately, taking seventeen hours to reach FOB Duke.[13]

---

[10] I MEF (Forward) and 11th MEU (SOC), "Battle for An Najaf, August 2004," pp. 10–12.

[11] Intervs, Johnston with Badger, 7 Sep 04, pp. 4–5, and Sherry with Miyamasu, 3 Oct 07, pp. 15–16; E-mail, Lt Col Myles Miyamasu, DAMO-FMF, Pentagon, to author, 9 Sep 08, Historians files, CMH.

[12] Intervs, Johnston with Badger, 7 Sep 04, pp. 3–4, 7–9, and with Miyamasu, 8 Sep 04, pp. 11–13.

[13] Interv, Sherry with Miyamasu, 3 Oct 07, pp. 15–16; Sherry with Maj Kevin S. Badger, U.S. Military Academy, West Point, N.Y., 21 Sep 07, pp. 17–18, GWOT Collection, CMH.

The night of hurried preparation followed by a day and most of a night of driving left the soldiers tired, but there was little time to rest as 8 August dawned. The company had twenty-four hours to get ready to launch an attack. The men unloaded tanks and infantry fighting vehicles from heavy equipment transporters, performed maintenance checks on each vehicle, and arranged for more ammunition. Their efforts were slowed by the bare-bones facilities at the forward base and the lack of adequate staging areas for the newly arrived reinforcements. The heat of late summer also was in full force, with daytime temperatures averaging over 110 degrees and reaching 122 at one point during the ensuing battle. At night it did not drop below 90 degrees. That was warmer than Baghdad; one tank commander in Badger's 3d Platoon, Sgt. Joshua W. Beams, described it as "ridiculously hot." The heat placed a significant strain on men and machines. The lack of shade in the cemetery, hot exhaust gas blowing into open hatches, and frequent breakdowns in the air conditioning in the tanks turned the armored vehicles into furnaces. Aside from the physical debilitation and danger that posed to crewmen, Beams' gunner, Pfc. Thomas F. Cosby, discovered that it often caused the electronics, including fire-control systems, to malfunction, thus degrading main-gun accuracy.[14]

Once the company was ready, Badger moved it forward to Camp Hotel on the northern edge of Najaf and about eight kilometers from the mosque. There, the unit received a full load of ammunition and water; but there would be no ice for the next two days.[15] His force was the strongest element in the battalion. The 1st Platoon, led by 2d Lt. Douglas J. Schaffer, was mechanized infantry with four M2A3 Bradleys. Second Lt. James M. Goins' 2d Platoon had four M1A2 Abrams. The 3d Platoon had initially deployed to Iraq with four M1114 HMMWVs, but 1st Lt. Christopher S. Dunn's group acquired two tanks just before the battle. The company headquarters fielded three more Humvees, plus a Bradley fire support team vehicle.[16]

While Colonel Miyamasu's troops got ready, he was meeting with Col. Anthony M. Haslam, the 11th MEU commander. Haslam and the MEU staff briefed the battalion commander on the tactical situation and Task Force 1-5 Cavalry's mission. As they went over of the imagery of the cemetery, Miyamasu asked whether there was a written order for the upcoming operation. The answer was no (nor would the battalion receive many written directives for the duration of the battle). Haslam's verbal guidance was to move to the northern edge of the cemetery, designated Phase Line Harlem, and prepare to enter

[14] Johnston with Badger, 7 Sep 04, pp. 7–9; Intervs, Johnston with Miyamasu, 8 Sep 04, pp. 7–9, and Johnston with Stauch, 6 Sep 04, pp. 7–8. Interv, S Sgt Parker, 54th MHD, with Sgt Joshua W. Beams, Co A, 2d Bn, 12th Cav, TF 1st Bn, 5th Cav, 2d BCT, 1st Cav Div, 6 Sep 04, pp. 4–5; with Pfc Thomas F. Cosby, 3d Plt, Co A, 2d Bn, 12th Cav, TF 1st Bn, 5th Cav, 2d BCT, 1st Cav Div, 6 Sep 04, pp. 5–7; both at Camp Banzai, Iraq, GWOT Collection, CMH.

[15] Interv, Johnston with Stauch, 6 Sep 04, pp. 8–10.

[16] E-mail, Capt Kevin S. Badger to author, 22 Sep 08, Historians files, CMH.

the fight as soon as possible, attacking from north to south in coordination with BLT 1/4, which would be in the city on the cavalry's east, or left, flank.[17] Reliable elements of the Iraqi security forces cordoned off Najaf to prevent militia reinforcements from joining the battle.

Miyamasu planned a linear assault, initially with Companies B and C. Company A would move up to an attack position in a lightly populated, semi-agricultural area on the eastern border of the cemetery at a point where the burial ground expanded to its maximum width. When the assault reached this spot, designated Phase Line Bronx (later renamed Dodge), Badger's force would join in, putting all three maneuver companies on line.

Task Force 1-5 Cavalry launched its initial attack at 0500 on 9 August. It took the two mechanized companies, moving carefully through the densely packed cemetery, nearly five hours to cover the two-plus kilometers to Bronx. During the morning, Company A got into position and discovered the carnival in the process. As Badger's men peered through a tree line and across a highway, they got their first glimpse of the objective. They saw a hodgepodge of closely packed tombs and markers that stretched one-and-a-half kilometers wide just along their company's assigned front. The first thing the soldiers noted was the number and size of the above-ground mausoleums. Miyamasu was surprised that "there were mausoleums as large as 1100 square foot houses," some over two stories high.[18] Nine dirt lanes, each generally just wide enough for a tank, cut south through this portion of the maze. While they would provide a means for vehicular movement in the cemetery, there would be no space for maneuver except on foot. Observation and fields of fire would likewise be constrained, while there would be no shortage of good ambush positions for the insurgents. More than two kilometers away, the Americans could make out the gold dome of the mosque and the taller buildings marking the edge of the city.

Company A finally entered the burial ground in the early afternoon.[19] Once in the cemetery, Badger and his men found the strange terrain even more forbidding. The deeper they moved inside it, the denser the tombs were packed. More disturbing, they soon discovered the presence of subterranean catacombs that offered the enemy another place for concealment. Thereafter, in Colonel Formica's words, there was "lots of three dimensional fighting" from the roofs of mausoleums down into the crypts.[20] The task force ended up engaging in a peculiar permutation of military operations in urban terrain, with one substantial difference. In this case, there was no need for concern about collateral damage to the civilian inhabitants—they were already dead.

[17] Interv, Johnston with Miyamasu, 8 Sep 04, pp. 12–15.
[18] Ibid., pp. 8–9, 16–17; Interv, Johnston with Badger, 7 Sep 04, pp. 7–8, and with Dunn, 6 Sep 04, pp. 5–6.
[19] Johnston with Miyamasu, 8 Sep, 04, pp. 15–17; Intervs, Sherry with Badger, 21 Sep 07, pp. 19–22, and Johnston with Stauch, 6 Sep 04, pp. 8–10.
[20] Interv, Matthews with Formica, 21 Apr 06, p. 7.

The armor company soon was moving at an even slower pace than the mechanized units had earlier in the day, taking between one and two hours to move a hundred meters. The extreme heat played a role, as did enemy opposition, but the main factor was the need to search the crypts. Badger's company found weapons, mostly rocket-propelled and hand grenades, stored in small caches in several of the catacombs, which mandated a thorough inspection of each.

The Mahdi militia opened the battle with mortar fire. The canalized American vehicles presented good targets to the insurgents, who had excellent observation from the tops of buildings from which they could adjust their aim. The firing positions were often in the exclusionary zone around the mosque, making it difficult to hit back at the mortarmen. Luckily, the militiamen proved less than adept at actually hitting a point target but posed a danger nonetheless for troops outside their armored vehicles. Capable snipers also operated from the taller mausoleums and the rooftops of buildings beyond the eastern fringe of the cemetery, directing aimed fire against sights on tanks and fighting vehicles, as well as any exposed crewmen. Occasionally, the black-garbed insurgents worked in small teams of two to five employing fire and maneuver tactics. Their communications system consisted of simple but effective mobile telephones.[21]

Another threat was the insurgent mainstay—the improvised explosive device. The first one encountered was a 120-mm. mortar round, found by tracking back a wire that disappeared underneath a rock. The soldiers came across many IEDs, some daisy-chained in groups of up to fifty munitions, as well as several dug into crossroads. One of Lieutenant Schaffer's squad leaders, S. Sgt. William T. Menjivar, said that his unit's "biggest fear was that we would run into a booby trap" when checking tombs for militiamen and caches. Consequently, the infantrymen began to initiate each search of such spaces with a concussion or fragmentation grenade. The methodical clearing operations paid off, and Company A suffered no casualties from IEDs or booby traps.

That first afternoon, Company A made it a few hundred meters beyond the line of departure. The soldiers saw few enemy at close range and had no occasion to use the tank main guns, relying instead on small arms and coaxial machine guns.[22] Miyamasu was unclear how long the 11th MEU wanted his battalion to continue the attack and when BLT 1/4 and Task Force 2-7 Cavalry (2d Battalion, 7th Cavalry) would join the fray. As dusk approached, he sought and received permission to pull back and rearm; the battalion spent the night in an assembly area on the edge of the cemetery.

Task Force 1-5 Cavalry resumed the attack around 0600 the next day, 10 August, and fought its way back across Phase Line Bronx. Enemy opposition increased and, according to one soldier, "around 1000 that morning, the battle really started for us." The level of both sniper and indirect fire picked up. Sergeant Beams felt that mortar rounds were "falling like raindrops." Snipers shot out sights

[21] Interv, Johnston with Miyamasu, 8 Sep 04, pp. 9–10.
[22] Interv, Parker with Cosby, 6 Sep 04, p. 12.

Soldiers remove mortar rounds and detonating cord from a crypt in the cemetery. Insurgents had stashed munitions throughout the area, requiring painstaking searches that slowed the advance.

on an Abrams and a Bradley, forcing Company A to modify its practices by closing hatches and ballistic doors and scanning with auxiliary sights.[23] Militiamen launched rocket-propelled grenades (RPGs) from hiding places in crypts, behind tombstones, and on top of mausoleums.

Badger's company continued to press a linear assault past Phase Line Bronx. As the force moved farther south, the rigid requirements of the exclusionary zone began to seriously hamper operations and the security of the troops. Sergeant Beams estimated that it took an average of thirty minutes from requesting clearance to fire tank main-gun and Bradley 25-mm. rounds to receiving permission to fire. Miyamasu, emphasizing the need to rapidly engage insurgents that posed an immediate threat to his men and vehicles, secured more relaxed rules of engagement in the cemetery as the operation progressed. In one case, the 11th MEU gave a blanket clearance to the battalion to engage snipers on rooftops of 3-, 4-, and 5-story buildings (presumably because rounds fired at a higher angle would overshoot the mosque). From this second day onward, Company A also became increasingly adept at targeting snipers with thermal sights on tanks and Bradleys, and then engaging them with 25-mm. chain gun or with coaxial machine-gun fire. Badger believed that his company had begun to gain local superiority over the insurgents, averaging about twenty-five confirmed kills a day. His unit suffered no casualties during this first forty-eight hours of fighting.[24]

The situation changed dramatically on 11 August, as the Iraqi government opened negotiations with the Mahdi militia to stop the fighting in Najaf. In deference to the host nation, MNC-I ordered a halt to offensive operations in the city. Colonel Haslam placed Task Force 1-5 Cavalry on the defensive in the cemetery, with the object of restricting the ability of the insurgents to launch

[23] Ibid.; Interv, Parker with Beams, 6 Sep 04, pp. 4, 13.

[24] Intervs, Johnston with Dunn, 6 Sep 04, pp. 10–12; with Badger, 7 Sep 04, pp. 8–9; with Stauch, 6 Sep 04, pp. 10–12; Parker with Beams, 6 Sep 04, p. 11.

attacks against Coalition forces outside the burial ground. For this holding action, Colonel Miyamasu decided that one company would be enough and he would use the opportunity to rest his force in case the battle resumed. He established a rotation, with the companies shifting every twelve hours between a screening position on Phase Line Bronx/Dodge, the camp at Hotel, and FOB Baker. The latter, located about six kilometers to the east, had air-conditioned barracks, thus giving the tired troops at least a temporary respite from the debilitating heat.[25]

Over most of the next two weeks, Badger's company settled into the new routine. During its turns in the cemetery, Company A maintained an active defense, often making limited forays several hundred meters in front of its position. These operations sought out and destroyed snipers and small teams of insurgents that occasionally moved close to the line to engage the Americans. Badger's armored vehicles also took out insurgents at ranges up to fifteen hundred meters with direct fire. Enemy mortars continued to be a factor, with one large-caliber round landing directly on top of a Bradley turret and wounding the gunner. Throughout this battle of attrition, the soldiers inflicted far more casualties than they suffered.[26]

The low point for Company A at Najaf occurred on 15 August. The unit's standard procedure when the hatches of an Abrams were open was for the tank commander to keep watch over the ten to four o'clock quadrant while the loader covered the opposite direction, facing backward in his hatch. Lieutenant Goins was in his tank on the western end of the cemetery aiming the main gun toward an insurgent mortar position near the exclusionary zone. He had sought permission over the radio to engage the target, then turned his attention back down into his gunsight. That distraction left the front of the tank unguarded for just a moment, and a watching insurgent seized the opportunity. Springing toward the tank, he leapt up onto the front of it, climbed onto the turret, shot both Goins and the loader (Spec. Mark A. Zapata) at pointblank range with an AK47 and then ran off. Alarmed at the gunfire, the driver attempted to back up; but without direction from another crewman who could see, the Abrams veered off the narrow road and backed into a mausoleum that collapsed on the tank, immobilizing it.[27]

Upon hearing over the radio that one of the M1A2s was out of action, the executive officer, Lieutenant Stauch, and the first sergeant raced to the scene in a Bradley fighting vehicle. The two of them took charge of the recovery effort, evacuating the two casualties in the battalion's medical track back to Hotel and extricating the tank with an M88 recovery vehicle. Stauch and the

---

[25] Interv, Johnston with Miyamasu, 8 Sep 04, pp. 19–21; I MEF (Forward) and 11th MEU (SOC), "Battle for An Najaf, August 2004," p. 12.

[26] Intervs, Johnston with Badger, 7 Sep 04, pp. 11–14; with Stauch, 6 Sep 04, pp. 10–12, 40–41; with Miyamasu, 8 Sep 04, pp. 24–25, 46–47. E-mail, Sfc William T. Menjivar to author, sub: An Najaf, August 2004, 1 Apr 08, Historians files, CMH.

[27] Intervs, Johnston with Stauch, 6 Sep 04, pp. 13–15; with Miyamasu, 8 Sep 04, p. 36; with Badger, 7 Sep 04, pp. 22, 24–27.

vehicle's gunner, Sgt. Jesse Mock, then drove the tank back to the base camp for repair. Goins and Zapata did not survive their wounds.[28] The casualties caused Miyamasu to alter the battalion's tactics. He directed the companies to push task organization farther down the line by establishing what he dubbed hunter-killer teams—mixed sections of one Abrams and one Bradley each. Each tank would now have accompanying infantrymen who could dismount as required to provide better security for both armored vehicles.[29]

Although the task force was inflicting casualties on the enemy and capturing munitions in the cemetery, in Miyamasu's opinion the operations were far from decisive. The Mahdi militia continued to occupy key areas of Najaf, including the sanctuary provided by the exclusionary zone around the mosque. Nor had the Iraqi government's negotiations with the insurgents produced any tangible results. To resolve the standoff, Miyamasu and other commanders urged a further reduction of the size of the exclusionary zone and a resumption of offensive operations that would liquidate the threat lurking in the old city.[30]

Colonel Haslam approved a probing attack by Task Force 1-5 Cavalry for the night of 21 August. Miyamasu selected Badger's Company A for a raid against the underground parking garage, now designated Task Force Objective C, which intelligence sources identified as the militia's main weapons cache. Higher headquarters also authorized the soldiers to return fire against enemy in the hotels to the north and south of the garage. Company B, Task Force 1-5 Cavalry, would provide overwatch from the cemetery during the movement to contact and support Badger's operations when he met resistance. On-call fires would be available from an Air Force AC–130 gunship, call sign Basher, and AH–64 Apache and AH–1 Cobra attack helicopters. This would be the first foray by American forces inside the road that ringed the old city and the mosque. In addition to testing and degrading the enemy's strength, the operation would allow the Coalition force to assess the trafficability of Route Apple, a dirt road in the wadi on the western boundary of the cemetery. To that end, the command group from BLT 1/4 would follow in trace of Company A, as the marines would use this avenue of approach if the 11th MEU attacked into the old city with all three battalions.[31]

Company A moved out in the dark down Route Apple with 6 tanks, 4 Bradleys, and 4 M1114 up-armored HMMWVs. As Sfc. John P. Roberson's

---

[28] 11th MEU Cmd Chron, 1 Jul–31 Dec 04, Encl 1, pp. 13–14; Interv, Parker with Beams, 6 Sep 04, pp. 17–19.

[29] Intervs, Johnston with Schaffer, 6 Sep 04, p. 14, and Sherry with Miyamasu, 3 Oct 07, pp. 30–31.

[30] I MEF (Forward) and 11th MEU (SOC), "Battle for An Najaf, August 2004," pp. 12–13; Interv, Johnston with Miyamasu, 8 Sep 04, pp. 25–26.

[31] Intervs, Johnston with Miyamasu, 8 Sep 04, pp. 25–28; with Badger, 7 Sep 04, pp. 12–14; with Stauch, 6 Sep 04, p. 13. Maj Kevin S. Badger, "Battle of An Najaf: U.S. vs. Mahdi Army, August 2004, Imam Ali Shrine Cemetery," Power Point Presentation, n.d., copy in Historians files, CMH; 11th MEU Cmd Chron, Encl 1, p. 16.

On 15 August, Lieutenant Goins and Specialist Zapata died when a Mahdi militiaman raced from cover, sprang onto their tank, and shot them. In the chaotic moments that followed, the driver backed the Abrams into a tomb, which collapsed.

lead tank, Blue 4, emerged from the wadi at 0119, it identified a daisy chain of eleven IEDs blocking its path. Badger ordered a Bradley into position and had it engage the devices with its 25-mm. chain gun until there was a gap wide enough to permit the rest of the company to proceed single file toward the old city. At 0129, Roberson's tank and the lead infantry fighting vehicle opened fire on enemy-held hotels on both sides of the parking garage. As Company A moved forward, it began drawing both machine-gun fire from the southwest and mortar fire from around the Imam Ali shrine itself. Miyamasu turned to his tactical air control party, asking Basher to take out the mortar. The aircraft located the target and requested authority to engage. Twenty minutes later, the AC–130 had permission to fire and attacked and silenced the gun.[32]

Badger's unit had not waited for the results of the airstrike but had kept pushing toward its objective. Insurgents in the hotels fired down at the armored vehicles, launching barrages of RPGs. In thirty minutes of intense combat, Company A responded with 68 tank main-gun rounds, approximately 1,200 rounds from its 25-mm. chain guns, and 8 tube-launched, optically tracked, wire-guided (TOW) antitank missiles. With that heavy firepower paving the way, Badger's men reached the entrance to the parking garage without casualty. The tanks pumped a number of main-gun rounds into the structure but got no expected secondary explosions in return for the effort. The garage was

---

[32] Intervs, Johnston with Schaffer, 6 Sep 04, pp. 15–16, and with Dunn, 6 Sep 04, pp. 12–13; 11th MEU Cmd Chron, Encl 1, pp. 16–17.

so large, however, that only a risky attack into its inner recesses would have determined whether it harbored fighters and weapons. Having achieved its limited objectives, Company A began withdrawing.[33]

The enemy finally drew blood as the retrograde got underway. An RPG round impacted the sponson box on the left side of the turret of Sergeant Beams' tank, Blue 2. The jet from the exploding warhead burned a hole into the first few inches of armor behind the sponson but did not penetrate all the way through. The round was probably one of the newer RPG18s, which posed more of a threat than the RPG7s generally used in Iraq prior to this time. The blast, Beams recalled, "kind of rocked us a little bit and we heard a thud." He noticed that one of the Halon fire extinguisher bottles had gone off and stopped his tank to find out if it was on fire. The accompanying Bradley in the hunter-killer team, Lieutenant Schaffer's Red 1, pulled alongside. The platoon commander exited his vehicle to run over to inform Beams that his tank had been hit and to ask about casualties. The blaze enveloping the sponson box began to cook off the machine-gun ammunition therein. Schaffer's infantrymen and the tank crew ignored the danger and put out the flames with portable extinguishers. Blue 2 then rejoined the company as the raid force fought its way back toward Route Apple.[34]

As the company withdrew, enemy RPG and machine-gun teams followed and engaged the column. Colonel Miyamasu requested air cover for the retrograde. Basher fired its 105-mm. howitzer and 25-mm. Gatling gun at one group of several militiamen moving in on Badger's trail element. As the AC–130 pulled out, attack helicopters dove in and destroyed another two-man RPG team to the southwest of the parking garage. The raid force made it back to friendly lines with no further damage.[35]

The probe set the stage for a deliberate attack on the old city on 25 August designed to decisively defeat the Mahdi force in Najaf. To prevent the insurgents from shifting their manpower to meet a single threat, the 11th MEU proposed a simultaneous assault by all thee U.S. battalions, which would converge on the mosque from the northwest, north, and southeast. Colonel Haslam presented the plan at a rehearsal of concept drill held at Duke on 22 August with Lt. Gen. Thomas F. Metz (commanding general of MNC-I) and Lt. Gen. James T. Conway, U.S. Marine Corps (commanding general of I MEF/MNF-W) in attendance. Miyamasu's Task Force 1-5 Cavalry would push down Route Nova, a main paved road heading due south through the cemetery and leading right to the Imam Ali Mosque. To his right (west) flank, BLT 1/4 would advance into the northwestern corner of the old city toward the line of hotels on the north side of the parking garage. Task Force 2-7 Cavalry would approach the

[33] Interv, Sherry with Badger, 21 Sep 07, pp. 42–51.
[34] Intervs, Johnston with Badger, 7 Sep 04, pp. 13–14; Parker with Cosby, 6 Sep 04, pp. 16–18; with Beams, 6 Sep 04, pp. 14–16; Johnston with Dunn, 6 Sep 04, pp. 12–13.
[35] Interv, Johnston with Miyamasu, 8 Sep 04, p. 28.

An RPG round hit Sergeant Beams' tank during the 21 August night raid on the parking garage. The resulting blaze in the sponson box cooked off machine-gun ammunition but otherwise inflicted no significant damage.

old city from the southeast. A battery of Marine artillery, Air Force AC–130 gunships and jets, and Army and Marine helicopter gunships would provide fire support. Haslam garnered approval from MNF-I to reduce the no-fire area around the mosque, now designated MEU Objective A, to a square of roughly two hundred meters per side. Once American troops surrounded the religious site, Iraqi troops would go in to clear it.[36]

Task Force 1-5 Cavalry pulled out of the cemetery on 24 August to refit and prepare for the upcoming operation. The marines and Task Force 2-7 Cavalry launched the first phase of the attack on the night of 25 August, gaining footholds in the old city. (*See Map 5.*) Task Force 1-5 Cavalry crossed its line of departure in the cemetery at 0200 on 26 August. It was a conventional-style assault, with Army 120-mm. mortars and Marine 155-mm. artillery providing suppressive fire along the boundary between the old city and the cemetery. Company A led the battalion, still pairing an Abrams tank with a Bradley infantry fighting vehicle, but now with a platoon of North Dakota

---

[36] I MEF (Forward) and 11th MEU (SOC), "Battle for An Najaf, August 2004," p. 14; Badger, "Battle of An Najaf: U.S. vs. Mahdi Army"; Interv, Johnston with Miyamasu, 8 Sep 04, pp. 31–32.

The densely packed neighborhoods of the old city of Najaf surround the Imam Ali Mosque, leaving few avenues of approach. The double line of hotels and the parking garage between them extend to the left of the mosque. *Below:* On the morning of 26 August, American forces push down Route Nova toward the gold-domed Imam Ali Mosque. Although Iraqi units were prepared to assault the complex, one of the most revered shrines in Iraq, that became unnecessary when the Mahdi militia agreed to a peaceful handover to authorities.

Army National Guard engineers also attached to the unit. The initial objective was a hotel on the eastern side of Route Nova near the mosque.[37]

When the lead vehicles reached the hotel, they found that it had been bombed the preceding night and was abandoned by the insurgents. Badger decided to continue the mounted advance as far as the first defended building, his implied objective, where he planned to dismount his infantrymen to clear it. The attack did not go unopposed, as the enemy kept up a continuous fire from a distance on the company, forcing the tanks and fighting vehicles to stay buttoned up. Private First Class Cosby thought his unit was attracting a lot of RPGs; his tank "took one that almost blew our track off." The platoon sergeant from the 2d Platoon was in the lead when he spotted what looked like a two- or three-story building being used as a militia strongpoint. Badger directed Lieutenant Schaeffer's 1st Platoon to dismount and clear the building, which was located only one hundred thirty meters from the Imam Ali Mosque.[38]

Schaffer's platoon, down to three working Bradleys, rolled up close to the hotel where two squads dismounted. It was still night, and smoke from a burning building nearby further obscured the seventeen soldiers as they plunged inside at the ground floor. They soon discovered that what looked from the outside like a three-story building at most, actually had seven levels and about three hundred rooms, each of which would have to be painstakingly cleared with traditional urban-warfare tactics. They set about the task room by room using hand grenades, rifles, shotguns, and squad automatic weapons, all in darkness and at close quarters with an enemy force that Sergeant Menjivar estimated at twenty to thirty insurgents. The platoon killed about six militiamen and captured another four on the first floor. Lieutenant Stauch's Bradley took the detainees back to the casualty and enemy prisoner of war collection point.[39]

Given the size of the hotel, Schaffer realized he needed more troops to help clear and hold it, so he radioed Badger and requested the use of the engineers. The 1st Platoon leader, knowing these soldiers were less skilled at clearing operations, employed them to secure access points and other key sites in the building. His infantrymen continued to methodically sweep the structure, moving from the ground floor up to the roof and then working their way back down. Sergeant Menjivar was often in the lead and reemphasized to his men that they should capture rather than kill insurgents whenever possible. About 0530, Company B, commanded by Capt. Darren F. Keahtigh, arrived with reinforcements. His snipers went up on the roof, and other soldiers helped in

---

[37] Intervs, Johnston with Miyamasu, 8 Sep 04, pp. 31–32; with Badger, 7 Sep 04, pp. 14–16; Sherry with Badger, 21 Sep 07, pp. 51–53. 11th MEU Cmd Chron, Encl 1, pp. 18–19.

[38] Intervs, Johnston with Stauch, 6 Sep 04, pp. 16–17; with Schaffer, 6 Sep 04, pp. 16–18; Parker with Cosby, 6 Sep 04, p. 16.

[39] Intervs, Johnston with Badger, 7 Sep 04, pp. 16–17, and with Schaffer, 6 Sep 04, pp. 16–18; E-mail, Menjivar to Sherry, 1 Apr 08.

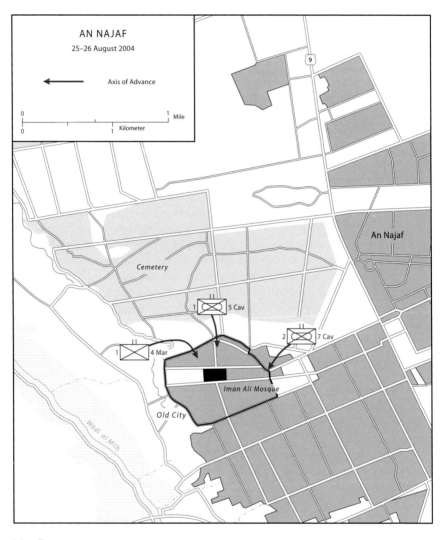

MAP 5

clearing the hotel. When the assault was done, Company A had suffered no major casualties, only minor wounds.[40]

Keahtigh organized his men to continue the attack on the next building to the south, a five-story hotel that dominated the approaches to the mosque.

---

[40] Intervs, Johnston with Schaffer, 6 Sep 04, pp. 18–19, and with Stauch, 6 Sep 04, pp. 17–19; E-mail, Menjivar to Sherry, 1 Apr 08; Interv, Sherry with Badger, 21 Sep 07, p. 61.

Company B moved out at 0830 with Company A supporting with fire.[41] The soldiers cleared the structure within a few hours, and the way was open for an attack on MEU Objective A. Task Force 2-7 Cavalry meanwhile had pushed farther north into the old city; by 1500, the mosque was surrounded. Fifteen minutes later, as Iraqi forces prepared for the final assault, MNF-I suspended all operations to allow another opportunity to negotiate a cease-fire that would peaceably remove insurgents from the Imam Ali Mosque as well as the rest of Najaf. Ayatollah Sistani, who had returned to Najaf that day from medical treatment in Great Britain, personally conducted the talks with Sadr's representatives. This time, given Sistani's moral authority and with the Mahdi militia facing certain defeat, the parties reached an agreement. The insurgents symbolically handed the keys to the mosque to Sistani on 27 August, Coalition troops permitted the remaining fighters to leave peaceably, although Task Force 1-5 Cavalry manned several traffic control points on the northern edge of the city to confiscate weapons. The battalion loaded up on 3 September to return to Baghdad, and the 11th MEU relinquished tactical control over the unit on 4 September.[42]

In some respects, this action was not uncommon for an Army battalion in Iraq in 2004. The unexpected and rapid redeployment from one area of operations to another, the transfer from one chain of command to another, the overnight switch from low-level counterinsurgency operations to a more-conventional type of combat, the requirement to work jointly with Marine forces at the battalion level (not seen to this degree since the Vietnam War), and the extreme heat—each constituted a hurdle to overcome. In addition, Task Force 1-5 Cavalry had to deal with the peculiarities of fighting in the strange terrain of a dense cemetery and the severe restrictions on the use of weapons around the mosque. Taken together, these factors created one of the most challenging environments a unit could face. Under those circumstances, the effectiveness of the battalion, and Captain Badger's Company A in particular, was a testimony to the training, discipline, decision making, and professionalism of the soldiers and their leaders. More important, the effort in Najaf had lasting consequences, since the successful offensive forced the Mahdi militia to take a less confrontational approach in the city and was a major factor in turning the large urban center into one of the more peaceful in the country.

---

[41] Intervs, Johnston with Capt Darren Keightigh, CO, Co B, TF 1st Bn, 5th Cav, 2d BCT, 1st Cav Div, Camp Banzai, Iraq, 7 Sep 04, pp. 22–28, GWOT Collection, CMH; Johnston with Miyamasu, 8 Sep 04, pp. 32–35.

[42] 11th MEU Cmd Chron, Encl 1, p. 18–19; I MEF (Forward) and 11th MEU (SOC), "Battle for An Najaf, August 2004," p. 13; Intervs, Johnston with Badger, 7 Sep 04, pp. 16–19, and with Miyamasu, 8 Sep 04, pp. 36–38.

CHAPTER FOUR

ENGINEERS AT WAR

JOHN R. MAASS

A platoon of combat engineers conducts a deliberate breach of a defensive belt and doubles as infantry in the all-out assault to regain control of an enemy-held city.

Fallujah—November 2004

As night settled over the city of Fallujah in western Iraq on 8 November 2004, a few thousand insurgents awaited a Coalition assault they expected to begin at any moment. The Iraqi rebels, reinforced by a large contingent of foreign fighters, had spent months readying their defenses, turning buildings into strongpoints, and emplacing improvised explosive devices (IEDs) and obstacles. Just to the north of town, several thousand U.S. troops and supporting Iraqi battalions moved into attack positions and made final preparations for the offensive. A dirt berm topped by railroad tracks separated the opposing forces. While tracked vehicles would have no trouble crossing it, trucks would find it difficult. On the enemy side, an open area sprinkled with mines and IEDs extended roughly one hundred meters to the first row of houses, some of which were fortified. Before the attackers could advance into the city, they would have to breach this substantial defensive belt. On the northeastern edge of Fallujah, this mission fell to the Army's Task Force 2-2 (2d Battalion, 2d Infantry) and its attached 2d Platoon of Company A, 82d Engineer Battalion.[1]

Obscured by rain, darkness, and a smoke screen and covered by suppressive artillery, tank, and machine-gun fire, the engineers moved forward that evening under incoming small-arms rounds and occasional mortar shells. They deployed their initial weapon, an M58 mine clearing line charge (MCLC, or "micklick"). This device consisted of a trailer bearing a rocket and 1,750 pounds of C4

---

[1] Interv, Matt Matthews, Combat Studies Institute (CSI), with Lt Col Peter A. Newell, 2d Bn, 2d Inf, 23 Mar 06, Operational Leadership Experiences Project, p. 7, CSI, Fort Leavenworth, Kans.

explosives fashioned into a rope 350 feet long. At 1915, the engineers fired the rocket, which arced over the berm pulling the line behind it. After it fell to the ground, the engineers electrically detonated the powerful charge, setting off mines and IEDs near its path. The main blast and secondary explosions of enemy ordnance produced "an awesome sight" and an accompanying shockwave that rolled over the battlefield. "It was this gigantic mushroom cloud," a soldier observed, "and it was just thunder and fire."[2] Another witness thought of it as "fireworks."[3] Like a Fourth of July show, it drew cheers from many of the soldiers and marines keyed up for the pending assault. The second Battle of Fallujah was underway.

Located thirty-five miles west of Baghdad in Anbar Province, Fallujah was known as the city of mosques. Its estimated prewar population of two hundred fifty thousand was mostly Sunni and thus a bastion of support for Saddam Hussein's Ba'ath Party. Many political and religious leaders in the region continued to back Hussein even after U.S. forces ended his regime in 2003. Others, seeking a counterweight to the rising national dominance of the Shi'ite majority, espoused armed opposition to the Coalition Provisional Authority and its plans to establish a new Iraqi government with elections in January 2005.[4] During 2004, the city evolved into "the dark heart of the insurgency."[5]

The first military attempt to eradicate the growing threat from Fallujah occurred in April 2004, triggered by the killing of four American contractors and the hanging of their burned bodies from a bridge. The U.S. Marine attack, hampered by a lack of armored forces and the specter of heavy civilian casualties in a large urban area, came to an unsuccessful end in the first week of May. Bowing to political reality, the Marine command pulled back and sought to control the city with the Fallujah Brigade, a newly created unit consisting of former Iraqi soldiers and other volunteers. This ill-conceived outfit soon became "indistinguishable from the insurgency" in the eyes of American observers. After

[2] Telecon, author with Spec Mark Sauve, 2d Plt, Co A, 82d Engr Bn, 11 Oct 07; Interv, Matthews with Capt James Cobb, 2d Bn, 2d Inf, 2 Jun 06, Operational Leadership Experiences Project, pp. 7–10, CSI; Interv, John McCool, CSI, with S Sgt Jimmy Amyett, 3d Bde Reconnaissance Troop, 31 Jul 06, Operational Leadership Experiences Project, p. 8, CSI; David Bellavia, *House to House: An Epic of War* (New York: Free Press, 2007), pp. 78–79; Center for Army Lessons Learned, *Newsletter*, November 2003, pp. 85–87.
[3] Interv, Matthews with Cobb, 2 Jun 06, p. 10.
[4] Interv, Laurence Lessard, CSI, with Lt Gen Richard F. Natonski, CG, 1 Marine Expeditionary Force, 5 Apr 07, Operational Leadership Experiences Project, pp. 3–4, CSI; Thomas E. Ricks, *Fiasco: The American Military Adventure in Iraq* (New York: The Penguin Press, 2006), pp. 138–39; Bing West, *No True Glory: A Frontline Account of the Battle for Fallujah* (New York: Bantam Books, 2005), pp. 13–14; John R. Ballard, *Fighting for Fallujah: A New Dawn for Iraq* (Westport, Conn.: Praeger Security International, 2006), pp. 2–4; GlobalSecurity.org Sum of Opn AL-FAJR (DAWN), Opn PHANTOM FURY [Fallujah], n.d., Historians files, U.S. Army Center of Military History (CMH), Washington, D.C.; Transcript of PBS *Frontline*: "The Insurgency," 21 Feb 06, Historians files, CMH.
[5] Transcript of Michael Ware Interv on FM WNYC 93.9, 24 Nov 04, Historians files, CMH.

the marines withdrew, the insurgents consolidated their control, bolstered by the appearance that they had defeated U.S. forces in a major battle. The city became a symbol of resistance and a magnet for volunteers from around the Middle East eager to battle American troops. By early November, perhaps as many as three thousand Iraqi and foreign insurgents had gathered there. Their influence spread even wider as they provided vital support to opposition elements around the country.[6]

The approaching national ballot raised the stakes even higher.[7] Maj. Gen. Richard F. Natonski, commander of the 1st Marine Division, believed that "As long as you had a base like Fallujah, where the enemy could rest, rearm, train, refit and launch its attacks from and return to, we could never hold a successful election." Referring to the city as "a real hotbed of the insurgency," U.S. Ambassador to the United Nations John C. Danforth spelled out the American position clearly: "If the elections are going to happen in a timely fashion, which is exceptionally important, then Fallujah has to be taken care of."[8]

Marine commanders began planning a new attack on the city in early September that would be an "aggressive, rapid, offensive maneuver."[9] Initially called Operation Phantom Fury, with the addition of several Iraqi battalions it took on the name al-Fajr (New Dawn) to reflect the multinational composition of the effort. "Our intent was to make this attack as quick as we could," said General Natonski, in part by employing overwhelming firepower against the enemy.[10] To facilitate that goal, the marines bombarded the city with warnings of the pending offensive. As expected, most civilians fled their homes, leaving much of the urban landscape a ghost town except for the insurgents "bound to stay [there] until . . . killed or captured."[11]

Another key change from the first assault was the decision to beef up the attacking force with additional armor and firepower. As one Marine officer observed: "We needed more combat power to thwart the enemy and their

---

[6] Matt M. Matthews, *Operation Al Fajr: A Study in Army and Marine Corps Joint Operations,* Global War on Terrorism Occasional Paper 20 (Fort Leavenworth, Kans.: Combat Studies Institute Press, 2006), pp. 2, 9–10; Ballard, *Fighting for Fallujah,* pp. 1–2, 12–15, 17–24; West, *No True Glory,* pp. 53–220; Ricks, *Fiasco,* pp. 343–45; Telecon, author with Sauve, 11 Oct 07.

[7] "Fighting in Fallujah," U.S. Department of Defense Office of Public Affairs, 8 Nov 04, Historians files, CMH.

[8] Interv, Lessard with Natonski, 5 Apr 07, p. 5; Trans of CNN, "American Morning," 9 November 2004, Historians files, CMH.

[9] Matthews, *Operation Al Fajr,* p. 11; Matt M. Matthews, "Shootout on Objective Wolf, 10 November 2004," in William G. Robertson, ed., *In Contact! Case Studies from the Long War,* vol. 1. (Fort Leavenworth, Kans.: Combat Studies Institute Press, 2006), p. 5; "Fighting in Fallujah," 8 Nov 04; Toby Harnden, "Phantoms Close in on Ghost Town," *The Sunday Telegraph,* 7 November 2004, copy in historians files, CMH.

[10] Matthews, "Shootout," pp. 5–6; Matthews, *Operation Al Fajr,* p. 20; Interv, Lessard with Natonski, 5 Apr 07, p. 6.

[11] Telecon, author with Sauve, 11 Oct 07.

defenses."[12] The I Marine Expeditionary Force headquarters requested and received two Army mechanized battalions to bolster the two reinforced Marine infantry regiments available for the offensive. Planners assigned Task Force 2-7 to support Regimental Combat Team (RCT) 1 and Task Force 2-2 to work with RCT 7.[13] Lt. Col. Peter A. Newell commanded Task Force 2-2, composed primarily of Company A of the 2d Battalion, 63d Armor (2-63); Troop F, 4th Cavalry; and Company A, 2d Battalion, 2d Infantry (2-2), a mechanized unit. The battalion's 14 M1A2 Abrams tanks, 16 M2A2 Bradley infantry fighting vehicles, 2 M109A6 Paladins (155-mm. self-propelled howitzers), and 4 M120 120-mm. mortars could deliver a heavy punch. The 2d Battalion of the Iraqi Intervention Force also supported Newell's soldiers and would follow the American advance.[14]

Capt. Sean P. Sims commanded Company A of Task Force 2-2. Task organized like its parent outfit, it had two mechanized infantry platoons, a tank platoon, and a platoon from Company A, 82d Engineer Battalion, led by recently commissioned 2d Lt. Shawn P. Gniazdowski. The twenty engineers fielded 2 M9 armored combat earthmovers, 3 M113A3 armored personnel carriers, 2 D9 armored bulldozers and their 2-man crews borrowed from the marines, and 1 M58 MCLC with two reloads. In addition, they were well supplied with explosive charges for blowing doors and destroying obstacles.[15]

The engineers and the rest of Task Force 2-2 had arrived in the Fallujah area on 5 November, coming from Forward Operating Base (FOB) Normandy seventy-five miles northeast of Baghdad. They made final preparations for the assault at Camp Fallujah, twenty miles outside the city.[16] The platoon practiced techniques for breaching obstacles and taught the rest of the company basic classes on demolitions. The engineers assembled explosive charges, even attaching the fuses beforehand, which raised the risk of an accident but would save time later when the men were under fire. Although the unit was trained and equipped to perform standard combat engineer missions, the soldiers also would double as infantry during the coming battle, so they practiced urban tactics such as clearing buildings.[17] The engineers'

---

[12] Matthews, *Operation Al Fajr*, p. 14.

[13] Matthews, "Shootout," pp. 5–6.

[14] Matthews, "Shootout," p. 6; Patricia S. Hollis with Maj Gen John R. S. Batiste, "Task Force Danger in OIF II: Preparing a Secure Environment for the Iraqi National Elections," *Field Artillery Magazine* (July-August 2005): 4.

[15] Matthews, "Shootout," pp. 6–7; Interv, Capt Laura Neal, 46th Military History Detachment (MHD), with 2d Lt Shawn P. Gniazdowski, 2d Plt, Co A, 82d Engr Bn, 7 Feb 05, p. 7, Global War on Terrorism (GWOT) Collection, CMH; Telecon, author with Sauve, 11 Oct 07; Interv, Neal with Sgt Blain P. Bart, 2d Plt, Co A, 82d Engr Bn, 1st Inf Div, 8 Feb 05, p. 9, GWOT Collection, CMH; Interv, Matthews with Capt Jeff Emery, 1st Plt, Co A, 2d Bn, 2d Inf, 17 Jul 06, p. 6, Operational Leadership Experiences Project, CSI.

[16] Matthews, *Operation Al Fajr*, p. 21.

[17] Intervs, Neal with Bart, 8 Feb 05, p. 2, and with Sfc Reginald Clayton, 2d Plt, Co A, 82d Engr Bn, 7 Feb 05, p. 20, GWOT Collection, CMH; Telecon, author with Sauve, 11 Oct 07.

An M113 armored personnel carrier and an M9 armored combat earthmover of the 2d Platoon, Company A, 82d Engineer Battalion, on a road near Fallujah. The unit's M9s were instrumental in breaching the city's outer ring of defenses at the beginning of the battle.

additional role was critical, since the task force had only a single mechanized company with less than a hundred infantrymen. A Marine battalion, in contrast, fielded more than five hundred grunts.

The task force rehearsed the opening moves of the operation on 6 and 7 November. The plan called for the joint force of soldiers and marines to attack Fallujah from the north while a blocking force, the Army's "Blackjack Brigade" of the 1st Cavalry Division, would seal off the city from other quadrants.[18] Newell's Task Force 2-2 would advance on the far left flank of the assault with the objective of reaching Highway 10, a six lane east-west roadway that bisected the city.[19] (*See Map 6.*) Designated Phase Line Fran, this major traffic artery was to serve as the operation's main supply route.[20] Along the way, the soldiers would clear their zone of the enemy. Most of this area consisted of adjacent one- and two-story houses built of concrete or masonry and often having walled courtyards. Each one had the potential to be a mini fortress. The insurgents also had barricaded the streets with cars, dirt-filled HESCO baskets, concrete Texas barriers, shipping containers, and anything else that might slow the movement of American troops and vehicles.[21] But first, the soldiers would have to cross the berm and fight their way into the city. The engineers, critical in this role, started off almost at a disadvantage. Initially, Marine commanders

---

[18] Matthews, *Operation Al Fajr*, pp. 1–2.

[19] Ibid., pp. 15–19; Interv, Matthews with Newell, 23 Mar 06, pp. 3–5.

[20] Matthews, *Operation Al Fajr*, p. 19; Interv, Matthews with Newell, 23 Mar 06, pp. 5–6; Telecon, author with Sauve, 11 Oct 07.

[21] HESCO baskets are steel-mesh reinforced fabric containers that can be rapidly filled with dirt or sand at the point of use to serve as a defensive barrier. The British corporation HESCO Bastion manufactures them.

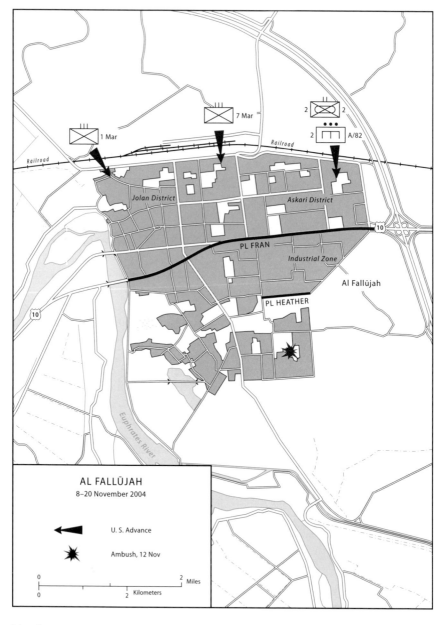

AL FALLŪJAH
8–20 November 2004

◄■ U. S. Advance

✸ Ambush, 12 Nov

0 — — — — 2 Miles
0 — — — — 2 Kilometers

Map 6

were hesitant to authorize use of the MCLC, considering it inappropriate in an urban environment. Colonel Newell, however, argued for it: "If I've got to go into this place, I have to be able to go in without fighting IEDs to break the ring to get into the city." He ultimately won his point.[22]

The marines and soldiers expected to meet stiff resistance since the insurgents had been preparing for a rematch for several months. Equipped with small arms, rocket-propelled grenades (RPGs), and machine guns, the enemy typically operated in groups of four to twelve men with minimal coordination. They customarily fought from inside buildings rather than in the street, gaining some protection against the heavier weapons American troops brought into the fight. Lacking night vision equipment, they tended to operate during the day but also used the supposed cover of darkness to reposition, resupply, or take potshots at Coalition forces.[23] The latter tactic would prove suicidal given U.S. dominance of the night. American troops did not underestimate their foe, in particular believing that the foreign fighters were "pretty good and . . . had some level of training."[24] Nevertheless, the soldiers were eager to go in. As they readied themselves to attack, the 2d Platoon listened to Colonel Newell's final exhortations: "That pile of crap has got to be cleaned out . . . keep hammering targets and if you see a guy with an AK47, I expect you to hose him with a .50 caliber machine-gun." Newell pointed out that the enemy fighters did not "give a rat's ass about civilians, morals or the ethics of war."[25] The task force commander's wishes were clear: "I expect you to pile in and kick someone's ass."[26]

Early on the morning of 8 November, Task Force 2-2 left the base camp and moved into its attack positions near the city. The enemy saw the movement and fired a few mortar rounds, inflicting a minor wound on one soldier in Company A. While leaders made a visual reconnaissance of their objectives, Troop F orchestrated a daylong preparatory bombardment with both direct and indirect fire to knock out the strongpoints on the edge of town. Most of the soldiers in 2-2 hunkered down for a long wait until nightfall, when the main assault would commence. For fourteen hours, the engineer platoon "just sat and waited to go to war," one man remembered. "Everyone was a little on edge. And we all wanted to do it. We all wanted to get it done with."[27] The 2d Squad kept busy making last-minute operational checks on the line charge, leaving nothing to chance.

---

[22] Interv, Matthews with Newell, 23 Mar 06, p. 6.

[23] Maj. A. R. Milburn, "Lessons Learned; Operation PHANTOM FURY," 5 Jan 05, p. 2, Marine Corps Center for Lessons Learned, Quantico Marine Corps Base, Va.

[24] Interv, Matthews with Cobb, 2 Jun 06, p. 15.

[25] Toby Harnden, "Cash on the Spot—If They Tell Us Where the Weapons Are," *The Telegraph*, 8 Nov 04, copy in historians files, CMH.

[26] Toby Harnden, "Hey, Hurry Up. You're Holding Up My Men," *The Telegraph*, 21 November 2004, copy in Historians files, CMH.

[27] Interv, Neal with Bart, 8 Feb 05, p. 8.

Late in the afternoon, the tanks of Company A, 2d Battalion, 63d Armor, moved into their attack-by-fire position and added their main guns to the fray. A dreary day, already marked by occasional rain showers and chilling wind, got darker as night fell. Shortly before 1900, the task force began firing artillery smoke rounds at the edge of the city, raising a cloud to further obscure enemy vision. Right on the hour, Company A, Task Force 2-2, crossed the line of departure and moved up to the berm. As the insurgents blindly fired rifles, machine guns, and 60-mm. mortars into the area, S. Sgt. Bryan J. Lockwald's squad of engineers moved up in their M113 armored personnel carrier, towing the M58 into place and deploying it. Both the trailer and the engineer vehicles loaded with prefused explosive charges posed an extreme hazard—a random hit could have dealt a devastating blow to the breach operation and the platoon. But the smoke and suppressive fire minimized the risk and the rocket went arcing downrange on schedule. The ensuing blast at 1915 seemed to take out a number of IEDs judging by the secondary explosions that accompanied it.[28]

The line charge theoretically cleared an area one hundred meters long and fourteen meters wide, but it was not effective against every type of mine. Amidst the billowing smoke and dust, the engineers rushed over the berm to proof the lane. One of the armored earthmovers led the way, since it "could take the bulk of the fire coming in." Its dozer-like blade plowed through the ground churned up by the line charge, pushing out or detonating any remaining mines. In the process, it set off two explosions but suffered no damage.[29] Sgt. Blain P. Bart's 1st Squad had the job of following behind and marking the path with engineer tape, flags, and chemical lights so the rest of the task force could see the left-hand boundary the entire way to the city's edge. Bart had his men lay out the cleared approaches to the breach while he grasped a handful of flags, crossed the berm, and ran down the lane, sticking the markers in the ground at intervals. All the while, enemy small-arms fire peppered the area and a covering force of snipers, Bradleys, and tanks responded with suppressive fire. The engineers finished their task in ten minutes, and Company A's armored vehicles poured through to secure a foothold. The rest of Task Force 2-2 followed soon after to launch the main assault and begin to "break up the scorpion's nest" in the city.[30]

As the infantrymen and tankers seized their initial objectives, Gniazdowski's platoon continued to widen and improve the lane through the minefield. The

---

[28] Intervs, Neal with Gniazdowski, 7 Feb 05, pp. 4–5, and with Spec Russell Joslin, 2d Plt, Co A, 82d Engr Bn, 8 Feb 05, pp. 8–9, GWOT Collection, CMH; Bellavia, *House to House*, pp. 79–81; Interv, Matthews with Cobb, 2 Jun 06, p. 10.

[29] Intervs, Matthews with Newell, 23 Mar 06, p. 9; Neal with Clayton, 7 Feb 05, pp. 11–12; Neal with Bart, 8 Feb 05, pp. 8–10. Telecon, author with Sauve, 11 Oct 07; Center for Army Lessons Learned, *Newsletter*, November 2003, pp. 85–87.

[30] Bill Powell, "War by Fits and Starts," *Time* (14 November 2004), copy in Historians files, CMH.

On the streets of Fallujah, engineers move warily and keep an eye out in all directions. Bypassed insurgents represented a threat in nominal rear areas early in the battle.

trucks of the supporting Iraqi battalion could not negotiate the railroad berm, so the engineers blew out a section of rails and then plowed through the dirt mound to accommodate them. Just before midnight, the adjacent Marine battalion sent its tanks through following a failed attempt to establish a breach in its own zone.[31]

Once inside the city, Task Force 2-2 drove south with Captain Sims' company in the lead. The Abrams and Bradleys met small-arms and RPG fire, some of it coming from rooftops, as well as occasional IEDs; but none of it slowed their steady progress through the darkened streets.[32] The infantrymen dismounted occasionally to clear buildings as they easily seized assigned objectives. When the engineer platoon completed its work at the breach, it moved out to catch up with the main body. The D9s and the excavators cleared obstacles in the roads as they advanced. They had covered about a mile by 0415, when a bypassed insurgent launched an RPG that struck one of the Marine bulldozers and injured one of its operators. (Earlier that night, the battalion's command sergeant major had died from a gunshot in a similar incident well behind the supposed frontline.) The platoon withdrew to the breach site to

---

[31] Interv, Matthews with Newell, 23 Mar 06, p. 10; Michael Ware, "Into the Hot Zone," *Time* (14 November 2004), copy in Historians files, CMH; Telecon, author with Sauve, 11 Oct 07.

[32] Interv, Matthews with Newell, 23 Mar 06, p. 11.

evacuate its casualty and wait for first light. The engineers endured a couple more hours of random small-arms fire until dawn broke.[33]

In the morning, the unit headed south again to link up with the rest of the task force. Navigating the urban terrain, the soldiers observed that it was mostly unoccupied. After a brief pause to refuel and rearm, Company A moved out at roughly the same time to cover the last few blocks to Phase Line Fran. The battalion met its heaviest fire there, where insurgents had occupied the buildings on the south side of the highway, taking advantage of the wide open area's clear fields of fire to establish a defensive belt similar to that at the northern edge of the city. The soldiers pounded the structures with artillery and direct fire until the enemy response dwindled to nothing. The engineer platoon sergeant, Sfc. Reginald Clayton, noted: "They were better fighters than we'd seen before. When they shot, they usually hit their targets."[34]

The engineers received the mission of clearing the streets throughout the task force sector. The dozers got busy pushing rubble, civilian vehicles, and other obstructions off the roadway. If a car looked like it might be rigged with an IED, the soldiers could usually get a tank to destroy it first with a main-gun round. The engineers used their own explosives to deal with mines and other IEDs scattered along the routes. One of the other platoon leaders noted that "their main job was to become the bomb squad."[35] Sergeant Bart later recalled: "We . . . just dropped charges and ran—drop charge, and run, drop charge—you keep going until we cleared most of the stuff."[36]

Just to the west of Task Force 2-2, the Marine battalion was fighting house to house and making slower progress, in part because it still lacked the heavier punch of the Army mechanized battalion. Some insurgents took advantage of the gap between the two American units to sidestep out of the way of the approaching marines and into the vacuum behind the soldiers. Other enemy fighters had simply hunkered down during the previous night's rapid onslaught and let the battle pass them by. During the course of 9 November, Colonel Newell established control over his portion of Phase Line Fran and swept it clear of IEDs then ordered Captain Sims' company to turn back north on the morning of the tenth and root out these pockets of resistance.[37]

Sims assigned each of his platoons a sector. The engineers, reinforced by the battalion scout platoon, were responsible for the easternmost blocks just north of Phase Line Fran. The squads worked together in a rotating fashion to check out houses and provide cover in the street. Clearing buildings room to room was dangerous, grueling work and initially created "high anxiety" among

---

[33] Interv, Neal with Bart, 8 Feb 05, pp. 9–10; Telecon, author with Sauve, 11 Oct 07.

[34] Interv, Neal with Clayton, 7 Feb 05, p. 9.

[35] Interv, Matthews with Emery, 17 Jul 06, p. 9.

[36] Interv, Neal with Bart, 8 Feb 05, p. 11.

[37] Interv, Neal with Gniazdowski, 7 Feb 05, p. 15; GlobalSecurity.com Sum, Opn al-Fajr (Dawn) Operation Phantom Fury [Fallujah]; Intervs, Matthews with Emery, 17 Jul 06, p. 8, and with Newell, 23 Mar 06, p. 12.

A soldier of the 82d Engineer Battalion observes as a Marine Corps D9 armored bulldozer aids in clearing a building in Fallujah. The wire cage around the cab was a defensive measure against rocket-propelled grenades.

the soldiers. There was no telling which structure or which room within might be an enemy position. Often, the insurgents simply fired as the Americans approached and then fled to the next building where they had stocked weapons or ammunition. "By the time we could shoot back they were already gone," said Sgt. John A. Cassidy, who "never saw more than six at a time."[38] Even empty houses posed a threat, since some contained booby traps. To reduce the risk, the engineers often used small charges to blow the doors off structures, which simultaneously solved the problem of locks and hidden tripwires.[39] Immediately following the small blast, a squad rushed in to search for insurgents. Inside, they sometimes discovered bodies of "people who had been dead for a week, two weeks, a month, and it was just horrible. It smelled awful."[40] The platoon also destroyed numerous caches of heavy ordnance, but saved recovered small arms for use by Iraqi government forces.[41]

While holed up in one building with large windows, the engineers received accurate rifle fire from a structure across the street. Pinned down and unable to

[38] Interv, Neal with Sgt John A. Cassidy, 2d Plt, Co A, 82d Engr Bn, 8 Feb 05, untrans, GWOT Collection, CMH; Interv, Neal with Joslin, 8 Feb 05, pp. 6, 8–10; Ware, "Into the Hot Zone."

[39] Interv, Neal with Bart, 8 Feb 05, pp. 11–12.

[40] Ibid., p. 14.

[41] Ibid., pp. 29–30; Interv, Neal with Gniazdowski, 7 Feb 05, p. 9.

return fire from the exposed position, Sergeant Lockwald sent Specs. Mitch L. Sievers and Justin A. Oakley to get an AT4 light antitank weapon. Returning soon after with a missile in hand, the two soldiers fired it from a room on the second story of their position into the house across the road. The force of the back blast "rattled our cage a little bit," Lockwald recalled, and filled the building with clouds of dust; but the round eliminated all further enemy activity on the receiving end.[42]

The engineers cleared building after building all day long and into the night. Darkness made the task that much more difficult, since the soldiers relied on lights attached to their weapons to illuminate the pitch-black rooms. (Night vision goggles provided poor depth perception and too limited a field view for such close-quarters work; in any case, too little natural light filtered inside to make them fully effective.) The risk never lessened, but repetition dulled the sense of danger. One noncommissioned officer (NCO) recalled: "I forced myself to go in first.... I would just push myself in. And, it just gradually got easier. I stopped thinking so much."[43]

S. Sgt. Donaval A. Avilamartinez, Sergeant Cassidy, and Spec. Mark C. Sauve led the way into one house that proved memorable. Sauve alertly spotted a wet footprint at the entrance and pointed it out, so the soldiers knew "there was a strong possibility of someone being in there." The men proceeded to carefully clear the first room. They noted two additional rooms with closed doors and a staircase situated diagonally across from them, "which added another degree of danger." After Avilamartinez got his men in place to cover Sergeant Bart's movement into the house, he called for him.[44] Bart and Spec. Kyle E. Matus went inside and headed for one of the adjacent rooms. Their tactical drill was well rehearsed by now:

> There's always the threat that when you come into the foyer that somebody is going to shoot you from the stairwell, and so what we usually do is run across the foyer as fast as we can into the other room because the rule is that when you open a door you keep going. You never stop because if you stand in a doorway and somebody's in there, it's easy to hit you.

In the lead, Bart ran across the space and forced open the door in a corner on the opposite side. As he lifted his weapon and attached light to search the room, he and Matus saw an insurgent four feet away kneeling with an RPG and another enemy fighter laying on the floor with a machine gun. "These guys

[42] Interv, Neal with S Sgt Brian Lockwald, 2d Plt, Co A, 82d Engr Bn, 8 Feb 05, p. 14, GWOT Collection, CMH.

[43] Interv, Neal with Bart, 8 Feb 05, p. 21.

[44] Comments by S Sgt Donaval Avilamartinez, 2d Plt, Co A, 82d Engr Bn, 1st Inf Div, 15 Jan 08, Historian's files, CMH.

Pvt. Russell Joslin and other soldiers of the 2d Platoon, Company A, 82d Engineer Battalion, enter a room during the battle. The unit cleared hundreds of structures room by room.

were point blank" and both weapons were "staring directly at our faces," Matus recalled. The two soldiers had only seconds to react in what was a very small room. The man with the RPG screamed in shock upon Bart's appearance in the doorway, "and the second my light hit him, I shot him and I killed him." For the sergeant it was a moment of "utter terror," in which his first reaction was to "shoot the guy that was in front of me . . . it was entirely reflex. I think if there was any thought that had to go into that, I would have been dead."[45]

Matus also opened fire then quickly stepped back from the door. The insurgent with the machine gun let loose with a wild burst that missed both Americans even at that close range. Bart's vision "just went red because it was muzzle flashes right in front of me." Matus saw "the room going red from all the tracers." The sergeant stood in the doorway for what "felt like a lifetime" but backed out after a moment of hesitation. He sprinted down a dark hallway; as he ran, he saw tracer fire going through the wall and past him. Bart thought, "That's the last thing I'm ever going to see."[46]

Fueled with adrenalin, the sergeant burst into the kitchen, saw a dark object in the corner, and fired, only then realizing it was just the stove. Matus, who had followed, pointed out a door to the outside and yanked down a curtain that

---

[45] Telecon, author with Sauve, 11 Oct 07; Interv, Neal with Bart, 8 Feb 05, pp. 15–19; E-mail, Spec Kyle Matus, 2d Plt, Co A, 82d Engr Bn, 1st Inf Div, to author, 12 Mar 08, Historians files, CMH.

[46] Interv, Neal with Bart, 8 Feb 05, pp.15–19; E-mail, Matus to author, 12 Mar 08.

A squad of engineers cautiously moves upstairs while searching for enemy fighters. Clearing buildings was exhausting, dangerous work.

covered it. Bart saw a figure and raised his rifle to shoot; but in a split second, he caught the glint of his light off the reflective tape on a fellow soldier and held fire.

Bart regrouped, reloaded, and cautiously advanced back down the hallway toward the occupied room. He and another soldier fired through the doorway and wall. Seconds later, Sergeant Cassidy ran up with a hand grenade and hurled it in. After the explosion, the men kicked the door all the way open and charged into the smoky space. Their eyes were drawn to a wooden wardrobe with one of the doors open and blood dripping out. The insurgent machine gunner had sought cover in it and subsequently been killed by return fire or the grenade. Although in Bart's estimation the entire action had lasted less than two minutes, "it seemed like forever."[47]

After a few short hours of rest, the 2d Platoon and the rest of Newell's command received orders to attack south of Highway 10 into "an industrial wasteland," an area roughly two kilometers wide and two deep, primarily consisting of warehouses and factories.[48] This section of Fallujah was "the heart of the school for terrorists" and considered "the most heavily defended" part of the city.[49] Foreign fighters had taken it over months before and set up several IED factories and training sites. The task force spent much of the day handing over positions to a Marine battalion, refitting, and preparing to launch the new assault.

Task Force 2-2 crossed the line of departure at 1400. The engineers followed in trace of the other Company A platoons with their more heavily armored Abrams and Bradleys. The enemy seemed more experienced and better trained

[47] Telecon, author with Sauve, 11 Oct 07; Interv, Neal with Bart, 8 Feb 05, pp. 15–19, and with Clayton, 7 Feb 05, p. 16.

[48] Interv, Neal with Bart, 8 Feb 05, p. 3.

[49] Interv, Matthews with Newell, 23 Mar 06, p. 14; Toby Harnden, "This Is Where the Foreign Fighters Hang Out," *The Sunday Telegraph*, 10 Nov 04; Ware, "Into the Hot Zone." Intervs, Lessard with Natonski, 5 Apr 07, p. 6; Matthews with Emery, 17 Jul 06, p. 11; Matthews with Capt Doug Walter, 3d Bde, 1st Inf Div, 21 Jul 06, Operational Leadership Experiences Project, CSI, p. 9. TF [Task Force] 2-2 Inf Opn PHANTOM FURY Sum, n.d., GWOT Collection, CMH.

than those they had faced north of Highway 10.[50] And the fire was heavier, keeping the engineers mostly inside or near their vehicles. In addition to small arms, hand grenades, and RPGs, the insurgents brought to bear a new weapon: 40-mm. Chinese rockets fired from homemade launchers consisting of plastic pipe and handles attached with hose clamps. The fighters also attempted to slip past the frontline infantry along back alleys or via rooftops. The engineers came into contact with a few of these infiltrators and brought to bear their M203 grenade launchers and the .50-caliber machine guns mounted on their personnel carriers.[51]

The movement continued until 2000, when the entire task force halted at Phase Line Heather, the southern edge of the industrial area. The pause allowed the Marine battalion on the right flank to catch up and also gave the 1st Marine Division headquarters a chance to sort out who was responsible for the battlespace farther south. Just after 2330, the advance resumed. Newell's battalion crossed an open area a few hundred meters wide and entered the Shohada District, a residential sector in the southeast corner of the city that was less densely packed than the northern neighborhoods. By daylight on 12 November, the task force had reached its limit of advance at Phase Line Jenna, nearly fifteen hundred meters south of Heather. The vehicles of the battalion tactical command post pulled into a dirt lot about one hundred fifty meters wide and two hundred fifty meters long and parked close together. The left-flank elements of Company A, including the engineer platoon, were also in and around the area. Captain Sims spotted a few insurgents shifting in the darkness to a different building and sent Sergeant Lockwald's squad to clear it. The engineers found no one but began to set up a strongpoint on the roof as the first rays of dawn came up.[52]

Throughout the battalion, the men began pulling off their night vision devices, adjusting their eyes, and stretching their muscles after long hours of movement and combat. Most had slept little in the past four days, and all were "dead tired."[53] With perfect timing, the enemy initiated an ambush at that vulnerable point of transition. "All hell broke loose," recalled Company A's senior NCO, 1st Sgt. Peter L. Smith, "we engaged 360 degrees."[54] Dozens of foreign fighters had lain in wait in the surrounding buildings and in numerous spider holes dug into the ground and topped by dirt-covered sheets of metal that blended into the terrain. Small-arms and RPG fire poured in from all points of the compass. Some of the engineers were in the thick of

---

[50] Interv, Neal with Bart, 8 Feb 05, pp. 27–29.
[51] Ibid., p. 22.
[52] Interv, Neal with Lockwald, 8 Feb 05, p. 19.
[53] Interv, Neal with Bart, 8 Feb 05, p. 22.
[54] Interv, Matthews with Sgt Maj Peter Smith, Co A, 2d Bn, 2d Inf, 1st Div, 6 Jun 06, p. 9, Operational Leadership Experiences Project, CSI.

the ambush, surrounded in the open area, while others were taking fire in the streets nearby.

The first RPG struck the open hatch of a Bradley, mortally wounding the Company A executive officer, 1st Lt. Edward D. Iwan. Another hit a tank and started a fire on the turret. One rocket whooshed by within a foot of an engineer NCO's head. Sergeant Clayton used his vehicles to cover some avenues of approach at the edge of the kill sack and had his remaining soldiers dismount and take cover in a nearby building. They scrambled to the roof and returned fire at any target they could identify. Sergeant Bart saw insurgents moving from building to building in an attempt to surround his squad. His tired soldiers, however, "were just picking them off one at a time as they were coming up closer."[55] To add to the confusion, the battalion lost radio contact with the marines when the communications security measures changed at the scheduled daily time right in the middle of the battle. Since the soldiers were engaging insurgents to their north, there also was concern over fratricide with the supporting Iraqi battalion operating a few hundred meters behind the task force.[56]

After thirty minutes of intense combat, Colonel Newell ordered his companies to break contact and consolidate one block to the north.[57] Instead of fighting on the enemy's terms, the task force would regroup and prepare a deliberate assault on the hornet's nest. One RPG round had lodged in the tire of a high mobility multipurpose wheeled vehicle (HMMWV) but did not detonate. Sergeants Bart and Avilamartinez had to pull the dud out before the vehicle could move. Once the battalion had established its new position, Newell had his companies clear the buildings in the area to ensure that no other insurgents were lying in wait. Then each company rotated a platoon at a time to the rear to refuel and pick up ammunition and supplies. That night, AC–130 Spectre gunships and artillery "pounded" the southern part of Fallujah.[58]

The next day, 13 November, the troops readied for the new push. Company A and the engineers drew the eastern side of the battalion front where the number of bunkers and other defensive positions was greatest. As Captain Sims entered a house near the line of departure to establish an observation post, he was cut down by an insurgent and killed. The loss of another company leader struck the engineers hard. Specialist Sauve sensed from that point on that he and his fellow soldiers "had a different reason for fighting."[59]

---

[55] Intervs, Neal with Bart, 8 Feb 05, p. 24; with Clayton, 7 Feb 05, pp. 21–22; with Lockwald, 8 Feb 05, pp. 18–21.

[56] Matthews, *Operation Al Fajr*, p. 51.

[57] Toby Harnden, "Warriors Spare a Moment for the Ones Not Going Back," *The Sunday Telegraph*, 15 November 2004, copy in Historians files, CMH.

[58] Intervs, Matthews with Newell, 23 Mar 06, p. 16, and Neal with Clayton, 7 Feb 05, p. 23.

[59] Intervs, Matthews with Newell, 23 Mar 06, p. 16, and Neal with Joslin, 8 Feb 05, p. 17; Harnden, "Phantoms Close in on Ghost Town"; Telecon, author with Sauve, 11 Oct 07.

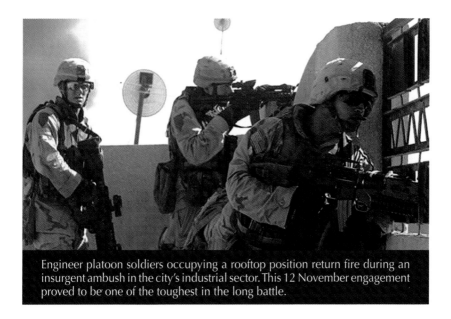

Engineer platoon soldiers occupying a rooftop position return fire during an insurgent ambush in the city's industrial sector. This 12 November engagement proved to be one of the toughest in the long battle.

At 1500, Task Force 2-2 again pushed forward into the southern sector of the city "to destroy the remaining pockets of AIF [anti-Iraqi forces] in zone."[60] Assisted by air support, the company's Abrams and Bradleys swept in and "just laid waste to everything." "It was weapons-free" and, as one soldier described the action, "the gloves had been pulled off." The engineers again were last in the task force's marching order because they had the lightest-armor vehicles; but the D9 dozer kept busy leveling any house that seemed to have been used as a strongpoint.[61] The soldiers saw few enemy fighters, as the insurgents had either died in the preparatory bombardment or slipped away to avoid a set-piece action against the stronger American armored force. After barely an hour, Newell's men had reached the southern outskirts of the city.

The Army task force pulled back for a quick refuel and resupply then conducted a passage of lines with the adjacent Marine battalion to assault south in that zone. By now, the soldiers had refined their tactics based on experience and they moved rapidly but methodically in a style reminiscent of a World War I attack. They liberally used air support and artillery and kept shifting it ahead of them as they progressed, a form of walking barrage that a doughboy would have instantly recognized, except for the speed of the advance. The tanks followed close behind the artillery, using their main guns against any remaining resistance. The Bradleys came next, then the engineers. After all that firepower, the soldiers met no opposition when they searched the buildings that were

---

[60] TF 2-2 Inf Opn Phantom Fury Sum.
[61] Intervs, Neal with Bart, 8 Feb 05, p. 27, and with Joslin, 8 Feb 05, p. 16; Sgt Kimberly Snow, "Task Force 2-2 Fights for Fallujah, *Danger Forward*, 1 (2004): 12.

still standing. "This was some of the best movement we had," Sergeant Clayton thought.[62] The engineers also had to help extricate two of the company's tanks, which had become stuck in holes in the roadway caused by collapsed insurgent tunnels. Alerted to nearby enemy activity on the ground by an unmanned aerial vehicle flying above them, platoon leaders called in artillery on insurgents as they assisted with the extraction of the tanks. At 2300, the battalion reached its limit of advance, having killed an additional twenty-eight foreign fighters.

For the next six days, the task force and the engineers searched every building in the industrial area and the eastern sectors of the city. They discovered numerous weapons caches, including heavy 57-mm. antiaircraft guns that would have been a serious threat to all vehicles but the tanks, had the enemy gotten them into action. The troops also uncovered more IED factories, one of them with an assembly line converting 500-pound bombs.[63] In addition to clearing structures, Lieutenant Gniazdowski's soldiers swept the major roads in their sector, particularly Phase Line Fran. As part of this mission, the platoon fired another MCLC on Highway 10 to clear IEDs and booby traps in buildings.[64] Shot down a city block, the powerful charge blew out all windows and doors and expelled some of the contents of the buildings out the back openings.[65] The device wasn't designed for urban combat, but Sergeant Lockwald reflected: "You know, think outside the box. It worked well."[66] The engineers found many more IEDs as they investigated every object that looked out of place on or near a roadway. Once the men identified a device, they traced the wires back to their source, usually a car battery, then used a charge to destroy the IED.[67] The work was tedious but dangerous, and two HMMWVs from other companies suffered damage from mines.[68]

After nearly two weeks of bombardment, armored combat, and the destruction of IEDs and weapons caches, much of the urban area was reduced to rubble. In most respects, this battle came closer than any other action in Iraq to more traditional urban fighting in the mold of Stalingrad. In such a realm, American advantages in armor, firepower, and training proved even more dominant than usual. It was no surprise then that resistance had faded to the point that Colonel Newell boldly stated he could "walk anywhere I want in the city."[69] The engineers were amazed when a puppy emerged unscathed from

---

[62] Interv, Neal with Clayton, 7 Feb 05, p. 28.

[63] Intervs, Neal with Bart, 8 Feb 05, p. 30; with Clayton, 7 Feb 05, pp. 28–30; with Cassidy, 8 Feb 05; with Lockwald, 8 Feb 05, p. 18; Matthews with Emery, 17 Jul 06, pp. 13–15. Telecon, author with Sauve, 11 Oct 07.

[64] Interv, Neal with Gniazdowski, 7 Feb 05, pp. 22, 31–32; Telecon, author with Sauve, 11 Oct 07.

[65] Telecon, author with Sauve, 11 Oct 07.

[66] Interv, Neal with Lockwald, 8 Feb 05, p. 22.

[67] Intervs, Neal with Gniazdowski, 7 Feb 05, p. 18, and with Lockwald, 8 Feb 05, p. 17.

[68] TF 2-2 Inf Opn PHANTOM FURY Sum.

[69] Toby Harnden, "Fighters' Leaders Run as Fallujah Falls to US Troops," *The Sunday*

the ruins; the company adopted it and named it Fallujah. On 20 November, the task force handed over its zone to a Marine battalion and headed out of the city.[70]

American forces had achieved the immediate goal of wresting control of the city from the insurgents; but it would take years before excessive violence by al-Qaeda in Iraq, coupled with Coalition pacification efforts, turned the population in Anbar away from rebellion and toward support of the Iraqi government. Nevertheless, the belief that insurgents could stand toe to toe against U.S. units and hold their ground was now thoroughly shattered. Henceforth, the war in Sunni areas devolved into a more typical guerrilla-style campaign relying on stealth and pinprick attacks designed to wear down American will. Instead of asserting active and visible control of terrain and people, al-Qaeda in Iraq and its Iraqi confederates would exert such influence as they could primarily through intimidation and terror.

For the 2d Platoon, Company A, 82d Engineer Battalion, as well as the other troops involved, the Second Battle of Fallujah had been grueling and dangerous. Sergeant Clayton, with eighteen years in the Army, appraised it as "the heaviest fighting that I've ever seen, the most destruction I've seen." While he thought the battle had been "pretty hard" and wanted to "forget most of it," the contribution of the platoon had been an important component in the victory.[71] From the breaching operation that had eased the entry of the task force into the city to the removal of deadly explosives strewn throughout the urban zone and the clearing of all the buildings in their secondary mission as infantrymen, the engineers had accomplished all that was expected and more. Capt. Douglas R. Walter, who succeeded to command of Company A, summarized their value in the understated fashion of a warrior: "A great bunch of guys, very capable, very competent, and they knew a lot about demolitions."[72]

Telegraph, 15 November 2004, copy in Historians files, CMH.
[70] Interv, Neal with Clayton, 7 Feb 05, pp. 35–36.
[71] Ibid., p. 31.
[72] Interv, Matthews with Walter, 21 Jul 06, p. 10; Matthews, *Operation Al Fajr*, p. 1.

CHAPTER FIVE

UNANTICIPATED BATTLE

MARK J. REARDON

A dispute between a corrupt official and an illegal militia ensnares a task-organized armor battalion in a daylong urban battle.

Musayyib—July 2006

Musayyib, a majority Shi'ite city of about two hundred thousand located sixty kilometers south of Baghdad, reflected many of the divisive issues that arose in Iraq after the toppling of Saddam Hussein's regime. On Saturday evening, 17 July 2005, al-Qaeda in Iraq targeted the town as part of a regional wave of suicide attacks. A propane tanker truck exploded in a fireball just as shoppers crowded a marketplace and worshippers departed an adjacent Shi'ite mosque. A hundred civilians perished in the inferno, making it one of the deadliest terrorist operations up to that point in the conflict.[1] Angry crowds blamed local authorities for not doing enough to prevent the horrific attack, while national legislators criticized the prime minister for repeated failures by Iraqi security forces.[2] Moqtada al-Sadr ordered his Mahdi militia to begin patrolling neighborhoods, calculating that he would garner popular support by doing so. The Baghdad government responded to the bombing by replacing the city's chief of police with Col. Ahmed Mijwal, a Shi'ite.

The colonel would prove to be a corrupt official who did little to soothe tensions between the religious sects. He was soon competing with Sadr's militia for money and influence. The two sides eventually clashed over the receipts from the gas station located in Tahir, a suburb of Musayyib. The urban area straddled the Euphrates, with Tahir on the western bank and Musayyib across a bridge to the east. Mijwal had assigned Mohammed Jassim, a Sunni who served with him in Hussein's army, to collect a share of the money at the end of

---

[1] Andy Mosher and Saad Sarhan, "Death Toll Rises to 100 in Suicide Blast: Relatives Seek Missing After Attack That Took Shiite and Sunni Lives," *Washington Post*, 18 July 2005, copy in Historians files, U.S. Army Center of Military History (CMH), Washington, D.C.

[2] "Carnage in Iraq, Fuel Truck Bomb Kills 98," *Turkish Daily News*, 18 July 2005, copy in Historians files, CMH.

each day. The militia, which was also extorting money and free gasoline from the station's owner, apparently was incensed at a Sunni interfering with a major source of revenue.[3]

On the morning of 22 July 2006, the Mahdi militia snatched Jassim from the gas station.[4] The kidnappers encountered a police patrol as they drove back to the mosque in Musayyib that served as their headquarters. The gunmen disarmed the Iraqi police and disabled their patrol vehicle by firing several rounds into the engine. Learning of the incident, an incensed Colonel Mijwal stormed over to the mosque to confront the militia leaders. After trading heated comments for a few minutes, Mijwal reportedly blurted out: "If you mess with me, I'll have the Americans bring this mosque down on your head!"[5] His words were more prophetic than he knew. Just then a patrol from Company D, 1st Battalion, 67th Armor, 4th Infantry Division, led by 2d Lt. C. Ryan Kelley, was en route to Tahir to teach Iraqi police officers the finer points of manning a roadside checkpoint. As the American patrol neared its destination, Sgt. Stanley R. Sneathen overheard shots coming from the east.[6] Kelley decided to detour to investigate.

The 4th Infantry Division was well into its second tour in Iraq. During its period of refitting back at Fort Hood, Texas, the outfit had converted to the new modular structure. The reorganization added a fourth brigade and pushed the combined-arms concept down to battalion level.[7] The 2d Brigade Combat Team's (BCT's) 1st Battalion, 67th Armor, for example, switched from an all-tank force to a mix of companies: 2 mechanized infantry, 2 tank, 1 engineer, and 1 multifunctional support.[8] Combat experience in Iraq dictated other changes. M1114 up-armored high mobility multipurpose wheeled vehicles (HMMWVs, or Humvees), better suited to lengthy mounted patrols and narrow streets, replaced many of the M1A2 Abrams and M2A3 Bradleys. The mechanized and tank companies also traded platoons to provide a flexible mix of combat systems.

While a large percentage of the division's soldiers had seen combat prior to its second tour, they would find the political situation, insurgent tactics, and area of operations different from previous experiences. The 4th Division's latest deployment coincided with escalating sectarian violence instigated by the

---

[3] Interv, Mark J. Reardon, CMH, with Lt Col Patrick J. Donahoe, CO, 1st Bn, 67th Armor, and Cmd Sgt Maj Ernest Barnett Jr., 1st Bn, 67th Armor, 30 Nov 06; Ltr, Capt Irvin W. Oliver Jr., Commanding Officer (CO), Co D, 1st Bn, 67th Armor, to author, 4 Feb 08; both in Historians files, CMH.

[4] After Action Review (AAR), 1st Bn, 67th Armor, n.d., sub: Bn Actions—Dealer, Archangel, Carnivore, Historians files, CMH.

[5] Interv, Reardon with Donahoe and Barnett, 30 Nov 06.

[6] Sworn Statement, Sgt Stanley R. Sneathen, Co D, 1st Bn, 67th Armor, 25 Oct 06, copy in Historians files, CMH.

[7] William M. Donnelly, *Transforming an Army at War: Designing the Modular Force, 1991–2005* (Washington, D.C.: U.S. Army Center of Military History, 2007), pp. 44–45.

[8] Ltr, Lt Col Patrick J. Donahoe to author, 19 Jan 07, Historians files, CMH.

al-Qaeda–inspired bombing of the Samarra mosque in February 2006. The 2d BCT inherited the so-called Triangle of Death. Situated between Baghdad and Karbala, the religiously mixed region gained notoriety when both Sunni and Shi'ite death squads began dumping increasing numbers of victims alongside major roads or tossing their bodies into the Euphrates River. The 1st Battalion, 67th Armor, took over Forward Operating Base (FOB) Iskandariyah, which surrounded a smoke-belching power plant several kilometers north of Musayyib in the heart of the triangle.

Four months to the day after the February bombing of the Samarra mosque, Lieutenant Kelley and his men were about to gain firsthand experience with the simmering tensions in Musayyib when they crossed the Euphrates River bridge from Tahir. The patrol consisted of four up-armored Humvees commanded respectively by Kelley, Sgt. Jahmali E. Samuel, Sgt. Brandon O. McDaniel, and S. Sgt. Carlos Garcia Jr.[9] The vehicles drove a couple hundred meters beyond the bridge and into the traffic circle in front of the mosque serving as the local Mahdi militia headquarters. It was a little after noon when Kelley saw Mijwal out front arguing with several militiamen. The Iraqi police colonel broke off the discussion and walked over, asking the Americans to "come with me."[10] Without another word, Mijwal departed. The patrol followed him to the main Musayyib police station located one-half mile southwest of the mosque. For better or worse, the small American unit had just become tied unwittingly to one side in the dispute over skimming gasoline receipts.

Colonel Mijwal asked Kelley to remain with him for awhile as he sought out the kidnappers and the situation in town calmed down. After an hour, Sergeant McDaniel noticed several Iraqi police preparing to depart the station and queried them on their mission. They replied that they were going to investigate reports of militia carrying rocket-propelled grenades (RPGs).[11] Iraqi citizens were authorized to carry small arms but prohibited from possessing heavier weapons. Kelley relayed the information to higher headquarters, prompting the battalion operations center to direct him to verify the report.[12] He told Mijwal that the patrol had to go investigate but promised that he would return as soon as possible.

The Humvees departed, with Kelley's vehicle in the lead, shortly before 1400. As the lieutenant headed toward the mosque, he noticed that there were no cars or trucks on the road. All of the shops and houses appeared to be closed. As the patrol entered the traffic circle, Kelley saw armed men perched in nearby windows and atop the mosque. The unprecedented open display of

[9] Sworn Statement, 2d Lt C. Ryan Kelley, Plt Ldr, 2d Plt, Co D, 1st Bn, 67th Armor, 25 Oct 06, Historians files, CMH.

[10] Interv, Reardon with 1st Lt C. Ryan Kelley, Plt Ldr, 2d Plt, Co D, 1st Bn, 67th Armor, 28 Nov 06, Historians files, CMH.

[11] Sworn Statement, Sgt Brandon O. McDaniel, Veh Cdr, Co D, 1st Bn, 67th Armor, 24 Oct 06, Historians files, CMH.

[12] Interv, Reardon with Donahoe and Barnett, 30 Nov 06.

Sergeant Samuel and Lieutenant Kelley stand in front of the mosque that was the center of the battle in Musayyib. Earlier that day, a dispute between Mahdi militia and a corrupt police chief had drawn American forces into an unexpected fight.

weapons raised in his mind the specter of ambush.[13] The black-clad militiamen for their part probably assumed the Americans were coming to carry out Mijwal's threats. Within moments, five Mahdi fighters standing on the roof of the mosque opened fire with assault rifles. Kelley's turret gunner, Sergeant Sneathen, shot back, killing at least one insurgent.[14] The Humvees continued into the traffic circle and started taking more fire from a building to the left of the mosque.[15]

At a point opposite the mosque, the patrol stopped and all four turret gunners began spraying the Iraqi fighters with bullets. Everyone else dismounted to add their individual weapons to the fight. Most of the Iraqi fire was inaccurate, but two rounds cracked Sergeant McDaniel's windshield as he exited his Humvee. A third bullet ricocheted from the turret shield that protected his gunner, Pfc. Philip R. Adams. Adams hunched a little lower as he continued to trigger controlled bursts at the enemy. As the skirmish escalated, Sergeant Garcia radioed a situation

---

[13] Interv, Reardon with Kelley, 28 Nov 06.
[14] Statement, Sneathen, 25 Oct 06.
[15] Ibid.

report to the company command post. Informed of the firefight, Capt. Irvin W. Oliver Jr., the company commander, ordered Kelley to disengage and meet up with friendly forces at the first major road intersection north of town. The battalion headquarters in turn ordered a patrol consisting of four HMMWVs from the mortar platoon to converge on the same spot.[16]

Although the Americans were directing a large volume of suppressive fire against their opponents, Kelley estimated that thirty to forty individuals were still shooting back. A sudden explosion near the lieutenant's vehicle, followed by the whooshing sound of additional incoming RPG rockets, marked an escalation in the battle. The patrol had confirmed the hard way that the reports of militia carrying antitank weapons were accurate. Kelley got his men mounted up, and the patrol moved out. As the unit left the traffic circle, Sergeant Garcia's gunner, Cpl. Ryan C. Rupprecht, noticed a two-man RPG team approaching from the rear. His M240 machine gun jammed, forcing the corporal to engage the insurgents with his M4 carbine.[17] His accurate fire bowled over both Iraqis.

Still trading shots with the militia, the four Humvees headed southwest. That was the opposite direction from the linkup point, but the patrol would not have to fight its way through the insurgents around the mosque. Kelley also calculated that he would avoid potential ambushes by taking the less-direct route back toward the base. Mahdi gunmen were almost certainly already moving to close off the likely avenue of reinforcement. Although the patrol dodged several more RPGs while passing through an industrial sector, Lieutenant Kelley reached the intersection north of the city, marked on battalion maps as Checkpoint 11, without suffering casualties. He joined forces there with four Humvees from the mortar platoon led by S. Sgt. Todd M. Tagami. Kelley ordered McDaniels, whose HMMWV engine was running roughly, back to the base, with Sergeant Garcia's team as an escort. The remaining six vehicles established a defensive perimeter. (*See Map 7.*)

Back at Iskandariyah, Oliver told Sfc. Jeffrey A. Mask, Kelley's platoon sergeant, and the 1st Platoon leader, 2d Lt. Keith G. Angstman, to send "every single soldier that we could get outside the wire . . . to Checkpoint 11."[18] Mask directed two of his tank commanders, S. Sgt. David Teran and Sgt. Brian J. Steffani, to ready their crews for combat.[19] Sergeant Teran immediately felt the sense of urgency:

> I just got back from the shower after a night patrol when my
> platoon sergeant screamed at me to get ready to move out with

[16] Interv, Reardon with Capt Irvin W. Oliver Jr., CO, Co D, 1st Bn, 67th Armor, 27 Nov 06, CMH.

[17] Statement, Kelley, 25 Oct 06.

[18] Interv, Reardon with Oliver, 27 Nov 06.

[19] Sworn Statement, Sfc Jeffrey A. Mask, Plt Sgt, 2d Plt, Co D, 1st Bn, 67th Armor, 25 Oct 06, Historians files, CMH.

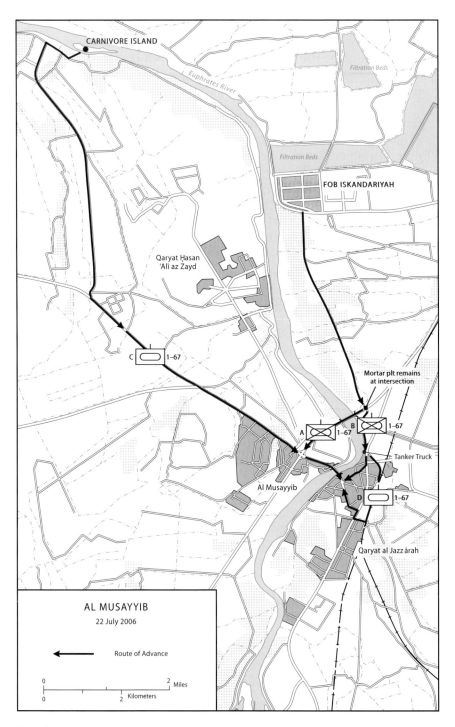

CARNIVORE ISLAND

Euphrates River

Filtration Beds

Filtration Beds

FOB ISKANDARIYAH

Qaryat Ḥasan
'Alī az Zayd

C ⬭ 1–67

Mortar plt remains
at intersection

A ⊠ 1–67 B ⊠ 1–67

Tanker Truck

Al Musayyib

D ⬭ 1–67

Qaryat al Jazzārah

AL MUSAYYIB
22 July 2006

⟵ Route of Advance

0   2 Miles
0   2 Kilometers

MAP 7

the platoon's remaining gun trucks. As I headed for the motor pool I met Capt. Oliver who told me to prep the platoon's tanks rather than more Humvees. His statement surprised me because we had rarely taken tanks into Musayyib. In the past six months the company had only driven tanks at night around the outskirts of the town. Usually we try to keep the tank commanders and drivers available. But that day I actually had two infantry guys in my crew, one who drove and one who loaded. The infantry guy [Spec. Sean L. Creighton] who was driving had never operated a tank until that day.[20]

Although Kelley had extracted his patrol from the city, Lt. Col. Patrick J. Donahoe, the commander of 1st Battalion, 67th Armor, did not consider the matter resolved. He began preparing for a coordinated counterattack against the militia. He planned to use Captain Oliver's company, augmented by Iraqi Army troops collocated with his battalion at Iskandariyah, to launch an assault into Musayyib from the southeast.

To ensure the attack did not simply drive off the insurgents, Colonel Donahoe moved to seal off possible escape routes. The force at Checkpoint 11 was in position to initially cover the north side of town. Donahoe instructed Capt. Bradley J. Maroyka's Company A to secure the sole bridge between Tahir and Musayyib, thus closing off the west side of the city. Most of Maroyka's men, however, manned guard towers situated at regular intervals along Iskandariyah's four-kilometer perimeter. The captain realized he would need more personnel to execute the blocking mission than the only readily available infantry section belonging to 2d Lt. Matthew F. Dusablon's 3d Platoon. So Maroyka ordered his platoon leaders to swap off-duty mechanics for infantry soldiers manning the fence line and to rouse from sleep those soldiers who had finished the night guard shift. S. Sgt. Brian L. Jenkins awoke to the words, "Company D just got hit in Musayyib." Jenkins had no other information but quickly understood the gravity of the situation: "We started loading everything up on the Humvees. Then we were told to bring armored vehicles. That is when I realized something serious was going on." Ultimately, Maroyka mustered just three Humvees and two Bradleys (both with their 25-mm. chain guns nonoperational).[21]

Colonel Donahoe ordered Capt. Stefan R. McFarland's Company C to take up a blocking position at the Tahir police station and assist Company A in sealing off the western exit from Musayyib. Two of McFarland's platoons were conducting changeover at a patrol base on an island in the Euphrates

---

[20] Interv, Reardon with S Sgt David Teran, Veh Cdr, Co D, 1st Bn, 67th Armor, 29 Nov 06, Historians files, CMH.

[21] Interv, Reardon with S Sgt Brian L. Jenkins, Sqd Ldr, Co A, 1st Bn, 67th Armor, 28 Nov 06, Historians files, CMH.

River located several miles northwest of Musayyib. McFarland assigned the Tahir mission to 1st Lt. Ken Nguyen and his 1st Platoon. Half of the platoon became stranded, however, when a five-ton truck slipped off a narrow causeway linking the island with the riverbank.[22] Nguyen departed with the remaining vehicles—his own up-armored Humvee and another under Sgt. James L. Freeman, plus two Abrams tanks commanded by Sfc. Samuel Del Pilar and Sgt. Gregory T. Wright.

Conforming to standard operating procedures discouraging use of a single avenue for entry and egress into an objective area, Donahoe tasked Company B with safeguarding the road leading from Checkpoint 11 to the traffic circle at the mosque. This would also help seal the city from the north. Once Company D completed the counterattack from the southeast, Captain Oliver's force would depart the city using the northern route secured by Company B.

Donahoe notified the Company B executive officer, Capt. Barry E. Wiley II, of the unit's mission.[23] The departure of the regular company commander on midtour leave had left Wiley temporarily in command. He summoned the platoon leaders to his command post and ordered them to start recalling everybody.[24] His initial plan called for a platoon of up-armored Humvees to secure the egress route for Company D. This conformed with previous practice that stressed avoiding damage to the streets by limiting the size and number of combat vehicles sent into Musayyib. The radio traffic coming over the speakers in the company command post, however, indicated that the fighting was more intense than in past incidents. The task organization soon evolved into a mix of Bradleys and gun trucks and then changed again when Wiley settled on employing all of the tanks and Bradleys he had available.[25] His scheme of maneuver called for Company B to hold north of the Checkpoint 11 intersection until Company D moved out in the assault. Then Wiley would head south to secure the designated egress route.[26]

Company B faced difficulties similar to others when it attempted to marshal its personnel. Two platoons had just returned to Iskandariyah after conducting gunnery training. They were busy unloading vehicles, showering, and cleaning weapons when the word came to mount up. Despite the absence of his 2d Platoon, which manned a combat outpost, Captain Wiley succeeded in assembling 7 Bradleys, 2 tanks, and 45 soldiers.[27] The 3d Platoon, commanded

[22] Sworn Statement, 1st Lt Ken Nguyen, Plt Ldr, 1st Plt, Co C, 1st Bn, 67th Armor, 24 Oct 06, Historians files, CMH.

[23] Interv, Reardon with Capt Barry E. Wiley II, Exec Ofcr, Co B, 1st Bn, 67th Armor, 28 Nov 06, Historians files, CMH.

[24] Interv, Mark J. Reardon with 1st Lt Jeffrey W. Donahue, Plt Ldr, 1st Plt, Co B, 1st Bn, 67th Armor, 29 Nov 06, CMH.

[25] Ibid.

[26] Interv, Reardon with Wiley, 28 Nov 06.

[27] Sworn Statement, S Sgt Jerry W. Holcomb, Sqd Ldr, Co B, 1st Bn, 67th Armor, 22 Oct 06, Historians files, CMH.

by 1st Lt. Jeffrey W. Donahue, one of the company's most experienced officers, formed the column's vanguard. The 1st Platoon, led by the newest officer, 2d Lt. Nathan A. Brown, brought up the rear. As Company B lined up at the forward operating base's front gate, Wiley notified the battalion executive officer, Maj. Ty D. Bonner, that his unit was ready to enter the fight.

Moments later, Company D departed FOB Iskandariyah with four tanks and seven Humvees.[28] Captain Oliver left behind two partially manned Humvees, under Lieutenant Angstman's command, with instructions to join up once they had full crews. The quartet of Abrams formed the point element, with the tank commanded by Sfc. Corey E. Stevenson, Angstman's platoon sergeant and the company's acting first sergeant, in the lead. S. Sgt. Arthur H. Castro, Sergeant Teran, and Sgt. Brian J. Steffani followed in that order. Company D headed south toward the road intersection held by Kelley and Tagami.[29]

While the 1st Battalion prepared for battle, Colonel Donahoe contacted Capt. James P. Cook, an American adviser with the 2d Battalion, 4th Brigade, 8th Iraqi Army Division, also located at Iskandariyah. Cook passed on the request for assistance to Lt. Col. Shahed Mohammed Jalel. The Iraqi battalion commander assembled two infantry companies in a few minutes, mounted them on vehicles, and sped off to link up with Captain Oliver. Donahoe and Oliver were impressed by the performance of the Iraqi unit. Only later did it dawn on the Company D commander: "The Iraqi Army was kind of expecting something to happen. Everybody was expecting it except for us."[30]

Captain Oliver's unit arrived at Kelley and Tagami's position without encountering resistance. A few moments later, the column of pickup trucks bearing the Iraqi soldiers and Captain Cook pulled up behind Company D. Oliver instructed his tanks to set up a hasty security perimeter between the intersection and the city and then started preparing an operations order to issue to the units assembled at the intersection. After mulling over possible courses of action while examining a map of the city, Oliver radioed for all leaders to assemble at his Humvee. He explained to the group that Company D, along with the Iraqi units, would move south along the eastern outskirts of Musayyib, bypassing a suspected militia strongpoint on the northern edge of town. Once the column reached the southeast corner of the city, it would head northwest up a main road to assault the mosque. The tanks would lead the attack, followed by the American Humvees and Iraqi Army vehicles. Turning to Cook and Jalel, Oliver explained that the Iraqi contingent had three important missions. First, it would clear out the industrial area where Lieutenant Kelley had taken fire as his patrol departed the city. Then the Iraqis would move forward on foot alongside the American vehicles during the final assault on the objective. After

---

[28] Interv, Reardon with Oliver, 27 Nov 06.
[29] Interv, Reardon with Teran, 29 Nov 06.
[30] Interv, Reardon with Oliver, 27 Nov 06.

Colonel Jalel (*middle*) is accompanied by Captain Cook (*right*), an American adviser with the 2d Battalion, 4th Brigade, 8th Iraqi Division. Jalel's troops, mounted in pickup trucks, supported the subsequent American push into the southeastern portion of the city.

the militia had been defeated, Company D would provide security for the Iraqis while they searched the mosque for documents and weapons. Captain Oliver closed by reminding everyone that they would depart Musayyib using the route secured by Company B.[31] Partway through the briefing, Lieutenant Angstman arrived with his two Humvees. He received the mission of providing rear security behind the Iraqi units.[32] Sergeant Tagami's mortar platoon would remain at Checkpoint 11 while Kelley joined the assault.

Oliver was wrapping up his operations order when a tanker truck unexpectedly appeared. Since it was virtually the only vehicle operating in the city at that time, two AH–64 Apaches on station over Musayyib had been following its movements. The pilot of the lead helicopter, call sign Longbow 62, broke into the battalion radio net to report: "I have a white fuel truck about a kilometer and a half from the tanks at Checkpoint 11. I am concerned that it is a Vehicle Borne Improvised Explosive Device [IED]. If he crosses the canal, I am going to fire."[33] Oliver asked the Apache pilot to go ahead and engage the vehicle, but the latter replied that he could not fire unless authorized by higher headquarters. Alerted by the radio call, Sergeant Teran moved his Abrams into the road to prevent the truck from entering the company perimeter. The truck stopped when it saw that and then reversed for

---

[31] Ibid.

[32] AAR, 1st Plt, Co D, 1st Bn, 67th Armor, n.d., p. 1, Historians files, CMH.

[33] Apache Longbow Video, "221508Jul06 PVBIED (White Tanker) Engagement in Musayyib 418," Historians files, CMH.

Captain Oliver briefs the hasty plan to seize the area around the mosque. *Left to right*: Sergeants Tagami and Stevenson, Captain Oliver, Sergeant Samuel, and Lieutenant Kelley. Oliver's choice to employ tanks rather than the usual HMMWVs would prove crucial in the coming fight.

a short distance before backing into the courtyard of a large building adjacent to Company D's intended route of advance.[34]

Grabbing a radio handset, Captain Oliver voiced concerns to Colonel Donahoe over the potential danger and stated that he did not want to start the counterattack until the truck had been destroyed.[35] Seconds later, the radio crackled with a transmission from the battalion commander: "Longbow 62 this is Dealer 6, engage the white fuel truck on [Route] Jennifer. My initials Poppa Juliet Delta (PJD)." The pilot acknowledged Donahoe's order. Less than a minute later, a Hellfire missile smashed into the cab of the truck, which burst into flames and sent a large column of smoke into the air.[36]

The immediate threat eliminated, Company D moved out but quickly met other resistance as soon as it passed the burning tanker. A lone gunman atop a water tank opened fire on the Humvees trailing behind the four Abrams. Captain Oliver ordered: "Take out the tower." Unsure where the fire was coming from, one of the tanks blasted a cell-phone tower. The mistake had an unintended but beneficial consequence. The Mahdi militia communicated via cell phone—when the hub went down, "they couldn't talk."[37] A few moments later, an Abrams main-gun round took out the correct target.

---

[34] Interv, Reardon with Teran, 29 Nov 06.
[35] Interv, Reardon with Oliver, 27 Nov 06.
[36] Apache Longbow Video, 221508 Jul 06.
[37] Interv, Reardon with Oliver, 27 Nov 06.

Other militiamen joined in the fray as Company D advanced, spraying various parts of the column with small-arms fire. Lieutenant Angstman's gunners at the rear responded with hundreds of rounds from their M240 machine guns.[38] The insurgents directed most of their attention to the lead tanks as they approached the outskirts of the city. Sergeant Stevenson's gunner, Sgt. Jess C. Thompson, identified four militiamen in a car firing AK47s at the first Abrams. The car disappeared in a ball of flame after Thompson hit it with a 120-mm. high-explosive antitank round. The sergeant quickly found new targets:

> I was scanning to the left when [I noticed] more small arms fire. . . . I shot down a couple of insurgents then traversed [the turret] to the left after Red 4 [Stevenson] called out "Identified Car" [pinpointing a potential vehicle-borne IED]. I replied "Identified Car," then shot a high-explosive round and blew it up. We continued our movement, but [now more] slowly because of irrigation ditches and soft terrain.[39]

Company B trailed Oliver at a distance, until Company D turned east to cross over a set of railroad tracks and then angled sharply south again. The column led by Captain Wiley continued down the main road from the north into Musayyib. He had an Abrams in the lead, followed by three 1st Platoon Bradleys, his own Bradley, a trio of Bradleys from Lieutenant Brown's 3d Platoon, and the second M1A2 bringing up the rear. That trail tank had orders to halt before it lost sight of Sergeant Tagami's platoon. Likewise, Brown's last Bradley would stop before it moved out of visual contact with the tank. The process would be repeated until Company B was stretched along the entire length of the route between the intersection occupied by the mortar platoon and the traffic circle.[40]

Company B initially ran the same gauntlet as Company D, though the opposition was now much reduced. Lieutenant Donahue was in the middle of the action: "We rolled past the burning truck suspected of being a vehicle borne IED. The lead tank was about 100 yards in front of my vehicle. As he passed a building on the edge of town, the M1A2 Abrams was engaged by an insurgent rocket propelled grenade team in an alleyway."[41] The blast caused the Abrams' gunner, Sgt. Brian A. Craycraft, to briefly lose control of the turret. It spun crazily; but he got it settled, and his tank resumed the advance.[42] Donahue's Bradley rolled up slowly and scanned down the alley. When the gunner reported he could not see anyone there, the remainder of Company B continued.

---

[38] AAR, 1st Plt, Co D, 1st Bn, 67th Armor, p. 1.
[39] Sworn Statement, Sgt Jess C. Thompson, Tnk Gnr, Co D, 1st Bn, 67th Armor, 25 Oct 06, Historians files, CMH.
[40] Interv, Reardon with Wiley, 28 Nov 06.
[41] Interv, Reardon with Donahue, 29 Nov 06.
[42] Sworn Statement, Sgt Brian A. Craycraft, Tnk Gnr, Co B, 1st Bn, 67th Armor, 25 Oct 06, Historians files, CMH.

On the western side of the river, Lieutenant Nguyen's platoon arrived in Tahir shortly before Captain Maroyka's company. Nguyen noticed a throng of Iraqi Army and police around the gas station, with a gaggle of Humvees and law enforcement vehicles parked nearby at the police station. (*See Map 8.*) When bullets began ricocheting in the platoon's vicinity, Nguyen sought and received permission to return fire from the most senior Iraqi he could find. The tanks opened up with their coaxial machine guns, forcing the militiamen to scramble for cover. Sergeant Wright's gunner, Cpl. Edwin J. Rodriguez, chased four gunmen with his 7.62-mm. bursts, but they escaped into a three-story building.[43] The Iraqis were safe for the moment, since Nguyen decided to withhold use of the tank main guns until he got Iraqi bystanders out of the line of fire. The arrival of the Babil Province police chief, Brig. Gen. Abbud Hamza al-Mamouri Qais, and the Hillah police Special Weapons and Tactics (SWAT) team solved Nguyen's dilemma. After the American lieutenant expressed to Qais his concern about possible fratricide, the Iraqi police general ordered everyone to move back.[44]

In the meantime, the pair of Company C tanks marooned on the island patrol base arrived in Tahir. Nguyen waved C10, commanded by Sgt. Robert K. Curry, and S. Sgt. Richard D. Phillips' C13 into position near the other pair of Abrams.[45] The company's senior noncommissioned officer, 1st Sgt. Charles M. King, accompanied by a fuel truck and two more up-armored Humvees, also linked up with the platoon.[46] King's Humvee disgorged a sniper team that scrambled up to the police station roof.[47] Colonel Donahoe's forward headquarters element arrived shortly afterward. Donahoe directed his top enlisted soldier, Cmd. Sgt. Maj. Ernest Barnett Jr., to position the battalion command vehicles near General Qais' command post.[48]

Once on the scene, Colonel Donahoe decided to send Maroyka's Company A across the bridge linking Tahir with Musayyib. The new assault from the northwest would take some of the enemy pressure off Company D's advance from the opposite direction. Receiving the order via radio while still en route, Maroyka passed the change in mission along to his unit. The path to the bridge went right through the major intersection where the Iraqi security forces and Nguyen's platoon were already engaged with Mahdi forces. From there, Company A would have to fight its way under fire across the exposed and narrow bridge over the Euphrates before it entered Musayyib.

---

[43] Interv, Reardon with Cpl Edwin J. Rodriguez, Tnk Gnr, Co C, 1st Bn, 67th Armor, 28 Nov 06, Historians files, CMH.
[44] Sworn Statement, Nguyen, 24 Oct 06.
[45] Interv, Reardon with S Sgt Richard D. Phillips, Tnk Cdr, Co C, 1st Bn, 67th Armor, 28 Nov 06, Historians files, CMH.
[46] Sworn Statement, Sgt Gregory T. Wright, Tnk Cdr, Co C, 1st Bn, 67th Armor, 21 Oct 06, Historians files, CMH.
[47] Statement, Nguyen, 24 Oct 06.
[48] Interv, Reardon with Donahoe and Barnett, 30 Nov 06.

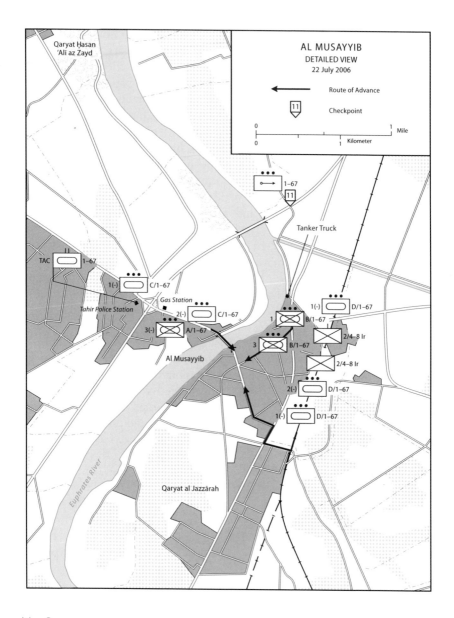

MAP 8

As Captain Maroyka neared the Tahir police station, he could hear heavy small-arms fire. Rather than continue leading with up-armored Humvees, he sent his two Bradleys to the front of the column. Dusablon's M2A3 Bradley assumed the lead, followed by Sergeant Jenkins' armored vehicle and then the trio of gun trucks commanded by S. Sgt. Chadwick R. Decker, Sgt. Trevor T. Lord, and Sgt. John P. Norton. At the intersection, the company turned left onto the road leading to Musayyib. Two hundred meters farther, the assault force began receiving small-arms and RPG fire. Bulling forward, Maroyka's men soon found themselves showered with "massive amounts of small arms fire, RPG's, and frag[mentation] grenades thrown on top of their BFVs [Bradley fighting vehicles] and next to their gun trucks."[49] Corporal Rodriguez watched the four insurgents he had earlier fired upon scramble to the building roof where they began tossing grenades at Company A's Humvees. Although he now had permission to fire his main gun, the tank commander could not engage the militiamen without endangering Company A.[50]

In Maroyka's column, Sergeant Jenkins noted the increasing opposition: "An RPG went between the slowly moving Bradleys. A second hit and exploded to the right of my vehicle. A volley of three RPGs sailed in. One hit some overhead power lines and spun away trailing sparks. The other two slammed into the front of Lieutenant Dusablon's Bradley."[51] One of those rockets ricocheted off the lieutenant's headlight and detonated against his thermal sight. Enveloped by the heat of the blast and a shower of fragments, he dropped down into the turret, surprisingly unhurt.[52] The explosion tripped the Bradley's electrical circuit breakers, shutting down the turret power and radios. The engine and the intercom system remained operable. Dusablon ordered his driver to halt. The lieutenant and his gunner popped open their turret hatches and began firing at the enemy RPG teams with M4 carbines. Fixated on the most dangerous threat, both men did not realize militiamen on nearby roofs were firing down at them. It was only after the battle that Dusablon would notice the bullet holes in the top of the Bradley's antisniper netting.[53] Unable to bring the Bradley's coaxial machine gun to bear with a dead turret, the lieutenant ordered his driver to reverse back up the street.

By this time, Sergeant Jenkins had pulled in front to suppress the RPG teams. The Humvees closed up behind Jenkins' M2A3, and the rest of the column resumed inching forward. The American vehicles drew heavy small-arms fire from a school on the right side of the street and a multistory building on the left. Other militiamen began popping out of alleyways to

[49] Statement, Wright, 21 Oct 06.

[50] Interv, Reardon with Rodriguez, 28 Nov 06.

[51] Interv, Reardon with Jenkins, 28 Nov 06.

[52] Interv, Reardon with 2d Lt Matthew F. Dusablon, Plt Ldr, 3d Plt, Co A, 1st Bn, 67th Armor, 28 Nov 06, Historians files, CMH.

[53] Ibid. Antisniper netting was a field expedient system using standard camouflage netting draped on a frame above the turret. It partially obscured the view of potential snipers, making it more difficult for them to target crewmen exposed in the hatches.

loose off bursts from automatic weapons. Sergeant Jenkins' Bradley, which had been firing at insurgents on nearby rooftops, experienced a coaxial machine-gun malfunction. When his effort to repair it under fire proved unsuccessful, his M2A3 and the trio of Humvees backed up the road until they reached Nguyen's position.[54]

The militia's apparent victory was short lived, as it opened them up to retribution. Lieutenant Nguyen's tanks were now able to engage targets without fear of injuring their comrades. When Maroyka's force pulled behind Corporal Rodriguez's Abrams, he brought his 120-mm. cannon to bear on the three-story building occupied by the four men who had earlier outrun his machine gun: "The insurgents were still on the balcony after Company A backed up. I lased [to obtain range information for the fire control computer] and hit the balcony with four main gun rounds. When the smoke cleared, there were no more grenades being thrown from the building."[55] The other tanks destroyed several more enemy positions. The battalion's next push into western Musayyib would meet with less resistance.

Maroyka's ill-fated attack made it clear to Colonel Donahoe that another assault from Tahir would require tank support. He believed the bridge could not support the weight of an Abrams, but he wanted the M1A2s to clear a passage to the riverbank and then take up firing positions that would support Company A's second attempt to get into Musayyib. Donahoe shared the new plan with Captain McFarland, the Company C commander, and Maroyka. MacFarland ordered Sergeant Del Pilar to switch to the battalion radio frequency and coordinate directly with the Company A commander. Maroyka told the section leader that his two tanks would lead.

Del Pilar moved out as the point, followed by Sergeant Wright's Abrams, Lieutenant Dusablon's hastily repaired vehicle, and Sergeant Jenkins' Bradley bringing up the rear. A few hundred yards up the road, Del Pilar noticed an Iraqi police vehicle: "It kind of looked like it had been shot up. The doors were open, you know, tires flat and bullet holes in it."[56] He had come upon the scene of the original confrontation between the police and militia kidnappers.

The armored column did not encounter significant opposition until Del Pilar reached the near end of the bridge, when heavier small-arms fire and a few RPGs began impacting near the tanks. Convinced that it was unwise to remain stationary in the face of this increasing fire, the sergeant ordered his driver to cross the bridge. Colonel Donahoe heard Del Pilar broadcast his intentions over the battalion net and immediately told him to stay off the bridge. It was too late. The driver already was gunning the engine and racing onto the structure.[57] The second

---

[54] Interv, Reardon with Jenkins, 28 Nov 06.

[55] Interv, Reardon with Rodriguez, 28 Nov 06.

[56] Interv, Reardon with Sfc Samuel Del Pilar, Plt Sgt, 1st Plt, Co C, 1st Bn, 67th Armor, 28 Nov 06, Historians files, CMH.

[57] Apache Longbow video [Classified], viewed by author, 28 Nov 06.

Mahdi gunmen on the roof of this schoolhouse and other nearby buildings temporarily delayed the advance of Bradleys and HMMWVs from Company A, 1st Battalion, 67th Armor. The unit subsequently provided suppressive fire to support a dash by two Company C tanks across a bridge spanning the Euphrates River.

Abrams followed its section leader without hesitation. Lieutenant Dusablon and Sergeant Jenkins paused for a moment to ascertain whether the bridge had been damaged by the tanks. Then the two Bradleys followed the tanks across.[58]

The pair of Abrams continued up the street until they entered the traffic circle where Lieutenant Kelley's patrol had been fired upon. Del Pilar paused for a moment to gain his bearings. Even with the engine roaring and commander's hatch lowered, he could hear bullets ricocheting off the turret. His gunner returned fire with the coaxial machine gun against any winking muzzle flash he could see. Realizing even a tank should not remain exposed in the traffic circle indefinitely, Sergeant Del Pilar ordered his driver to head southeast to link up with Company D. Sergeant Wright followed behind and to the left of the lead Abrams. After traveling several hundred yards, both tanks came to an abrupt halt when Del Pilar's driver yelled over the intercom: "I've got to stop. I've got an IED right in front of me."[59] The Abrams' turrets began traversing left and right to spot militia RPG teams that might be lurking in ambush.

---

[58] Interv, Reardon with Dusablon, 28 Nov 06.
[59] Interv, Reardon with Del Pilar, 28 Nov 06.

By this time, Company D was nearing the industrial area in southeast Musayyib. The column turned right onto a main road and began crossing over a bridge spanning a large irrigation canal. Captain Oliver was not surprised at the reaction provoked by the lead tank: "All hell broke loose. There were multiple enemy fire teams firing at us with AK47s, machine guns, and RPGs. We engaged them and killed some, while others withdrew."[60]

Oliver asked Captain Cook to have Colonel Jalel bring up his troops to clear the buildings on either side of the bridge. The four tanks slowed to a crawl to allow the Iraqi soldiers to make their way to the front. At that speed, Sergeant Castro spotted an IED emplaced in the road and told his driver to back away from it. An Iraqi soldier, Saed Dakhel Nuwaier, walked forward and began following the command wire in an effort to pinpoint the triggerman.[61] As he approached the building that it snaked into, an insurgent hiding inside shot him dead. Sergeant Castro fired at the IED with his .50-caliber machine gun, and it exploded. Three Iraqi soldiers then ran forward to recover their fallen comrade.[62] Seconds later, Castro spotted an RPG team lurking on a nearby rooftop. He pointed out the targets to his gunner, Cpl. Mark E. Baldwin, who blew them away with a 120-mm. high-explosive round. The loader, Sgt. Roberto Burgos, saw an Iraqi with an antitank rocket launcher attempting to crawl behind Sergeant Stevenson's tank. Burgos killed the militiaman with a short burst from his M240 machine gun.[63]

At the rear of the stalled column, the four Humvees began drawing enemy fire from a white, two-story house two hundred meters to the north. Lieutenant Angstman ordered his section to dismount: "We took cover behind our vehicles and a stone fence to our rear and began returning fire. We fired about two magazines per dismount and three 40-mm. high-explosive grenades, along with the Humvee's turret machineguns, but [that] didn't seem to have much effect on the house."[64] Meanwhile, Sgt. Daniel A. Lewandowski alerted the platoon commander to several gunmen firing from behind a car parked in a nearby alleyway.[65] Angstman ordered half of his element to turn their attention to the enemy in the alley.

Sergeant Teran heard a radio call reporting the firefight at the rear of the column and asked Captain Oliver for permission to assist Angstman. The company commander assented. Locking one track in place while applying power to the other, both Abrams in Teran's section spun around on their axis

[60] Interv, Reardon with Oliver, 27 Nov 06.

[61] AAR, 1st Bn, 67th Armor, n.d.

[62] Sworn Statement, S Sgt Arthur H. Castro, Tnk Cdr, Co D, 1st Bn, 67th Armor, 25 Oct 06, Historians files, CMH.

[63] Sworn Statement, Sgt Robert Burgos, Veh Cdr, Co D, 1st Bn, 67th Armor, 25 Oct 06, Historians files, CMH.

[64] AAR, 1st Plt, Co D, 1st Bn, 67th Armor, p. 1.

[65] Sworn Statement, 1st Lt Keith G. Angstman, Plt Ldr, 1st Plt, Co D, 1st Bn, 67th Armor, 25 Oct 06, Historians files, CMH.

and then headed back the way they had come. As they approached the Humvees, Teran asked Angstman to move his vehicles out of the road so he could pass. Angstman complied and pointed out the building that was giving him the greatest trouble. Teran got into position and fired two 120-mm. high-explosive rounds at the house. Sergeant Steffani's Abrams added two more. Angstman dispatched Sergeant Lewandowski with a few men to search the structure. They found one dead militiaman and one wounded.

The tank section began retracing its path back toward the head of the column, but Sergeant Teran's M1A2 Abrams became stuck in an irrigation ditch. His crew dismounted under fire and hooked a tow cable to Sergeant Steffani's tank, which pulled the stranded Abrams free. The section resumed its journey to the front of Company D, which had halted again after spotting a second IED in the road leading to the mosque.[66] They were now close enough to the objective that Sergeant Stevenson could see the tanks from Company C, also hung up by an IED, several hundred yards to the north.

Captain Wiley's Company B, charged with securing the battalion's egress route, was encountering different challenges. Trailing in the wake of the lead Abrams, Lieutenant Donahue saw a wounded Iraqi lying on the sidewalk and instructed his driver to halt. The platoon commander started to climb out of the turret to investigate, throwing his load-bearing vest to the ground and grabbing his rifle. "As I was coming out, we started taking fire . . . my gunner could not traverse the turret because I was getting out . . . [so] I literally jumped right off the turret to the ground."[67] Donahue scrambled to the opposite side of the Bradley to gain cover. Realizing he could do little by himself, the lieutenant banged on the driver's hatch and told him to drop the ramp. Sgt. Mickey E. Brigman's team piled out the back of the Bradley moments later. With bullets pinging off the vehicle's armor, Donahue directed the men to seek cover at the base of a nearby courtyard wall. Moving in its shelter, the group got near the next Bradley and linked up with a second dismounted element under S. Sgt. Jerry W. Holcomb II. The platoon commander told the two team leaders to clear out nearby houses.[68]

Donahue's efforts to root out the gunmen were hampered by language barriers. One of the last units to depart Iskandariyah, Company B found that "everyone [else] grabbed all of the interpreters there were."[69] The soldiers found themselves reduced to communicating with the occupants of the houses using pidgin Arabic and pantomime. A desire to avoid harming civilians also slowed the process. Stepping onto the top of one building, Donahue and his men found themselves trading fire with militia shooting from an adjacent roof. It reminded him of "one of those games at the arcade with the target that pops up and you're

---

[66] AAR, 1st Plt, Co D, 1st Bn, 67th Armor, p. 1.
[67] Interv, Reardon with Donahue, 29 Nov 06.
[68] Ibid.
[69] Ibid.

The tail end of an American column (*far right*) stalled by an IED came under fire from the white house on the far left. The section of Humvees led by Lieutenant Angstman responded with small arms and an automatic grenade launcher, but it took main-gun rounds from a pair of Abrams tanks to silence the enemy position.

trying to knock it down, smack it back down before it pops up again ... [they] have a little wall, and they would just stick the gun over and spray."[70]

Monitoring the platoon's progress over the radio, Captain Wiley realized his dismounted elements were moving too far off the main street in pursuit of the gunmen. He ordered Donahue to return to the egress route and reminded the company to keep the road under observation to prevent insurgents from emplacing IEDs. He also sent medics to treat the wounded Iraqi, but the man had died.

While the enemy facing Company B refused to make a stand, the insurgents near the mosque swarmed around the American armor there. The Company A Bradleys had caught up with the Company C Abrams stopped in the road by an IED. The four stationary targets were a magnet for RPG teams, which rapidly converged on the site. The militiamen took positions in alleys, second-floor windows, and rooftops. The Americans laid down suppressive fire with their machine guns, the tanks taking on street-level targets while the Bradleys focused on upper-story windows and roofs. But it was not enough against a numerous and dispersed enemy.

A rocket soon hit Sergeant Jenkins' Bradley, sending a ball of fire up its left side, penetrating the hull about one foot behind the driver, and

---

[70] Ibid.

cutting electrical lines.[71] The Bradley lost turret power, radio, and internal communications. Damage to the cooling system also shut down the engine.[72] Jenkins ordered his gunner, Pfc. Matthew C. Bragg, to manually traverse the turret to bring the coaxial machine gun to bear. Fragments were jamming the turret, and it took several attempts before Bragg succeeded in freeing it. The crew also got the radio working; but a few moments later, while Jenkins relayed a status report to Captain Maroyka, another RPG slammed into the rear of the turret. The transmission ended abruptly in midsentence as the vehicle lost all power. The driver finally coaxed the Bradley's engine back to life, and Jenkins turned his damaged vehicle back toward the Tahir police station.[73]

The RPG teams now concentrated their efforts against Dusablon's M2A3.[74] The blast of several near misses repeatedly shook his Bradley. One finally struck home. The halon fire suppression system went off; a soldier in the rear compartment, Spec. Isaac Guiterrez, screamed out that he could not see anything. The lieutenant ordered his driver and gunner to assist the injured man while he took the turret controls and continued to engage targets. Dusablon reported the casualty to company headquarters. Asked whether the wounded man would require air or ground evacuation, he reflexively answered "air" because that was the standard for injuries threatening life, limb, or eyesight. Given the amount of incoming fire, he realized it would be impossible for a helicopter to land in the traffic circle. He thus ordered his driver to head back over the bridge. When the two Bradleys limped into the perimeter at Tahir, Lieutenant Nguyen sent his two other Abrams into Musayyib and also deployed his own and Sgt. James L. Freeman's Humvees to secure the bridge.[75]

Even before the reinforcements arrived, Sergeant Del Pilar's section of Company C tanks exacted a toll from the militia near the traffic circle in return for the damage inflicted on the Bradleys. He could see gunmen running to the scene, but also felt that the tide was turning. "We engaged them with our [automatic] weapons. . . . .50 caliber, M240, and coaxial machineguns. . . . We opened the hatches and were engaging from the top of the tank at that time, because we pretty much had control of the circle at that point."[76] Sergeants Curry and Philipp joined up soon after and added their firepower to the battle. Then General Qais ordered the Hillah SWAT unit to cross the river.

[71] Interv, Reardon with Jenkins, 28 Nov 06.

[72] Sworn Statement, Pfc Matthew C. Bragg, Veh Gnr, Co A, 1st Bn, 67th Armor, 25 Oct 06, Historians files, CMH.

[73] Interv, Reardon with Jenkins, 28 Nov 06.

[74] Interv, Reardon with Dusablon, 28 Nov 06.

[75] Sworn Statement, Nguyen, 24 Oct 06; Sworn Statement, Sgt James L. Freeman, Veh Cdr, Co C, 1st Bn, 67th Armor, 24 Oct 06, Historians files, CMH.

[76] Interv, Reardon with Del Pilar, 28 Nov 06.

Elements of Companies C and D link up in the traffic circle. In the face of these converging American columns, Mahdi militiamen retreated from the mosque and broke off the fight.

Company D still had to deal with the IED blocking its progress. Captain Oliver requested one of the Apaches circling overhead to take out the obstacle with its 30-mm. cannon. The helicopter missed on its first attempt, but the second strafing run detonated an unseen IED on the opposite side of the road.[77] It took a couple more time-consuming gun runs before the Apache destroyed the initial IED.[78] As the dust cleared from the explosion, Oliver asked Captain Cook to have Colonel Jalel's infantry companies push forward into the traffic circle.

The destruction of the final IED signaled the end of the Mahdi militia's confrontation with the 1st Battalion, 67th Armor. The convergence of two Iraqi infantry companies, Hillah SWAT, and several more Abrams took the fight out of the gunmen near the mosque. The insurgents began disappearing into nearby neighborhoods dragging their casualties with them. Within minutes, Company D and its accompanying Iraqi soldiers linked up with the four Company C tanks in the traffic circle. General Qais then ordered the Hillah SWAT to clear the mosque. The Coalition force recovered a number of documents but only a few weapons.

The battle for Musayyib, unplanned by either side, had concluded as fast as it began. But it had a lasting impact. Colonel Mijwal found himself transferred

---

[77] Interv, Reardon with Oliver, 27 Nov 06.
[78] Ibid.

to another job. The Mahdi militia treaded lightly around the Americans for the remainder of the 1st Battalion, 67th Armor's deployment, opting to target patrols with IEDs rather than engaging in open combat. And the 4th Division soldiers who fought that day gained an appreciation for their ability to handle a determined enemy in an urban environment.

CHAPTER SIX

THE BATTLE FOR SALEM STREET

BEN R. SIMMS AND CURTIS D. TAYLOR

A night raid by a reinforced armor platoon turns into a hasty urban defense when one tank is destroyed by a lucky hit.

Diwaniyah—8–9 October 2006

In October 2006, a reinforced American tank platoon from Company D, 2d Battalion, 8th Infantry, supported by a handful of Iraqi Army infantrymen, conducted a raid into a hostile section of the city of Diwaniyah. The combined unit came into heavy contact with a larger, well-equipped Shi'ite militia force. In a hectic and confusing battle that lasted more than four hours, the small Coalition element lost one M1A2 tank but suffered no casualties while inflicting on the enemy more than thirty dead. Despite the destruction of the Abrams, the engagement proved yet again how indispensable heavy armor is in urban warfare and also demonstrated the value of the combined-arms team. Most important, it showcased the bravery and versatility of American soldiers facing a determined foe.[1]

Diwaniyah, the capital of Qadisiyah Province, lies about fifty kilometers east of Najaf and a little more than one hundred fifty kilometers south of Baghdad. Astride the Baghdad-Basra railroad, Highway 8, and a branch of the Euphrates River, it is a commercial and market town for the surrounding agricultural region. (*See Map 9.*) Its population of roughly half a million is almost entirely Shi'ite and had a long history of opposing the Saddam Hussein regime. In one notable incident in December 2000, assailants fired rocket-propelled grenades (RPGs) at the provincial Ba'ath Party headquarters. Following the fall of Hussein, Diwaniyah became enmeshed, like the rest of the Shi'ite south, in factional jockeying for power. Tribal ties added

---

[1] This article is an expanded version of the essay that took first place in the U.S. Army Center of Military History (CMH) 2007 James Lawton Collins Jr. Special Topics Writing Competition and subsequently appeared in the Fall 2007 issue of *Army History*. It is based primarily on the direct observations of those who fought the battle.

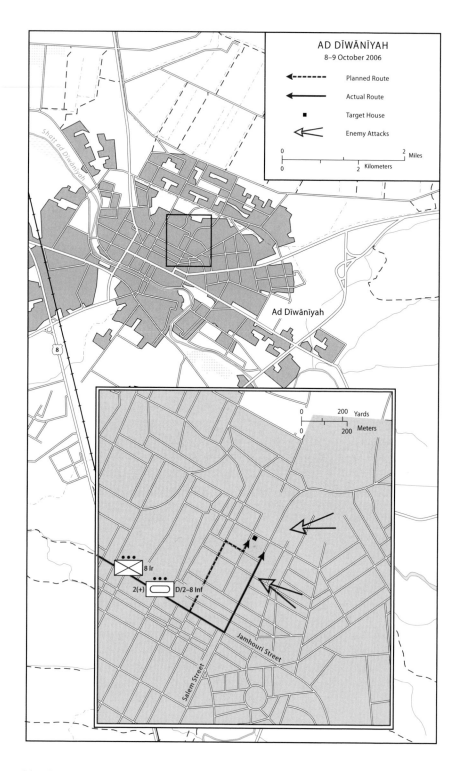

AD DĪWĀNĪYAH
8–9 October 2006

- - - → Planned Route

──────► Actual Route

■ Target House

⇐ Enemy Attacks

0   2 Miles
0   2 Kilometers

Shaṭṭ ad Dīwānīyah

8

Ad Dīwānīyah

0   200 Yards
0   200 Meters

8 Ir

2(+)   D/2–8 Inf

Jamhouri Street

Salem Street

Map 9

An Iraqi Army soldier standing on top of a Polish-model armored car cuts down a poster of Moqtada al-Sadr in Diwaniyah. Clashes between Sadr's Mahdi militia and Iraqi government forces would lead to the battle with American armor in October 2006.

another layer of complexity. Much of the population was from the Jabouri tribe, which generally did not back Moqtada al-Sadr, though some smaller tribes in the city did. For many people, party and tribe were less important than immediate safety—they avoided confrontation with whoever seemed most threatening at the moment. Two other emerging trends complicated the mix. One was the increasing tendency of some elements of Sadr's militia to operate independent of party control. The other was the appearance of the Iran-backed special groups.[2]

Since the fall of 2003, elements of the Polish-led Multi-National Division–Central South had overseen the area from Forward Operating Base (FOB) Echo, just to the southwest of Diwaniyah. The 8th Iraqi Army Division had a camp immediately adjacent to the Coalition facility. During 2006, insurgents, most likely Mahdi militia, mortared and rocketed the combined compound with growing frequency, destroying a warehouse, a mess hall, and other

---

[2] Patrick Gaughen, *The Fight for Diwaniyah: The Sadrist Trend and ISCI Struggle for Supremacy*, Backgrounder no.17 (Washington, D.C.: The Institute for the Study of War, 2007), Historians files, CMH.

132

TIP of the SPEAR

structures. Late on Saturday, 26 August, clashes broke out in the city between the Iraqi Army and insurgents, possibly instigated by the arrest of a senior Sadr supporter. Mahdi fighters rushed to Diwaniyah from other towns.[3] The battle resumed the next night and continued all through Monday, culminating in the militia overrunning an Iraqi Army platoon. The rebels publicly executed the seventeen survivors in front of a large crowd of onlookers. They further intimidated the security forces, nearly all locally recruited, by threatening the families of the policemen and soldiers. The police melted away, and the Iraqi Army elements withdrew from the urban area, effectively ceding control of the city to the militia.

Within hours of the outbreak of violence, the 2d Battalion, 8th Infantry, based eighty kilometers to the north at FOB Kalsu, received a warning order. On Sunday, units were on the move by road march and heavy equipment transporters, with the mission to restore order in Diwaniyah and enable the Iraqi Army to reassert control. Maj. David A. Segulin, the battalion executive officer, orchestrated the rapid repositioning. The battalion commander, Lt. Col. James A. Howard, deployed with a forward command post; Companies A and D; and Company A of the 1st Battalion, 67th Armor. The Americans began arriving in the city that night. The Iraqi Army also dispatched infantry companies from Najaf and Kut.[4]

The 2d Battalion, an element of the 2d Brigade Combat Team, 4th Infantry Division, had deployed from Fort Hood ten months earlier. One of the first permanent combined-arms battalions, it had two mechanized infantry companies, two armor companies, an engineer company, and other support elements. The subordinate units were task organized as well. Company D, nicknamed the Dragoons, had two tank platoons and one mechanized infantry platoon. In addition, for this deployment the outfit was equipped with enough high mobility multipurpose wheeled vehicles (HMMWVs) to allow each of its Abrams or Bradley crews to shift to the lighter wheeled vehicle when the mission required it. Most of the slightly more than one hundred men in the company had been together for nearly two years, and nearly all had served a previous combat tour in Iraq or Afghanistan. The company commander, Capt. Benjamin R. Simms, was an armor officer who had deployed to Kosovo in 2001 and Iraq during 2003–2004.

Company D's Abrams had the system enhancement package (SEP), which included a global positioning system, digital terrain maps, improved thermal sights, air conditioning, and other upgrades. Each four-man crew consisted of a commander, gunner, and loader in the turret and a driver forward in

---

[3] Thassin Abdul-Karaim, "40 Killed as Shiites, Iraqi Forces Fight," Fox News.com, 28 August 2006; "Iraqi Militia Kills 20 Soldiers, Seizes Key Town," Middle-East-online.com, 28 August 2008; U.S. Department of State, *Iraq Weekly Status Report*, 30 August 2006, p. 5; copies of all in Historians files, CMH

[4] E-mail, Col James A. Howard to Jon T. Hoffman, 14 May 08, Historians files, CMH.

An M1A2 SEP tank belonging to Company D, 2d Battalion, 8th Infantry, maneuvers down a street in Diwaniyah in August 2006. This type of urban terrain, composed of one- and two-story masonry buildings and low courtyard walls, was typical of the city.

the hull. Although this version of the M1A2 was ideal for operations in the buttoned-up mode, typically the crews worked with the hatches open. The tank commander not only had a better field of view standing with his head and upper body exposed, it was the only way he could employ his .50-caliber machine gun. Simms considered it one of his best weapons in an urban fight due to its power and ease of use. The loader had a pintle-mounted 7.62-mm. M240 machine gun at his hatch, while the gunner controlled another M240 mounted coaxially with the 120-mm. main gun.

When the American heavy armor arrived at Echo in late August, the militiamen disappeared from the streets. Based in part on that turn of events, Maj. Gen. Ali Salih Farhood Othman, commander of the 8th Iraqi Army Division, asked the 2d Battalion to remain outside the city while his own troops tried to reassert control. His forces initially seemed successful, but insurgent elements used the respite from American operations to gather reinforcements and bring in new weapons. These included Iranian-provided explosively formed penetrators (EFPs)—a deadlier form of improvised explosive device (IED)—as well as more modern and powerful RPGs. The 2d Battalion used the time to acquire intelligence on Diwaniyah from an American special operations team in the area and to assist the Poles with civil affairs and other noncombat activities. The neighborhoods around

Salem Street (pronounced with a soft "a") appeared to be the strongholds of antigovernment elements.

Within days, the strengthened insurgents attacked an Iraqi police unit. General Othman, acknowledging the failure of his first approach, authorized a large-scale operation to root out the enemy. The 2d Battalion, seven Iraqi companies, and two platoons from Coalition nations began clearing the city sector by sector, focusing on those areas that supported Sadr's militia. Government forces searched every house, and U.S. units conducted raids targeted against local Mahdi leaders and suspected weapons caches. The rebels avoided combat, but Sadr's supporters brought political pressure to bear on the Iraqi Ministry of Defense, falsely claiming that American forces were using heavy-handed tactics. After a single day of operations, an order came down to General Othman to pull Coalition units out of the city. The insurgents did not repeat their mistake; for the time being, they kept a low profile to avoid triggering a renewed, full-scale offensive against them. In contrast, citizens, especially those from the Jabouri tribe—it was their clansmen who had been executed in the August battle—had welcomed the presence of Americans and the order they promised to bring to Diwaniyah.

During the balance of September, the city generally remained peaceful. The 2d Battalion continued to assist the 8th Iraqi Army Division, conducting occasional joint raids and patrols and providing training. The military operations supported the work of Iraqi national police units, which set up and manned around-the-clock checkpoints throughout Diwaniyah. Howard noted that the Iraqi companies from other cities were more determined and active than their Diwaniyah counterparts, since the former faced little concern over threats to their families. Given the relative calm, Colonel Howard and two companies redeployed north to Kalsu, leaving the Dragoons behind to assist the Iraqi forces in killing or capturing the militia leaders responsible for the massacre of the Iraqi soldiers. The battalion forward command post, now under Maj. Curtis D. Taylor, the battalion operations officer, also remained at Echo. An armor officer with twelve years' service, Taylor had a tour in Afghanistan under his belt.

Late in the month, Company D had its most serious engagement to date in Diwaniyah. Captain Simms was leading a mixed unit of American HMMWVs and M1A2s and Iraqi armored cars on a night sweep to monitor police-manned security checkpoints and to check out suspected locations of wanted militia leaders. The group stopped to search one house, finding nothing. Afterward, although Simms intended that a tank always lead, the narrow streets made it impossible for the patrol to move out in the desired order, so an Iraqi vehicle ended up at the head of the column with the captain's HMMWV next in line. There was no room to pass an Abrams to the front until they reached the next major intersection, site of a friendly checkpoint. As the force approached the cross street, it became apparent that the police had abandoned the position. Just then, an array of daisy-chained IEDs exploded against the lead vehicle. The force of the blast, far larger than anything Simms had experienced to date, shattered all the nonballistic glass in his HMMWV and gave the driver a concussion. Of the six Iraqis in the armored car, two died immediately and the others lost a total of six limbs. The rest of the force found and destroyed two more IEDs and stabilized the casualties. There was no landing zone for an aerial medical evacuation, but the Iraqi command dispatched vehicles that arrived quickly and got the wounded back to Echo for airlift to a hospital. Within two hours, two companies of Iraqi infantry appeared at the scene and searched every house in the area. Tracing back the command wires of the IEDs, they found and arrested two suspects. The responsiveness and effectiveness of the Iraqi soldiers in this and other instances gave Simms some confidence in their capability. The deadliness of the ambush and the enemy's use of EFPs also made him reluctant to send out his men in wheeled vehicles on any future high-risk mission.

Shortly after this engagement, the 2d Battalion initiated a swap of units at Echo. One platoon of Abrams from Company C arrived to start the handover, while Captain Simms sent two-thirds of his outfit back to Kalsu, keeping his 2d Platoon of tanks. The latter was a veteran unit. The platoon leader, 1st Lt. Andrew J. Merchant, had been in the Army two years, while the NCOs commanding the other tanks each had served for more than a decade. All had participated in dozens of raids and had been under fire before. The only experience they lacked was actually fighting from their tanks in an urban area. While they had considerable training in this realm back at Fort Hood, the limitations of that simulated environment did not reveal the full power of an Abrams in a city.

On the evening of 8 October 2006, the Dragoons received credible intelligence on the location of a prominent sheik accused of ordering the execution of the Iraqi soldiers. A videotape had shown him brandishing a pistol he had taken from the platoon commander killed in the August fight. A local Iraqi offered to lead Coalition forces to the house and positively identify the sheik. The target was one block west of Salem Street. The source thought the best approach would be via a side road to avoid the most dangerous part of the neighborhood. Recent aerial photography seemed to confirm this route was viable.

The 2d Battalion forward command post planned an immediate raid. The U.S. unit conducted most of its operations at night in any case, and time was essential with such fleeting information. Lacking any infantry of its own, it asked the 8th Iraqi Army Division to provide its strike platoon, a specially trained unit tailor made for an operation such as this. The American contribution would be five M1A2 SEP tanks—the 2d Platoon reinforced by the company commander, who would exercise overall control. For this mission, Simms brought along his interpreter and the local guide. To provide them the same protection accorded his own men (plus anonymity for the guide), the captain had each of them displace a loader, who would remain behind at the base, a calculated risk that decreased the combat effectiveness of two tanks.

The American force linked up at the Iraqi compound with the strike platoon, which on short notice turned out a dozen or so men and three up-armored HMMWVs. Simms briefed the lieutenant on the mission and scheme of maneuver right before departure, thus minimizing any threat posed by the Iraqis' sometimes-lax approach to operational security. The tanks, one section in front and the other in trace, would escort the wheeled vehicles to the target and then provide a cordon around it while the Iraqi soldiers entered the house and picked up the suspect. The strike platoon leader provided an Iraqi Army handheld radio to the interpreter, who would ride in Simms' Abrams and serve as the communications link between the two units. The plan maximized the respective strengths of both elements—the armored firepower and night capability of the Americans and the ability of the Iraqis to deal more effectively with the population. Together, the tanks and infantry also had the combined-arms versatility essential for urban operations.

The raid force rolled out of the Iraqi Army base shortly after midnight on 9 October and headed into the city. The temperature was a pleasant 60 degrees with a clear sky and a partial moon that provided little ambient light. The operation proceeded without incident until the column was moving along Jamhouri Street, approaching the turnoff to the road leading to the target house. (*See Inset, Map 9.*) Suddenly, all the lights in the city went out. Simms and his men could not determine whether this was a reaction to their operation or a random blackout. Both types of power outages had occurred frequently in this area and elsewhere in Iraq. Either way, the darkness was of little concern and actually gave the Americans an additional advantage due to their night-vision devices. The raiders continued forward without a pause.

When the lead tank reached the designated turn, its commander, Sfc. Jonce S. Wright, saw that the side street was narrow and choked with low-hanging wires strung between buildings. It was a poor avenue of approach for armor. The next option was Salem Street, less than six hundred meters farther down. Captain Simms approved the change in plans. Minutes later, as Sergeant Wright's Abrams, D24, turned north onto the broader avenue, an insurgent poked around the corner of a building and fired an RPG. The tank crew replied immediately with an M1028 canister round from the 120-mm. main gun. The casing disintegrated as designed and spewed its load of 1,200 quarter-inch tungsten balls in a shotgun pattern; but the militiaman already had ducked back out of sight. Wright, one of the most skillful armored fighters Simms knew, responded with classic counterambush tactics, charging up Salem Street to deny cover to the attacker. The RPG gunner leaned around the corner to fire a second time but again missed. While the crew of D24 reloaded the 120-mm., the tank commander engaged with his .50-caliber machine gun. As the tank moved into the intersection, an RPG struck its right side in a shower of sparks and flame. Wright already

Sergeant Wright and D24 depart Camp Echo on a mission. His quick response at the beginning of the ambush allowed the raid force to accomplish its mission of seizing an insurgent leader who had publicly executed Iraq Army soldiers.

had the turret trained over the side of the tank, down the road, and his gunner saw the RPG team as it fired. Two militiamen sought cover behind a car parked on the right side, while a rifleman hid behind a van across the street. The main gun spit out a high-explosive antitank (HEAT) round at the automobile. When the smoke from the blast cleared, the vehicle was a tangled wreck resting on the bodies of the two RPG gunners. The rifleman was lying dead in the street. Within moments, someone came out of a house and dragged his body away.

Meanwhile, at the intersection of Jamhouri and Salem Streets, the Iraqi Army platoon had heard the firing, stopped, and refused to move forward. Since the street was not wide enough to allow a tank to pass the HMMWVs, this cut the raid force in half and prevented it from proceeding the last several hundred meters to the objective. The Iraqi lieutenant was shaken by the ambush. Shouting over the radio to the interpreter, he frantically claimed he had orders to return to camp. Simms made several appeals and threats to get the Iraqi unit moving while simultaneously monitoring his company and battalion radio nets to determine what was happening with his lead section and to keep the forward command post informed of the situation.

While Captain Simms' attention was focused on the dispute with the Iraqi lieutenant, a militia rifleman approached the left rear of the company commander's tank, using a parked minibus to mask his movement. Lieutenant

Merchant, next in line in D21, saw the threat, engaged with his .50-caliber machine gun, and had his gunner join in with the coaxial M240. Their fire chewed up the vehicle, and the insurgent disappeared. Before they could ascertain whether they had killed or wounded the rebel, the strike platoon leader relented and agreed to resume the advance. The back half of the column moved out again.

Having dispatched the RPG team on Salem Street, the lead section of tanks reached the target building and took up positions covering the streets leading to it. The Iraqi Army soldiers arrived soon after and quickly entered the house. Within minutes they emerged, reporting that they had captured the wanted sheik and recovered the slain Iraqi officer's pistol.

While these actions proceeded at the objective, the trail tanks were passing the side street where the ambush had occurred. Another RPG team emerged at the same location and fired one hundred fifty meters down the lane at the last Abrams in line, S. Sgt. Russell E. Chapman's D22. The well-aimed rocket detonated against the side skirt. The force of the blast disabled the commander's optics, while a jet of hot gasses found a seam and penetrated to start a blaze in the engine compartment. Sergeant Chapman continued to operate the tank using night-vision goggles while his gunner shot a canister round back down the alley. The blast from the tank round obscured the narrow road and made it impossible to determine whether it had any effect. As the smoke and dust cleared, a second RPG from the same direction missed the wounded Abrams. For the next several minutes, Sergeant Chapman and his crew exchanged fire with RPG gunners located at the end of the alley. The tank's automatic fire-suppression system retarded the flames and bought time for D22 to continue fighting but could not put out the growing inferno. As the blaze got out of control, Chapman ordered his men to evacuate the vehicle. The gunner, Sgt. Jason Caroll, saw two men with an RPG at the end of the alley. He shot a final HEAT round dead on target and killed them before abandoning the burning tank.

By this time, the Iraqi Army soldiers were back in their vehicles. Captain Simms asked the forward command post at Echo to provide immediate close air support and armor reinforcements. S. Sgt. Jimmy M. Brown Jr., commanding D23, meanwhile smashed his tank through a compound wall, making his own shortcut to quickly secure a key alleyway and protect the team's northern flank. In the process, however, dead electrical wires ensnared the vehicle, wrapping around the turret ring and jamming it. For the remainder of the fight, Brown had to pivot steer the Abrams side to side to aim the main gun. At the same time, Lieutenant Merchant in D21 and Captain Simms in D66 headed back toward Sergeant Chapman, whose last report was that his M1A2 SEP was on fire, that he was engaging an RPG team, and that his crew was evacuating the damaged Abrams. As the two tanks approached, they could see Chapman and his men taking cover behind the burning hulk and firing with small arms at a rooftop. From a perch on top of the two-story

The crew of D22 (*left to right*): Sergeant Chapman, commander; Sergeant Caroll, gunner; and Spec. James Robles, driver. The three soldiers fought from their burning tank until the last possible moment.

building on the southwest corner of the intersection, a militia rifleman had the soldiers pinned down. But the sergeant's decision to stay inside the tank until the last possible moment probably saved his men by allowing them to destroy the RPG team. Otherwise, they would have been facing fire from two directions with no effective cover at all. The two supporting tanks added their coaxial M240 machine guns to the duel and quickly brought it to an end. The raiding force received no more interference from that rooftop the rest of the night.

The crew of D22 took advantage of the short-lived respite from incoming fire to split up among the four remaining tanks, adding a fifth man to each. In three cases they crammed, rifle in hand, into the loader's station with the man already there. This greatly complicated the work of the loader, who had to maneuver in an already cramped space, hit a knee switch, select a round from the ready rack, and then pivot and maneuver the fifty-pound shell into the breach. Both men then had to keep clear of the path of the gun's recoil in a space designed for one person. All this occurred while the tanks were in a quick-draw battle in close urban terrain, which left no margin for delay or error. Only Sergeant Brown's crew could operate normally, as the Iraqi civilian who had identified the target house voluntarily yielded his position in the loader's seat to Sergeant Chapman and moved to the top of the turret. For the remainder of the battle, the young man clung to the armor as the tank spun left and right to bring the main gun to bear then jolted in recoil as it fired each 120-mm. round. Deafened, dizzied, and dodging small-arms fire, he maintained his composure throughout the ordeal.

Following the rescue of Chapman's crew, the four other tanks were in the positions they would hold throughout the night. Sergeant Wright in D24 faced north on Salem Street while Sergeant Brown in D23 secured the northeast alleyway. The turret of D66 pointed north, covering the backs of the two sergeants, while Captain Simms trained his heavy machine gun over the side and down the southeast alleyway. Parked beside a low wall topped by a chain-link fence, he had defilade protection from RPGs but still had a clear field of fire over the top of the fence from his perch in the turret. Lieutenant Merchant in D21 parked just to the rear of Simms, aiming south toward the burning tank. The four Abrams were spread out over about two hundred meters.

The Iraqi strike force, which had performed well on the objective, now huddled in its HMMWVs in the middle of the American formation. Simms, having faced the challenge of getting the Iraqi lieutenant to move forward after the initial small ambush, realized that his partners had no firm leadership and that the unit would be only as brave as its commanding officer. He wanted the infantrymen to hold the rooftops or at least protect the rear of his tanks against infiltrators, but he was heavily engaged in a full-scale battle that consumed his attention and required his active participation as a tank commander. He was in no position to cajole the Iraqi soldiers into action. He bolstered his close-in defensive capability as best he could, passing his own 9-mm. pistol to the interpreter so the Iraqi could help deal with any militiamen trying to crawl onto the tank.

Simms had little time to make a decision on his next course of action. His situation bore eerie inklings of a remake of *Blackhawk Down*. In the October 1993 battle in Mogadishu, Somalia, the loss of two helicopters had turned a quick snatch-and-withdrawal operation into a static defense in a hostile urban zone. Rapidly surrounded by hundreds of enemy militia, that raid force had fought against heavy numerical odds while a relief column struggled for hours to get to the scene. Simms had one important advantage this night that the soldiers in Somalia did not—the armor and firepower of four Abrams. In the chaotic first minutes of the insurgent attack, the tanks were mobile fortresses that dominated the battlefield. (It was an asset he had nearly forgone a few hours earlier during the hasty planning phase when he had considered using HMMWVs to increase the odds of surprise. He now realized that would have resulted in disaster.) What the Dragoon commander lacked was the reliable infantry needed for a battle in a city. He had little concern about the ability of his tanks to fight their way back to base if it came to that, even though this militia force seemed more determined, more numerous, better trained, and better armed than any foe he had yet faced in the war. But the shocking loss of D22 to an RPG complicated the picture. If Simms abandoned the Abrams, the insurgents would undoubtedly exploit it

Sergeant Brown, commanding D23, smashed his tank through a wall, gaining position to dominate this alley leading into the Company D perimeter. He and his crew battled the enemy here throughout the night. *Below:* Sgt. Joseph Schumacher loads a HEAT round in preparation for a mission, while Sergeant Brown cleans a Browning M2 .50-caliber machine gun. Schumacher was the gunner of D23 during the battle.

to achieve a propaganda coup. Much more important, the technical secrets of the M1A2 SEP would likely make their way into the hands of enemies beyond the borders of Iraq. The captain thus determined that he had to accept the risk of remaining in place to defend the destroyed vehicle until help arrived to retrieve it.

The insurgents gave the Dragoons little time to dwell on their circumstances. It was impossible to tell whether the militiamen were operating under central control or merely reacting individually and moving to the sound of the guns. The flames from D22 were now reaching three stories high and seemed to draw Mahdi gunmen like moths. The result was a steady stream of fighters maintaining pressure on the small perimeter. The first probe came almost immediately after the rescue of Sergeant Chapman's crew. Sergeant Brown observed an individual carrying a sniper rifle at the end of the alley and killed him with a burst from the .50-caliber machine gun. An RPG team appeared next, and Brown's gunner fired a HEAT round. Another RPG gunner moved down Salem Street toward D24. Sergeant Wright employed a canister round, shredding the insurgent and detonating the rocket on his shoulder. Another militiaman maneuvered into position to launch a rocket at D23, but the tank commander again eliminated the threat with his machine gun. Several minutes later, yet another RPG team appeared and Brown wiped it out with a multipurpose antitank (MPAT) shell. A sabot-encased round primarily designed to penetrate light armor and destroy fortifications, the MPAT's fuse could be set for a proximity burst that turned it into a fragmentation weapon useful against soft targets such as personnel.

Approximately forty minutes into the battle, as Sergeant Brown remained engaged in a toe-to-toe fight on the north end of Salem Street, two Air Force F–15s arrived on the scene. The flight commander contacted the forward command post and the tank platoon on the battalion frequency. Using the burning tank as a reference point, the pilots reported directly onto the command net what they were seeing. The enemy was approaching from the northeast and staging along a road three hundred meters to the east that roughly paralleled Salem Street. From that cover, the militiamen could make a quick dash down the alleyways to attack the Coalition perimeter. Some of them were already moving over the rooftops to seize positions overlooking the tanks. One cluster at the north end of Salem Street seemed intent on trying to outflank Sergeants Brown and Wright to get into position for a clean RPG flank shot on either Abrams. A second group appeared to be boring in toward the D22 bonfire. Simms asked the jets to make repeated shows of force over Salem Street and five hundred meters to the east, hoping they would deter additional militiamen from joining the battle and changing the odds. Several low, ear-shattering passes from the F–15s had the desired effect, disorganizing the enemy and slowing his advance.

The near-simultaneous probes across a broad front, the enemy's equipment (sniper rifles and the latest RPG models), his sheer numbers and aggressiveness, and the fact that fighters already had scored two long-range rocket hits in darkness against moving tanks all indicated to Captain Simms that he was facing a tougher and more sophisticated opponent than usual. The danger would increase exponentially if the insurgents launched a large-scale coordinated attack and simultaneously blocked the approach of a relief force. Fortunately, the militiamen had no appreciation of the capability of American night-vision systems or of the futility of seeking cover behind vehicles or walls. Some of the insurgents moved in the open, thinking the darkness was all the concealment they needed. Others sought shelter that might have protected them from small arms, but the tank main guns simply obliterated the obstructions. The side-by-side townhouse-like structures that lined the alleys offered the enemy almost no place for concealment or cover, and the firepower of the 120-mm. smoothbores and the .50-caliber machine guns proved devastating in these open corridors. The varied heights of the buildings also limited the ability of the insurgents to move rapidly from rooftop to rooftop to gain position over the tanks. Still, the threat of envelopment was real and growing more serious with every minute.

While Simms focused on the close fight, the battalion forward command post worked to prevent the encirclement of the force and protect the long line of communications back to the compound. Clearly, the enemy's most logical course of action would be to lay deadly roadside bombs along the approach routes to ambush any reinforcements. To prevent this, Major Taylor sent out a quick reaction force of four tanks from Company C. The platoon moved rapidly into the city and established a strongpoint at the intersection of Salem and Jamhouri Streets, with one Abrams pointing in each direction. That formation provided all-around defense for the relief force and gave them a clear field of view (and fire) down the length of the two main thoroughfares, thus allowing them to defeat any attempt to emplace explosive devices on either route.

The platoon was barely in position when an RPG team appeared from a nearby alley. The soldiers ended that initial threat with a canister round. The F–15s then reported men on the rooftops immediately above the relief force and also near the flaming carcass of D22. The Abrams crews could not see the attackers above them, but the pilots illuminated the enemy positions with a directed infrared beam (known as Sparkle) that the tank commanders picked up with their night-vision goggles. The tankers opened up with their .50-caliber machine guns, aiming for the bottom of the bright beams of light. The armor-piercing rounds sliced easily through the light masonry or sheet metal of the upper floors of the buildings and then through the roofs, scattering the gunmen. The real-time situational awareness provided by the aviators protected the armor platoon in the potentially deadly urban canyon and denied the enemy positional advantage.

While the relief force fought to secure its intersection, the enemy kept up the pressure on the Dragoons. A small pack of dogs and several startled birds alerted D66's crew to the presence of a militia group even before it came into sight. Captain Simms thus already had his machine gun trained on a cross street down his alleyway when an RPG team turned the corner. The surprised gunmen disappeared among the flashes of .50-caliber armor-piercing incendiary rounds spraying the walls and pavement all around them. At the same time, an RPG gunner peered around a corner from the north on Salem Street and loosed a rocket at D24 that sailed wide of the mark. Sergeant Wright returned fire with a HEAT round and killed him.

With Sergeant Wright securing the northern approaches of Salem Street and the relief force holding Jamhouri Street to the south, the small American force had "refused right" and "refused left," giving the enemy no chance to maneuver around the flanks. On the other hand, without infantry and having to maintain control over D22 and the two main routes, the eight tanks were in no position to launch a counterattack to dislodge the militiamen staging in the parallel street to the east of Salem. The battle in effect had become a standoff.

About this time, the F–15 flight lead reported that he was leaving the net to refuel from a tanker. It was the last time the forces on the ground would hear directly from the jets, although they stayed in the air for several more hours. Before the aircraft returned from the tanker stop, Air Force ground control directed the flight to talk only on high-frequency radios and only to the nearest Air Force ground control team located eighty kilometers north at FOB Kalsu. To communicate with the pilots, Simms thenceforth had to contact the battalion forward command post, which would relay the message through an online chat system to the Kalsu ground control team, which would pass it by radio to the aircrew. This effectively ended the close coordination between the troops in contact and the F–15s, eliminating the critical reconnaissance and target-designation capabilities the airmen had been providing to the ground tactical commander.

Just after Sergeant Wright's engagement, Major Taylor arrived on scene with his tank, an M88 recovery vehicle, a company of Iraqi soldiers, and a contingent of the local fire department. The Iraqi unit immediately established a screen along Jamhouri Street to secure the exit route. The Abrams and the M88 pressed on to the burning wreckage that was once Sergeant Chapman's tank. The engine fire had grown to consume the entire vehicle. Flames reached high above the buildings, and the heat could be felt at one hundred meters. Small puddles of molten aluminum were beginning to form at the base of the tank as the tracks and road wheels melted into the asphalt.

Two Apache helicopters also arrived at the scene at the same time. As the gunships made their first pass, another RPG team attempted to maneuver down Sergeant Brown's alley to the northeast. He could see their rocket poking up into the air as they moved behind a low wall. A HEAT round eliminated both the masonry structure and the gunmen. Once the Apaches located the tanks, the pilots reported armed men on the street to the east. Since Iraqi

Army soldiers were now in the area, Captain Simms checked to confirm that there were no friendly dismounts in that vicinity. The Apaches reached the same conclusion almost simultaneously when they started taking fire. They requested clearance to engage, and Major Taylor approved the mission. The attack helicopters began a series of strafing runs down the axis of the street parallel to Salem, catching the enemy in enfilade. The Apaches relied solely on their 30-mm. chain guns, which were both precise and devastating against personnel in the open, thus limiting the potential for collateral damage. The pilots reported two to four enemy dismounts killed in the initial passes.

The attack aviation proved to be the ideal weapon at the perfect time, serving as the additional maneuver element needed to break the impasse. The enemy was now caught in a dilemma. If the militiamen remained on the parallel road, they were at the mercy of the helicopters. If they moved into the side streets, they fell under the guns of the tanks. Several insurgents chose the latter course and rushed to escape the aerial assault. Sergeant Brown took out one RPG team with a HEAT round and engaged another group of militiamen with an MPAT. The Apaches saw an RPG team hesitating and destroyed it with 30-mm. cannons.

That was the last contact with the enemy. Under attack from the air and the ground and with no tactical options left open, the survivors slipped into the nearest houses and blended in with the civilians. The engagement had lasted four hours from the opening ambush to the final shot. Suddenly, all was quiet and the battlefield was empty, even of casualties. Throughout the night, a steady stream of unarmed people had policed up enemy wounded and dead and the raiding force had made no move to interfere.

Near sunrise, with the battle over and the danger of ammunition cook-offs in the tank diminished, Iraqi firemen moved in to extinguish the flames. The Dragoons repositioned closer around the destroyed Abrams to provide better security from the crowds that started forming at first light. The Iraqi rifle company and the strike platoon began searching the surrounding neighborhoods. They found a rocket at a school on Salem Street and detained eight male suspects. The Coalition force owned the Mahdi-dominated area for the next several hours as a complex ballet of cranes and heavy equipment transporters retrieved the massive hulk of D22.

Large, unfriendly crowds gathered on all sides of the perimeter throughout the day. Periodically, groups of children would run to within fifty meters of the tanks and throw rocks at the men and equipment involved in the recovery mission. That nuisance took on a deadlier cast on two separate occasions when hand grenades came flying in from the rear ranks of the kids and detonated near the tanks. Fragments from one blast slightly wounded Captain Simms' interpreter in the arm. At one point, a sniper also fired from long range, the round smacking into a telephone pole just overhead. The sheer mass of the thousands of people hovering so close posed a significant risk. As dangerous and frustrating as this was, the soldiers never lost their composure and never resorted to force to clear the streets. Whenever the mob moved forward, the American and Iraqi troops shouted verbal warnings, brandished their weapons, fired warning shots into the air, or formed online and moved toward the civilians to intimidate them into retreating. Apaches also were on station throughout and occasionally made low-level passes. By midafternoon, the derelict tank was on the back of a heavy equipment transporter and the American force headed back to Camp Echo.

Both air and ground technology had helped achieve this victory, but the outcome had been decided largely by the ingenuity and bravery of the junior tank commanders and their men. Sergeant Chapman and his crew fought from a burning Abrams for almost fifteen minutes and then joined the remaining tanks to continue the fight. Sergeant Brown's decision to aggressively seize the key northeastern alley and his subsequent efforts to retain it while in close combat with the enemy most likely saved the unit from being overrun. He and his crew proved absolutely fearless in the face of wave after wave of attacks from what proved to be the enemy's most heavily used avenue of approach. All with a disabled turret and a civilian on the top of the tank whose identity and safety had to be protected. For the duration of the fight, Sergeant Brown and his crew were seemingly immune to defeat, fear, and enemy fire. The small but fierce battle along Salem Street prevented the Mahdi militia from taking control of a large city and enabled the Iraqi Army and police to regain dominance in the area. It also serves as a powerful reminder that the resourcefulness and courage of the American soldier remains the Army's greatest asset.

CHAPTER SEVEN

SHROUDED IN THE FOG OF WAR

MARK J. REARDON

A Stryker battalion, Special Forces elements, American advisers, and their Iraqi units come together to defeat a well-armed cult preparing to assassinate religious leaders and unleash a new wave of chaos throughout the country.

Zarqa—28–29 January 2007

During the night of 27–28 January 2007, a squad of Iraqi Army soldiers lounged around an armored high mobility multipurpose wheeled vehicle (HMMWV, or Humvee) and a Polish-model wheeled personnel carrier parked astride a road outside Najaf. The checkpoint was a few kilometers north of the city, the capital of Najaf Province, which the Coalition had turned over to Iraqi control just the previous month. Only a few U.S. Special Forces detachments and Military Transition Teams (MiTTs) remained in the region. The main force in the area was Lt. Col. Muhammed Hanoon Majeed's 2d Battalion, 1st Brigade, 8th Iraqi Army Division, stationed at Forward Operating Base (FOB) Hotel on Highway 9 on the northern outskirts of Najaf.

By midnight, most of the soldiers at the checkpoint were fighting off sleep and boredom. Those still alert peered suspiciously at a long string of approaching headlights. Nudging their fellow soldiers awake, the Iraqis fingered AK47s as the convoy came closer. A lieutenant motioned for the lead vehicle to halt and then stepped forward, shielding his eyes from the glare. Unsatisfied with the answers offered by the occupants, the officer told them to remain in their car while he contacted his headquarters. As he walked back to the Humvee, firing broke out and dozens of men clutching automatic rifles rushed forward from the convoy. Confronted with overwhelming odds, the Iraqi soldiers broke contact, most of them running back toward their base. The checkpoint overcome, the gunmen clambered back into their vehicles, commandeering the personnel carrier and Humvee in the process. The convoy turned onto a dirt road leading to a nearby farm

A Polish-built "Dzik" armored personnel carrier and an Iraqi Army Humvee sit in the cultist motor pool destroyed by American airstrikes. The capture of these two vehicles at an Iraqi Army checkpoint initiated the battle at Zarqa.

and village named Zarqa, situated in a narrow neck between Highway 9 and the Euphrates River.[1] (*Map 10*)

Diya Abdul Zahra Kadim, a forty-year-old Shi'ite from Diwaniyah, owned the Zarqa complex.[2] According to Shi'ite belief, the twelfth Imam (the supreme spiritual leader descended from Mohammed), disappeared as a child in the ninth century and would reappear in the future as a messianic figure, the Mahdi, to save mankind and usher in a perfect Islamic society.[3] Kadim had proclaimed himself the Mahdi and formed a small cult and militia. His Zarqa base gave him ready access to Najaf, the holiest city in the Shi'ite sect and home to its religious leaders, such as Grand Ayatollah Ali al-Sistani. Kadim planned to kill those senior clerics during the approaching holiday of Ashura, commemorating the death of the Prophet Mohammed's grandson during the battle of Karbala.[4] He would then step into the vacuum of leadership he had created.

At the farm, the cult had been training two hundred fighters to form the hard core of its military wing. All wore headbands proclaiming themselves Soldiers of Heaven.[5] The convoy, carrying two hundred members of the Hawatimah tribe from Diwaniyah, was arriving just prior to the attack on

---

[1] Ltr, M Sgt Thomas S. Ballard, former Noncommissioned Officer in Charge (NCOIC), Military Transition Team (MiTT) 0810, to author, 23 Apr 08, Historians files, U.S. Army Center of Military History (CMH), Washington, D.C.

[2] "Iraq Cult Leader Among Najaf Dead," *al-Jazeera*, 29 January 2007, copy in Historians files, CMH.

[3] Sumedha Senanayake, "Iraq: Al-Najaf Mystery Reflects Iraqi Division," *Radio Free Europe/Radio Liberty*, 2 February 2007, copy in Historians files, CMH.

[4] Haider al-Kaabi, "Najaf Curfew Raised Partially as Bodies of Recent Military Operation Buried," *Voice of America*, 2 February 2007, copy in Historians files, CMH.

[5] "Iraq Cult Leader Among Najaf Dead."

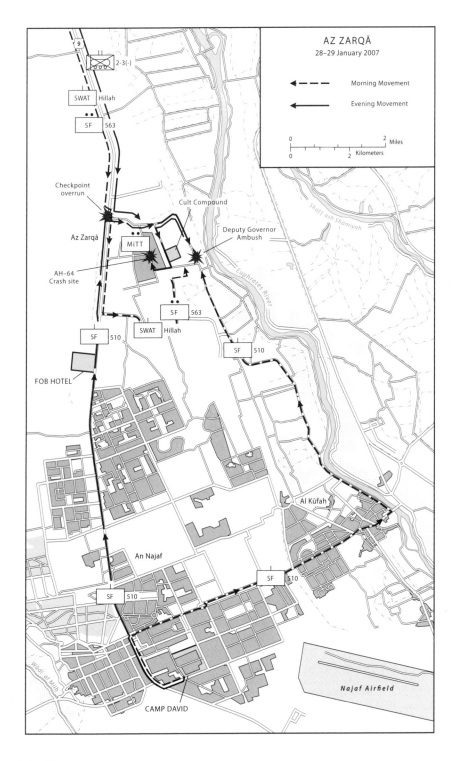

AZ ZARQÂ
28–29 January 2007

◀----- Morning Movement

◀───── Evening Movement

0 ————————— 2 Miles
0 ————————— 2 Kilometers

9

2-3(-)

SWAT Hillah

SF 563

Checkpoint
overrun

Cult Compound

Az Zarqâ

Deputy Governor
Ambush

MiTT

AH–64
Crash site

SF 563

SF 510

SWAT Hillah

SF 510

FOB HOTEL

Shatt ash Shamiyah

Euphrates River

Al Kûfah

An Najaf

SF 510

SF 510

SF 510

Najaf Airfield

Wadi al Milh

CAMP DAVID

MAP 10

Najaf to avoid raising the suspicions of Iraqi security forces.[6] Kadim rounded out his force with a wave of involuntary recruits. Having invited many Ashura pilgrims to stay in large tents at Zarqa, the cultists now informed the visitors they would join the ranks or be killed.[7] The draftees, numbering roughly another two hundred men, received brand-new AK47s and ammunition vests. Those displaying visible reluctance were chained together and placed under the direct supervision of a trusted cult member.[8]

Kadim expected a violent response from other Shi'ite groups seeking to avenge the death of their leaders. In preparation, his Soldiers of Heaven had turned the square-shaped complex, measuring about six hundred meters on each side, into an elaborate defensive network. His farm and the surrounding area already had numerous dirt berms separating the fields. The cultists had dug deep trenches behind some of these barriers around the perimeter. Supplementary trenches and individual fighting positions provided a defense in depth, with caches of weapons and ammunition pre-positioned throughout. The village just inside the western trench housed command, logistics, and medical facilities, all partially concealed by palm groves. Tree lines bordering the checkerboard layout of agricultural fields masked some defensive works. A mortar battery with a mix of eleven 60-mm. and 82-mm. tubes occupied the dead center of the square to maximize all-around coverage. A number of trucks mounted 12.7-mm. and 14.5-mm. heavy machine guns for both ground and air defense.[9] Most of the firepower was oriented to the south and east, the likely avenue of approach from Najaf. In addition, tall berms surrounding adjacent compounds to the east and south served as a vehicle barrier in those directions.

The encounter at the checkpoint, apparently unexpected by both sides, gave Iraqi security forces some hint of the impending danger. Colonel Majeed provided news of the encounter to his brigade commander, Col. Saleh Mushin Sa'adi, also based at FOB Hotel. Sa'adi ordered Majeed to prepare his battalion for combat operations and notified the deputy governor of Najaf Province, Abdul Hussein Abtan. The deputy governor, aware in part of Kadim's activities, contacted the intelligence chief of the Ministry of Interior. The two civilian officials decided that negotiation with the cultists seemed preferable to launching a full-fledged assault.[10] Abtan directed Colonel Sa'adi to deploy two companies of Colonel Majeed's battalion in a cordon around Zarqa. At dawn, the 2d Battalion's scout platoon, along with National Police from Najaf, would escort the deputy governor and the intelligence chief to Zarqa.

---

[6] "Iraq: Al-Najaf Mystery."

[7] Ltr, Ballard to author, 23 Apr 08.

[8] Marc Santora, "Missteps by Iraqi Forces in Battle Raise Questions," *New York Times*, 30 January 2007, copy in Historians files, CMH.

[9] 2d Bn, 3d Inf, Optimized Fallen Angel Storyboard, 28 Jan 07, copy in Historians files, CMH.

[10] Gregory Frye, "Special Forces Soldiers Earn Third Highest Combat Medal," *The Fort Campbell Courier*, 10 April 2008, copy in Historians files, CMH.

The first indication for American forces that something was afoot came at 0700 the next day. Operational Detachment Alpha (ODA) 566, a U.S. Special Forces team based at FOB David in southern Najaf, received a cell phone call from Majeed's scouts (whom the Americans had trained).[11] An Iraqi soldier shouted over heavy firing that his comrades faced annihilation if they did not receive immediate help. The Special Forces team leader alerted his men to prepare for combat, then shared what little he had learned from the call with Operational Detachment Bravo (ODB) 510. An element of the latter unit, consisting of portions of both ODA 512 and 513, was advising a fifty-man force of Iraqi commandos that had deployed from Baghdad to FOB David for the Ashura religious holiday. The senior American adviser, a Special Forces field grade officer in command of ODB 510, promised to follow ODA 566 as soon as the commandos were ready.

It did not take long for ODA 566's compact column of armed Humvees to reach Zarqa. The team pulled into a palm grove several hundred yards southeast of the farm, where they received an update from Colonel Sa'adi. The Iraqi officer explained that the deputy governor and the intelligence chief, along with the scouts and a police security detail, had been ambushed. The Iraqi Army scout platoon had been in the lead and borne the brunt of the attack. A pair of its Humvees had just gone through an opening in the berm surrounding the complex when the cultists opened fire and wounded the turret gunner in the first vehicle. The driver dismounted and fought back with his rifle. When he ran out of ammunition, Kadim's men captured him, forced him to kneel, and cut off his head. They shot and killed the wounded gunner as he attempted to drive away. The scouts and National Police suffered a number of other casualties. The Americans could see vehicles, many bearing signs of battle damage, strung along a dirt road leading into the southeast corner of the complex. The survivors of the ambush were pinned down all around the convoy.[12]

The Special Forces team wasted no time swinging into action. M. Sgt. Raymond A. Lancey opened up on the enemy fighters with his vehicle's .50-caliber machine gun. After loosing several accurate bursts, he turned over the weapon to another team member and huddled with M. Sgt. Petter Jacobsen and S. Sgt. Gregory A. Keller. Lancey explained that he intended to cross the open ground to reach the Iraqi scouts. The trio started out under the cover of their team's Humvee-mounted machine guns. Within minutes, the heavy return fire disabled one of the American gun trucks.

Undeterred, the three sergeants continued across the field. While Lancey and Jacobsen bounded forward in alternating rushes, Sergeant Keller employed an M203 grenade launcher to hit the enemy. Although an exploding rocket-propelled grenade (RPG) wounded Keller, he kept up his supporting

---

[11] Ibid.
[12] Ltr, Capt John R. Mitcha to author, 1 Feb 08, Historians files, CMH.

fire. The cultists also struck back with heavy machine guns of their own, and Lancey and Jacobsen had to go to ground just short of their intended goal.[13] When Kadim's men started lobbing volleys of RPGs at nearby Iraqi police and soldiers, the government forces began streaming away from the compound toward Najaf.

The Iraqi commandos and ODB 510 arrived as the rescue attempt began to falter. Their vehicles halted to the southeast of the ambushed convoy along a road within a dense palm grove. Making contact with ODA 566, the ODB 510 commander, whose force possessed much more combat power, offered to take over the fight. He suggested that ODA 566 focus on the reorganization of Iraqi security forces—the sooner they were steadied, the sooner they could assume responsibility for the situation. The ODA 566 team leader assented and signaled for his men to reposition themselves to the south of the commandos. The ODB 510 commander then placed the ODA 512 team leader in charge of tactical operations.

Moments after ODA 566 pulled back, a barrage of lofted RPGs slammed into the palm grove, making ODB 510 and the commandos think they were being targeted by mortars.[14] A sergeant in ODA 512 was wounded, and the newcomers quickly shifted their vehicles out of range.[15] Realizing that it would be unwise to mount a direct assault in the face of such firepower, the ODB 510 leadership decided to employ close air support to soften the enemy.

Accompanied by two Air Force combat controllers, the ODA 512 team leader crawled out to a small berm that offered a better view of the cultist positions. A pair of 332d Expeditionary Fighter Squadron F–16C Falcons already were orbiting to the east of Zarqa.[16] The combat controllers initially directed the fixed-wing aircraft in a strafing run against the Iraqi Army vehicles abandoned at the head of the deputy governor's convoy in order to prevent the enemy from adding those guns to their arsenal.[17] The Falcons zoomed in with 20-mm. cannon roaring. Although a cloud of sand and dust rose near the target, neither ground controllers nor pilots could confirm if the attack had been effective.

The combat controller began picking out other targets for the F–16 flight's 500-pound bombs. At least two exploded near an earthen berm sheltering a

[13] "Special Forces Soldiers Earn Third Highest Combat Medal"; 5th Special Forces Grp, Narrative, Award of the Silver Star to S Sgt Gregory A. Keller, n.d., Historians files, CMH.

[14] Comments by Operational Detachment Alpha (ODA) 512 Tm Ldr on 10 May 08 Ms Version, Historians files, CMH.

[15] "Special Forces Soldiers Earn Third Highest Combat Medal."

[16] Interv, Mark J. Reardon, CMH, with former Tm Ldr, ODA 563, 5 Feb 08, Historians files, CMH; T Sgt Jennifer Gregoire, "Air Force Combat Airpower Helps Turn Tide in Decisive Battle of An Najaf," *Air Force Print News Today*, 4 February 2007, copy in Historians files, CMH.

[17] Lt Gen Michael W. Wooley, "America's Specialized Airpower in the War on Terrorism," 24 Sep 07, U.S. Air Force Association National Symposium, p. 5, copy in Historians files, CMH. Copresenters included S. Sgts. Ryan A. Wallace and David Orvash.

large number of enemy fighters. During the lull between airstrikes, however, the cultists succeeded in driving the abandoned Iraqi Army Humvees into a grove of palm trees. Two 74th Expeditionary Fighter Squadron A–10 Thunderbolt II attack planes came on station and joined in the strafing and bombing runs.[18]

The cultists did not all hunker down under the aerial assault. In the midst of the bombardment, the ODA 512 team leader was astonished when he saw gunmen moving out from the northeast corner of the compound in an effort to get to the flank of the Iraqi commandos. During multiple tours in Iraq, the Special Forces captain had never encountered opponents who tried to aggressively maneuver against a Coalition unit. The ODA 512 team leader relayed a request through ODA 566 for Iraqi permission to use close air support against the enemy's flanking element, which had occupied the upper stories of a small mosque and opened fire on the Americans and the commandos. Colonel Sa'adi approved the request mere seconds after it had been made. Although the first bomb proved to be a dud, the second wiped out the building and the cultists.[19]

Their nearest antagonists dead or pummeled into silence, one by one the trapped officials, police, and scouts made their way to friendly lines. The cultists maintained constant harassing long-range fire from their positions within the palm groves surrounding the village and used the respite from aerial bombardment to reorganize. But with the fighting seeming to ebb, it looked like Colonel Sa'adi's troops had control of the situation, so ODB 510 and the commandos returned to their base to refit and rearm.[20]

Not everyone believed the battle was largely over. Earlier that morning, Col. Abbas al-Jeboury of the Babil Province Police Special Weapons and Tactics (SWAT) team appeared at ODA 563's quarters near Hillah, approximately sixty-five kilometers northeast of Najaf. A subordinate element of the same Special Forces headquarters unit that controlled the teams in Najaf, ODA 563 provided advisory support to Colonel Jeboury's unit. He told the American team leader that "something big was going down" north of the holy city. A short while later, the Special Forces detachment received a report that ODA 566 was in a firefight but did not require assistance. Reassured by the news, ODA 563 informed Colonel Jeboury that everything seemed well in hand. Jeboury departed, only to return a few minutes later saying, "We have to go NOW." The Iraqi police colonel emphasized his words by pointing toward the pickup trucks containing two full SWAT companies parked outside of the Special Forces team's compound. The Americans quickly readied their armed five-ton truck and turreted Humvee, and the combined convoy departed at 1000 for the hour-long trip. Based on the latest reports, however, ODA 563's team leader expected to find an "empty battlefield" upon arrival.[21]

---

[18] "Air Force Combat Airpower Helps Turn Tide."
[19] Wooley, "America's Specialized Airpower," p. 5.
[20] Ibid.
[21] Interv, Reardon with former Tm Ldr, ODA 563, 5 Feb 08.

Other American units were on their way to Zarqa. At 0800, the 4th Brigade Combat Team, 25th Infantry Division, passed on a report of the fighting north of Najaf to Lt. Col. Stephen Hughes, commander of its MiTT based at Diwaniyah.[22] The small group served as advisers to the 8th Iraqi Army Division and as a liaison element between that command and American forces at FOB Kalsu. When Hughes pressed for more details, a brigade staff officer told him that a dozen or so insurgents were fighting Iraqi troops backed by American airpower. The team already was scheduled for its regular weekly visit to Colonel Sa'adi. Hughes loaded his six officers and six noncommissioned officers plus a specialist from the support element into three up-armored Humvees and headed to Zarqa.[23]

A pair of AH–64 Apache attack helicopters belonging to Lt. Col. Timothy P. DeVito's 4th Battalion, 227th Aviation Regiment, also prepared to join the fight. CWO4 Johnny W. Judd and CWO2 Jacob R. Gaston flew the lead aircraft, call sign Big Gun 52. CWO3 Cornell C. Chao and Capt. Mark T. Resh piloted the second Apache, designated Big Gun 53. The two helicopters departed Taji at 1020 en route to Kalsu, twenty miles northeast of Hillah. They were accompanied by a pair of UH–60 Black Hawks loaded with spare parts, ammunition, ground crew, and mechanics. The Black Hawks would establish a base of support at Kalsu while the Apaches flew on to Zarqa.

Since Najaf Province was under Iraqi control and there were no major U.S. forces there, there was no American command structure to guide operations. The Iraqi security forces were still inexperienced in running complex undertakings, so they were not able to fill the gap. As a result, small American units were reacting to events on the ground on their own initiative, most did not know that others were doing the same thing, and no one had a clear picture of the enemy. This unintended piecemeal response and lack of good intelligence would characterize most of the battle and have an impact on its course.

The AH–64s arrived on the scene first. Chief Warrant Officers Judd and Chao received no enemy fire during their first hour on station, lending credence to the growing belief that the battle was over. The SWAT companies appeared next. They encountered a checkpoint on the main highway west of the complex, but the Iraqi security personnel there had no useful information and no other forces appeared to be in the vicinity. Colonel Jeboury announced his intention to sweep through Zarqa. His Special Forces adviser figured the Iraqi leader was out to score a public relations coup by presenting his unit as the victors of a battle that was already over, but the American captain decided to go along with the operation in order to maintain a good relationship. Working from a map, the two commanders decided to approach the complex from the southeast, unaware that was the site of the opening ambush.

[22] MiTT 0810, "Chronology for Najaf Battle, 28 Jan–5 Feb 07," p. 1, Historians files, CMH.

[23] Ltr, M Sgt Thomas S. Ballard to author, 30 Jan 08, Historians files, CMH.

ODA 563 and Hillah SWAT pause to assess the situation before moving against cult members holed up in their compound north of Najaf. On the far side of the berm are Iraqi government vehicles abandoned that morning when the cultists attacked local authorities arriving to negotiate.

As the convoy neared its destination, driving eastward parallel to and several hundred meters from the southern end of the farm, the SWAT personnel and ODA 563 watched as the Apaches began trading fire with the cultists. The Iraqi vehicles began to slow, prompting the ODA team leader's Humvee to assume the lead. The Special Forces captain spied a gap in the southeast corner of the berm, with armed Iraqis and a number of vehicles clustered there. Unsure of their identity, the team leader's turret gunner triggered short bursts of machine-gun fire off to one side as warning shots. The unknown individuals turned out to be Iraqi security forces, but no one knew that at the time. The Special Forces team leader and his team sergeant reacted with the same instinct and simultaneously gave the signal to turn left rather than continue eastward. The SWAT and ODA vehicles transitioned from a column into a line abreast, now heading north toward the berm. The convoy's abrupt change in direction triggered an immediate reaction from the cultists. On the far side of the long mound, the enemy began scrambling from their redoubt in the village to man the same rampart.

Hillah SWAT and ODA 563 won the race. On the far right, ODA 563's team leader climbed to the top of the berm. He could hear heavy gunfire but saw only a couple of gunmen dodging amongst the line of palm trees to his left front. Farther to the west, the Special Forces .50-caliber gunner on the armored five-ton spotted dozens of fighters swarming forward. From his high perch, he fired over the berm at the advancing cultists. Overhead, the AH–64s also saw the enemy movement and started strafing runs. Chief Warrant Officer Gaston's cannon had been damaged by enemy fire, but both Apaches mounted rockets and Hellfire missiles, which they employed with precision.[24]

---

[24] Sfc Rick Emert, "ACB Aviators Honored with Awards for Valor," *1st Cavalry Division News*, 14 June 2007, copy in Historians files, CMH.

Shortly after 1330, the Coalition troops were stunned to see a helicopter shot down by a truck-mounted 12.7-mm. heavy machine gun. ODA 563's Air Force combat controller, S. Sgt. Ryan A. Wallace, had just watched an Apache roll through:

> Then his wingman came in right behind him, pointed at the same target, and then his rotors just stopped. They completely froze up. No smoke, no sparks, no fire. The rotors froze and the helicopter fell out of the sky from 600–700 feet. As soon as it went behind the tree line, maybe fifteen seconds later, a big black cloud of smoke came up.[25]

The crash site, hidden from the Americans on the ground by intervening palm groves, was a few hundred meters west of the farm complex. Within seconds of Big Gun 53 going down, Chief Warrant Officer Judd contacted an incoming pair of AH–64Ds and warned them about the presence of enemy air defense weapons.[26]

Colonel Hughes' advisory team, now approaching Zarqa from the southwest, also witnessed the downing of the Apache. M. Sgt. Thomas S. Ballard, manning the turret weapon of the lead Humvee, saw a dark explosion against the side of the second helicopter and its rapid plunge to earth.[27] "When I saw the Apache go down, it immediately changed everything. . . . Everything was focused on the crash site; nothing else mattered. That's where we had to go and that's what we did."[28]

The MiTT Humvees reached the site only to find the shattered Apache had begun attracting heavy RPG and machine-gun fire. Two of the adviser gun trucks remained in overwatch while Sergeant Ballard's continued on to the downed helicopter. Dismounting from his vehicle, Ballard confirmed that both pilots were dead.[29] As the amount of incoming fire increased, Colonel Hughes ordered his team to fall back three hundred meters to defensible ground. From its new location, they could dominate the crash site until reinforcements arrived.

The MiTT displaced behind a low berm providing cover and clear fields of fire. The enemy took shelter behind another berm several hundred yards from the destroyed chopper, bobbing up to fire long bursts and RPGs before seeking cover once again. One of the Humvee turret gunners, M. Sgt.

---

[25] Wooley, "America's Specialized Airpower," p. 8.

[26] Ltr, Lt Col Timothy Zito, Commanding Officer (CO), 4th Bn, 227th Avn, to author, 11 Mar 07, Historians files, CMH.

[27] Interv, Reardon with M Sgt Thomas S. Ballard, former NCOIC, MiTT 0810, 2 Feb 08, Historians files, CMH.

[28] "Soldiers Lauded for Courage Under Fire," *Army News Service*, 20 September 2007, Historians files, CMH.

[29] Richard Mauer, "Grim Battlefield: Fort Richardson Paratroopers Fought Doomsday Cult," *Anchorage Daily Times*, 18 February 2007, copy in Historians files, CMH.

Christopher T. Crawford, replied to the incoming fire with his .50-caliber machine gun while Sergeant Ballard and Sfc. Cary M. Wallum joined in with their 7.62-mm. M240B machine guns. Crawford was hit by fragments but remained at his weapon.[30]

The team's fire inflicted losses on the cultists and also prevented them from overrunning the crash site. After a prolonged exchange, the shooting dwindled and petered out. The advisers were running low on ammunition, and the cultists apparently hoped that a lack of action around the downed Apache would bait American forces into the open. This separate fight in the west went unnoticed by the Special Forces teams to the south, who had no idea that another U.S. element was on the battlefield and defending the downed helicopter.

After the crash, the ODA 563 captain contacted his team sergeant, who reported that his half of the line in the west was pinned down by fire so heavy that the Hillah SWAT personnel there would no longer expose themselves at the top of the berm to shoot back. The NCO suggested a flanking assault to drive away the cultists and to recover the aircrew. Mulling over the advice for a few seconds, the team leader instructed the sergeant to organize a base of fire to support such a maneuver by the eastern elements of the Iraqi-American force.

The team sergeant directed two of his men to take a Carl Gustav 84-mm. recoilless rifle to the top of the berm in the hope that its heavier firepower would turn the tide. The soldiers lugged the heavy weapon and several rounds of ammunition into position; but as they rose up to shoot, the assistant gunner took a bullet to the head. The slug penetrated the helmet and creased his skull. Dazed and bleeding, he tumbled back down the mound. Before the gunner realized what had happened, he also was hit in the helmet and went sprawling. That example did nothing to buck up the courage of the Iraqis behind the berm. Aid men from SWAT and the Special Forces team tended to the two wounded, then the American medic retrieved the Carl Gustav and began lobbing high-explosive rounds over the berm at the enemy fighters in the palm grove.[31]

The flanking force, consisting of the ODA 563 team leader, his junior American medic, Air Force combat controller, and Iraqi interpreter, along with forty SWAT personnel including Colonel Jeboury, prepared for their assault. They would have to traverse open terrain before reaching a large berm a few hundred meters to the north. The U.S. captain decided to cover the exposed ground in several rushes, making use of a slight depression located partway to the objective. After receiving an acknowledgment from Colonel Jeboury, the team leader signaled for everyone to advance. Their first rush carried them to the vehicles abandoned by the deputy governor's entourage, where they began to receive well-aimed small-arms fire. A reprieve appeared in the form of a second flight of Apaches from the 4th Battalion, 227th

---

[30] Ltr, M Sgt Thomas S. Ballard to author, 4 Mar 08, Historians files, CMH.

[31] Interv, Reardon with Former Tm Ldr, ODA 563, 5 Feb 08.

Aviation Regiment. ODA 563's combat controller, Sergeant Wallace, called them in "about 200 meters to our front to get some heads down so we could get up and move."[32]

As the volume of incoming fire died down, the assault team pushed forward once again; but an enemy machine gunner opened up, sending the Americans and the SWAT personnel scrambling for cover. Bringing his M4 carbine to bear, Sergeant Wallace peered into the scope: "The guy popped his head up, I took off a couple of shots and hit the dirt right beneath his chin, so hopefully those armor piercing rounds skipped through [the berm] and hooked him up. I readjusted my aim on my scope and waited about 20 seconds. That guy didn't come back."[33]

The remaining distance to the assault team's final goal was even more flat and featureless, and it was apparent now that cultists occupied the objective. Sensing an impasse, Sergeant Wallace asked the ODA team leader, "Why don't I drop a bomb on them?"[34] The Special Forces officer realized the target was much nearer than the minimum safe distance for using ordnance in the proximity of friendly troops. However, he nodded assent before ordering the team's interpreter to tell the SWAT personnel to stay down until the bomb detonated. Immediately after, the assault team would sprint for the berm. Sergeant Wallace radioed the request to the F–16s circling overhead and signaled the team's position with a mirror. To minimize the chances of error, the inbound fighter flew on a course perpendicular to the direction of the ground attack.

The bomb whistled down and exploded on the enemy side of the berm. With debris still raining over the area, the Special Forces team and the interpreter ran forward. Glancing back, the soldiers discovered that none of the SWAT personnel had accompanied them. The Americans returned to rouse Jeboury and his men. With everyone finally in tow, the assault team sprinted across the open ground. After scaling the earthen rampart, the soldiers were surprised at what they saw. Another berm, constructed at right angles to the main one, extended off north into the distance. A deep trench backed both mounds, with a vehicle-mounted heavy machine gun anchoring the juncture. There were a dozen or more bodies near the site of the blast, but numerous other cultists occupying the position had merely been stunned by the concussion.

The team leader, medic, and combat controller, accompanied by Colonel Jeboury's deputy, Captain Ali, took position atop the berm. Already the dazed enemy fighters were stirring back to life. Captain Ali took a bullet in the upper lip that knocked him backward, and the Americans dropped back behind the mound. The ODA captain's first thought was to storm the trench with his

[32] Ltr, S Sgt Ryan A. Wallace to author, sub: Shrouded by the Fog of War Review and Comment, 9 May 08, Historians files, CMH; Wooley, "America's Specialized Airpower," p. 9.
[33] Wooley, "America's Specialized Airpower," p. 9.
[34] Interv, Reardon with former Tm Ldr, ODA 563, 5 Feb 08.

combined force. His medic pointed out that they had no hand grenades and that the SWAT personnel had no training in this type of combat. The Special Forces team leader nodded and then realized the weakness of the enemy position, which lacked the zigzag pattern of a proper defensive work. He decided to secure the junction of the northern and western berms and from that elevated position to sweep the straight, exposed enemy trench line by fire.[35]

The three Americans scrambled back up the earthen wall. Almost all of the cultists were facing south toward the team sergeant's location. Only the enemy fighter closest to the Americans appeared to realize that the position had been outflanked. Sergeant Wallace and the others opened fire before the gunman could sound the alarm: "Once we knocked him down, we just knocked down the next guy and the next guy and the next guy. I went through two and a half magazines. Everybody else went through a couple of magazines."[36]

The team's interpreter kept yelling down at the SWAT personnel to join the Americans. The Iraqis came up as the last cultists in the trench went down. When the shooting subsided, the ODA 563 team leader could hear the distinctive sound of American automatic weapons in the distance. Moments later, ODB 510's Humvees, along with the commandos and ODA 566, came into sight at the northeast corner of the cult compound. Having monitored reports of the Apache going down, the Special Forces teams had been ordered by their higher headquarters to secure the downed aircraft. The column had come in from the west, passing several hundred meters north of the crash site but not seeing the downed chopper. They now joined up with ODA 563 at the southeast corner of the Zarqa complex.

The ODA 512 and 563 team leaders linked up to develop a coordinated plan of action. As the two American officers conversed, the Iraqi commandos formed a firing line along the eastern berm and began engaging the cultists. The enemy returned fire, wounding a commando company commander in the head. The Special Forces captains decided the best course of action consisted of ODA 563 and the SWAT companies (still arrayed along the southern berm) fixing the enemy forces to their front while ODA 566, ODB 510, and the commandos maneuvered in their vehicles to secure the Apache.

No one on this side of the battlefield, however, knew just where the helicopter had gone down. When the ODA 512 team leader tried to obtain a precise location from gunships circling overhead, they were unable to provide coordinates. After the pilots rejected several alternate suggestions on how they could mark the Apache's location, the team leader persuaded one of the AH–64s to launch several flares as it flew directly over the crashed helicopter. That enabled the Special Forces captain to gain a rough approximation of its location using a compass azimuth and a quick map survey.[37] The combined force of ODB

[35] Ibid.

[36] Wooley, "America's Specialized Airpower," p. 10.

[37] Interv, Reardon with Tm Ldr, ODA 512, 30 May 08, Historians files, CMH.

Cultist casualties line a trench stormed by ODA 563 and Hillah SWAT. The barrel of a destroyed truck-mounted antiaircraft machine gun is visible behind the berm to the right. The number of enemy, their weapons, the strength of their defensive positions, and their tactical skill all surprised American and Iraqi forces.

510, ODA 566, and the commandos departed soon after, heading north and then west, back the way they had recently come. Once the Humvees left, ODA 563's team leader ordered his group to rejoin the rest of the unit along the main southern berm. Calling in several airstrikes to suppress the enemy, the assault group withdrew to friendly lines without loss.[38]

The ODB 510 Humvees and commando vehicles led the search for the Apache, with ODA 566 providing rear security. With only an educated guess to work from, the location of the downed helicopter seemed as elusive as the proverbial needle in a haystack. The column turned south down one dirt road that ended, forcing the vehicles to backtrack before continuing west again. The Humvees rounded the next left turn and headed south along a dirt road paralleling a large berm. As they did so, they were met by a tremendous burst of small-arms and RPG fire from pointblank range. The cultists were strung out in a long line on the other side of the berm, which transformed that particular section of road along the western edge of Zarqa village into a 400-meter kill zone. The ambushers were so close that RPG warheads hit home but did not detonate, having failed to travel the minimum arming distance. The Coalition force accelerated and returned fire, inflicting many casualties but also suffering losses. Gunshots killed two commandos manning turret guns and wounded several other Iraqi and American soldiers. The cultists also knocked out several of the automatic weapons mounted on the Special Forces Humvees.[39] Enemy fire did not abate, as more fighters

---

[38] Interv, Reardon with Former Tm Ldr, ODA 563, 5 Feb 08.
[39] Wooley, "America's Specialized Airpower," p. 13.

streamed out of the village toward the berm to take part in the fighting. Others took up positions on rooftops within the village that afforded them a clear view of the road.

Despite numerous casualties and extensive damage, all of the ODA and commando vehicles succeeded in fighting through the ambush. During the intense gun battle, the ODA 512 team leader had noticed the downed Apache to the west. As the battered Humvees exited the kill zone, they turned right and then right again to gain the cover of a large berm overlooking the crumpled helicopter from the west. As they made the second turn, the leading vehicles spotted the Humvees belonging to Colonel Hughes. The convoy pulled up near the advisory team to exchange information and coordinate a combined defense.

While many of the Special Forces soldiers and commandos took up positions along the berm, others began treating wounded, repairing weapons, changing tires, and sharing ammunition with those who were running out. Within a short period of time, the Americans realized they would be able to fully repair only four of ODB 510's damaged Humvees. Appraised of this sobering fact, the Special Forces major in command sent ODA 566's hastily patched vehicles, along with as many wounded as they could carry, back to Camp David to obtain repair parts, ammunition, and more crew-served weapons.[40]

Additional American troops were en route to Zarqa. (*See Map 11.*) Acting on ODA 566's request for a mechanized battalion, the 4th Brigade, 25th Infantry Division, sent Lt. Col. Barry F. Huggins' 2d Battalion, 3d Infantry (Stryker), from Kalsu to Zarqa. The outfit, temporarily detached from the 3d Brigade, 2d Infantry Division, had joined the 4th Brigade barely a week earlier following the 20 January insurgent attack against the Karbala Provincial Joint Coordination Cell that had left five American soldiers dead. The battalion employed the M1126 Stryker, a medium-weight wheeled vehicle that had less armor than a Bradley but more mobility in many situations.

The brigade staff informed Huggins that an AH–64 had been shot down, that a Special Forces team had secured the crash site, and that his battalion would assist in recovering the aircraft, sensitive items, and crew. With one company detached on another mission, Huggins had only Company B led by Capt. William W. Parsons and Company C commanded by Capt. Brent A. Clemmer. The battalion commander immediately dispatched Company C to the crash site, where it would establish the southern half of a perimeter centered on the helicopter. Company B, accompanied by the assault command post, engineers, a wrecker truck, and flatbed trailer, would follow twenty-five minutes behind and form the rest of the perimeter.[41]

---

[40] Interv, Reardon with Tm Ldr, ODA 512, 30 May 08.
[41] After Action Review (AAR), 2d Bn, 3d Inf, sub: Patriot Battalion Opns Near An Najaf (Zarqa), Iraq, 28–29 Jan 07, 11 Feb 07, p. 3, Historians files, CMH.

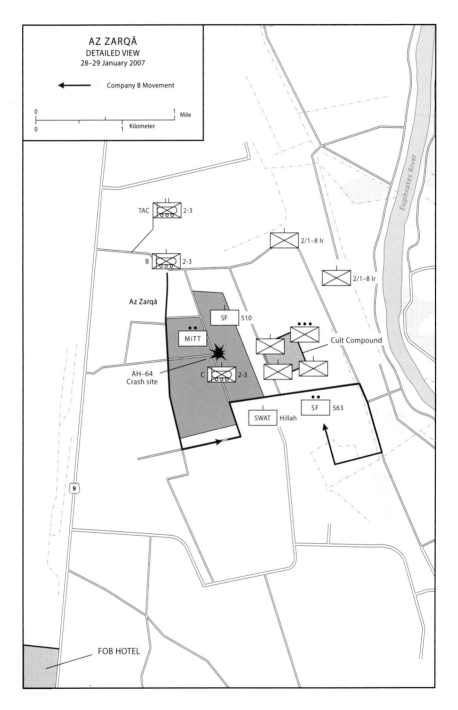

AZ ZARQĀ
DETAILED VIEW
28–29 January 2007

← Company B Movement

0 ──────────── 1 Mile
0 ──────────── 1 Kilometer

TAC 2-3

2/1–8 Ir

B 2-3

2/1–8 Ir

Az Zarqā

SF 510

MiTT

Cult Compound

AH–64
Crash site

C 2-3

SF 563

SWAT Hillah

Euphrates River

9

FOB HOTEL

Map 11

In the background, armed Humvees of ODB 510, ODA 566, and the Iraqi commandos depart the location of ODA 563 and Hillah SWAT en route to the downed Apache. Heavy enemy fire subsequently prevented the force from securing the crash site.

The lack of overall coordination of Coalition efforts at Zarqa reared its head again. Brigade headquarters had given Huggins the information it had, but he knew only a little about American units and nothing about Iraqi forces:

> We were aware of only one ODA on the scene. . . . The ODA [563] was in direct fire contact with an enemy force; they said they required no help and were using close air support to suppress the enemy. We used their location for our planning, assuming they were guarding the crash site. In fact, they were engaged with an enemy trench about one kilometer southeast of the crash site. The crash site was being over-watched by a second ODA, also in contact, but unknown to us at the time.[42]

To provide the battalion with some expertise on the area, the brigade staff loaned to Huggins Capt. John R. Mitcha, a seasoned veteran with a previous combat tour in Iraq. He was the officer-in-charge of the Najaf Provincial Joint Coordination Center, which had moved to Kalsu after the Karbala incident. His cell existed to bridge the communications gap between provincial officials, Iraqi security forces, and the U.S. chain of command and

---

[42] Ibid.

would prove to be a critical force multiplier in the confusing situation that had developed at Zarqa.[43]

Company C departed Kalsu at 1430 with Sfc. Shawn S. Martin's 1st Platoon leading the long column of vehicles. Studying the 95-kilometer stretch to Najaf, Martin knew he would have to push hard to arrive during daylight. Captain Clemmer chose the platoon as the point element because Martin had fought in the city in April 2004. Remembering Najaf as "not being a very friendly place," Sergeant Martin was not excited about returning there.[44]

Most of the Stryker soldiers were expecting to deal with twenty insurgents at most during the recovery operation. Captain Clemmer, who had earlier served with the 75th Ranger Regiment, mentally prepared himself for much worse: "Images went through my mind of what happened in Somalia and I was not going to let that happen if at all possible. . . . I told my soldiers when we drove down, over the radio, no one is going to touch our brothers but us."[45]

When Clemmer's outfit entered Hillah, halfway to the destination, it encountered a throng of religious pilgrims blocking the sole bridge spanning the Tigris. Emerging from the lead vehicle, several Americans ran up to a group of policemen to explain: "We're heading to Najaf to help other Iraqi police." The words spurred the officers to open a path through the crowd at the bridge and then guide the column through side streets to avoid the path of the pilgrims.[46] There were no more delays as Company C sped south on Highway 9.

As the force neared the objective and got ready to turn east onto a secondary road leading to the crash site, Captain Clemmer saw a parked Humvee. The ODA 512 team leader emerged from the vehicle, and the two officers conferred on the best course of action.[47] Clemmer directed Sergeant Martin's platoon, along with the company mortar section under S. Sgt. Scott M. Muetz, to remain in place, secure the road junction, and prepare to deliver supporting fire to the east.[48] Special Forces personnel then guided the company commander and the other Stryker platoons to the berm overlooking the downed Apache. There was a slight delay as the large armored vehicles mingled on the narrow trail with outbound damaged Humvees.

Colonel Huggins' assault command post and Company B appeared on the scene about thirty minutes later. On the way down, he repeatedly attempted to make radio contact with other American units near Zarqa. (This was the first effort by anyone to identify all friendly forces on the battlefield and coordinate

---

[43] Ltr, Capt John R. Mitcha to author, 21 Apr 08, Historians files, CMH.

[44] Interv, William J. Koziar, Fort Lewis Battle Command Training Center (FLBCTC), with Sfc Shawn S. Martin, 1st Plt Ldr, Co C, 2d Bn, 3d Inf, n.d., Historians files, CMH.

[45] Michael Gilbert, "Captain Awarded Silver Star for Najaf Battle," *The News Tribune*, 3 December 2007, copy in Historians files, CMH.

[46] Interv, Koziar with Martin, n.d.

[47] ODA 512 Tm Ldr, Written Comments on 10 May 08 Version of Draft Ms, Historians files, CMH.

[48] Interv, Koziar with Martin, n.d.

their efforts.) Huggins eventually received answers from several elements. One came from Xiphos 6, Colonel Hughes' advisers. Moments later, ODB 510 made its presence known. Then Blacksmith 63A chimed in, identifying himself as a Special Forces team leader. At first, Huggins thought, "I was linking up with him when I dismounted to make face-to-face with the ODA/MiTT force near the crash site."[49] Blacksmith soon explained by radio that he was ODA 563, located south of the compound, and the battalion commander realized:

> [A]nother force was still in the battlespace, still engaged. I asked him to describe the battlespace to me, and he did an excellent job painting the enemy picture. It was thorough, comprehensive, and accurate. . . . I came to understand that we were not merely securing the crash site until we could recover the crew and wreckage, but that there was a sizable force (it turned out, one that outnumbered us) . . . attempting to encircle the downed aircraft.[50]

At the MiTT berm, Clemmer coordinated a recovery mission with the ODA 512 team leader. The pair agreed to load several Special Forces soldiers aboard 1st Lt. Stephen C. Smith's 2d Platoon vehicles, which would conduct a mounted assault against the enemy fighters nearest the downed AH–64D. When the Strykers charged forward, they encountered surprisingly slight resistance. The Special Forces soldiers went to the helicopter as the Stryker platoon formed a hasty defensive line facing east toward the cult compound. The 3d Platoon under 1st Lt. Gregory S. Weber then moved forward to reinforce the initial assault element. Clemmer positioned Weber's troops to the right of Smith's platoon to expand the position. The ODA team, assisted by Sergeant Ballard of the MiTT, recovered the dead pilots and collected unexploded ordnance scattered over the area from the force of the crash.[51] Clemmer then brought up the rest of his company. The 1st Platoon occupied a position on Lieutenant Smith's right flank, while the mortar section and company headquarters, along with the 4th Platoon's three Strykers armed with tube-launched, optically tracked, wire guided (TOW) antitank missiles, settled down in a supporting position two hundred meters in the rear of the infantry platoons.

The Apache secured, Colonel Huggins now focused on what to do about the larger problem of the enemy that remained. The battalion commander knew that his opponent had few choices available. The Tigris River prohibited escape to the east. Apache helicopters from the 4th Battalion, 227th Aviation

---

[49] AAR, 2d Bn, 3d Inf, 11 Feb 07, p. 5.

[50] Ibid.

[51] Interv, Koziar with 1st Lt Stephen C. Smith, Plt Ldr, 2d Plt, Co C, 2d Bn, 3d Inf, 12 Sep 07; MiTT 0810, "Chronology for Najaf Battle, 28 Jan–5 Feb 07," n.d., p. 1; both in Historians files, CMH.

Regiment, patrolled to the north; Company C blocked any westward movement; and ODA 563 and Hillah SWAT covered the south. Given that the enemy was contained in an unpopulated area, Huggins opted to rely primarily on supporting arms rather than maneuver and assault to bring the battle to a conclusion. To that end, he decided to remove everyone from the field who did not have Force XXI Battle Command, Brigade and Below—a command and control system that provided real-time location of units and thus minimized the risk of hitting friendly forces. Learning that the cult possessed captured Iraqi Army vehicles only reinforced Huggins' concern about identifying friend from foe. He thus ordered a temporary halt to all airstrikes and directed all units aside from his Strykers to break contact and leave the area.

In accordance with that plan, ODB 510, ODA 566, the Iraqi commandos, and the MiTT extricated themselves with a minimum of problems. Coordinating the withdrawal of other Iraqi security forces, however, turned out to be a time-consuming and convoluted process. Fortunately, Huggins had Captain Mitcha on hand and put him to work on the problem. Mitcha began calling Najaf Province officials, who were soon issuing orders to the various Iraqi elements by cell phone, courier, and other means. One by one, the Iraqi units returned to their bases to refuel and rearm. The last detachment, however, did not leave until shortly after midnight.[52]

The team sergeant of ODA 563 questioned the order to withdraw immediately and suggested to his captain that they should remain in place to cover the southern flank and retain control of the berm that formed the key terrain on that side of the compound. The team leader concurred and relayed that consideration to Colonel Huggins, recommending the Special Forces unit hold until relieved by a Stryker company. The battalion commander agreed and assigned Company B to conduct the relief in place as soon as possible.[53]

While Huggins sought to gain control of the battlespace, the cultists decided to renew their push to capture the helicopter by using the cover of darkness to circle around the southern flank. They still enjoyed superior numbers despite their losses and were more familiar with the ground. Their determination became apparent to the Stryker soldiers as the volume of incoming fire picked up. When Captain Clemmer brought Sergeant Martin's 1st Platoon forward to reinforce the perimeter, the cultists increased their rate of fire. The Strykers, hulls protruding above the berm, drew the most attention. Bullets ricocheted from their armored sides, gashing the trunks of palm trees or tossing up small showers of sand. The vehicles replied with their turret-mounted .50-caliber machine guns equipped with thermal sights.[54]

---

[52] Interv, Maj Glynn Garcia, 90th Military History Detachment (MHD), with Capt John R. Mitcha, Ofcr in Charge, An Najaf Provincial Joint Coordination Center, 5 Feb 07, Global War on Terrorism (GWOT) Collection, CMH.

[53] Interv, Reardon with former Tm Ldr, ODA 563, 26 Feb 08, Historians files, CMH.

[54] Interv, Koziar with Sgt Brian Ross, Sqd Ldr, Co C, 2d Bn, 3d Inf, n.d., Historians files, CMH.

The enemy demonstrated a level of skill that surprised many U.S. soldiers, including Lieutenant Smith: "I realized very quickly [we faced] a highly trained element. They used tactics that we employed. One group would fire as another group was moving."[55] The Stryker soldiers had to begin coordinating their fires to try to pin down the enemy fighters. As the cultists drew closer to the crashed Apache, they also made it more difficult for the Americans to safely employ aerial supporting fires. The troops sheltering behind berms had adequate cover, but a portion of the company was posted on open ground. Sergeant Martin realized "we are going to have to dig in here."[56] As the word went down the line, it proved an unsettling experience for some soldiers. One of Martin's squad leaders incredulously asked, "Are we really digging in against Iraqis?"[57] Astonished men began rummaging through vehicles in search of entrenching tools.

The aggressiveness of the cultists had forced Colonel Huggins to resume airstrikes even though ODA 563 was still on the battlefield. He and the Special Forces captain hashed out boundaries delineating where supporting fires could be employed. Quite by accident, these control measures spared from air attack the portion of the village where Kadim's fighters had placed their families.[58] Sergeant Wallace and the Air Force combat controllers with the Strykers began directing AC–130 Spectre gunships, jets, and AH–64D Apaches against the enemy. A high priority was destroying the captured Iraqi Army Humvees. One by one, the American aircraft succeeded in hitting those vehicles. To stop the flanking movement, the controllers brought heavy ordnance ever closer to friendly lines. Lieutenant Smith felt the impact firsthand:

> It came to a point where we had thousand pound bombs landing danger close . . . some of the guys got knocked back and some had their [helmet-mounted] night vision devices knocked back . . . we had dirt flying on us from one of the last bombs dropped that stopped the final enemy advance on our position.[59]

Army aviation also played a significant role. The 4th Battalion, 227th Aviation Regiment, assisted by its sister Apache unit, the 1st Battalion, 227th Aviation Regiment, ensured that pairs of AH–64Ds were orbiting Zarqa throughout the night. At least eight teams belonging to the former, along with one team from the latter unit, took part in the aerial assault. S. Sgt. Brian D. Ross, a squad leader in Smith's platoon, welcomed the assistance: "The Apaches were [constantly] over us, shifting left and right, they were like our guardian angels that night."[60]

---

[55] Interv, Koziar with Smith, 12 Sep 07.
[56] Interv, Koziar with Martin, n.d.
[57] Ibid.
[58] Interv, Reardon with former Tm Ldr, ODA 563, 26 Feb 08.
[59] Interv, Koziar with Smith, 12 Sep 07.
[60] Interv, Koziar with Ross, n.d.

While the bombardment continued, ODA 563 kept an eye out for Company B. The Special Forces soldiers expected the Strykers to arrive from the south so the berm would shield the relief in place from the enemy. The team leader maintained a fruitless lookout in that direction until a gentle tap on his helmet, followed by a finger pointing to the west, revealed the approaching friendly force. The dozen or so blacked-out armored vehicles were moving along the road situated between the ODA 563/SWAT–held berm and the compound.[61] Confused by the maze of dirt trails weaving between the numerous farm plots, the Strykers had turned east too soon. The cultists, however, remained quiet in this sector and did not fire on Company B, probably because their attention was focused on the battle over the helicopter in the west and due to the aerial assault that pinned down many of them. The ODA team leader flagged down the column and conferred with Captain Parsons. Unable to drive over the steep berm, the Strykers continued east till they found the road that hugged the river, then turned south and then back west. Ninety more minutes elapsed before Company B was in position to begin the relief.[62]

When Captain Parsons' Stryker finally pulled up next to the ODA team leader's Humvee, the two officers began coordinating the handover. Since Company B had not seen the terrain in daylight, it took more time than usual for the Special Forces leader to share what he had learned. In addition, the Stryker soldiers were skeptical that they faced an enemy numbering in the hundreds. With the view partially obscured by dense palm stands, the Company B commander could not see for himself the midsized village replete with trenches, fighting positions, crew-served weapons, and vehicles that lay just to his north. Captain Parsons was unconvinced by the briefing of the Special Forces captain: "He was spouting off so many numbers that I thought the guy was inflating things. . . . I had him write it all down on a piece of paper so I could better understand. . . . I actually did not disseminate that information because I thought it was so inflated."[63]

Although Colonel Huggins shared a degree of skepticism regarding enemy strength, he planned as though the reports were accurate. He saw the east-west trench that ODA 563 had cleared earlier as the key to the cultist defensive system. Company B thus became his main effort with the mission of sweeping north to regain the trench and then move beyond it. Just prior, Company C would move forward in the west to gain positions from which its automatic weapons could support the attack from the flank. The two units would coordinate their efforts using a series of east-west phase lines

---

[61] Interv, Reardon with former Tm Ldr, ODA 563, 26 Feb 08.
[62] Ibid.
[63] Interv, Koziar with Capt William W. Parsons, CO, Co B, 2d Bn, 3d Inf, n.d., Historians files, CMH.

delineating the progress of Company B.[64] Anticipating a transfer of responsibility to the Iraqi Army and police once his unit secured the farm complex, Huggins assigned the task of coordinating that process to Captain Mitcha and Colonel Hughes.

In the predawn hours of 29 January, the 2d Battalion, 3d Infantry's attached engineer platoon finally finished its efforts to recover the downed Apache. It had required several hours of hard work and the use of the wrecker's crane to free the body of one of the pilots from the crumpled wreckage. The engineers then lifted pieces of the AH–64D onto two flatbed trucks. A Navy explosive ordnance disposal team gathered up rockets and cannon shells scattered around the crash site. The aircraft's 30-mm. cannon proved to be the only unrecoverable item, since it had live ammunition jammed in its feed tray. The sailors destroyed it in place with a demolitions charge.[65]

At daybreak, Colonel Huggins ordered his companies to initiate their assault. Captain Clemmer's unit moved first to secure its support-by-fire position, broadcasting surrender appeals over a loudspeaker as it closed on Zarqa. As the leading squads halted near the outskirts of the village, a secondary explosion signaled the destruction of an ammunition cache hit earlier by AC–130 gunships. Captain Clemmer, accompanying his center platoon on foot, watched as men prepared grenades for an assault into the village. The unexpected explosion, however, triggered the appearance of white flags among the buildings. The Company C commander was surprised:

> All of a sudden the flood gates start opening up and I get five, ten people coming out.... My assessment later is that these people were the bravest ones, I think they thought the Americans would kill them . . . but when everyone else saw nothing happened, other people started coming out . . . within ten minutes, we go from five people, to fifty, to one hundred.[66]

Colonel Huggins was wary of the enemy's motives for a few moments, his suspicions triggered by reports from ODA 563 that it had encountered enemy fighters displaying white flags in an attempt to lure Coalition forces out into the open. However, the surrender appeared genuine this time; the numbers mounted rapidly upward until several hundred cultists were in the hands of Company C.[67] Clemmer's men transitioned from preparing for an assault to collecting prisoners and constructing a makeshift confinement facility using concertina wire from the Strykers. The soldiers separated the captives into groups of women and children, seriously wounded fighters,

[64] AAR, 2d Bn, 3d Inf, 11 Feb 07, p. 8.

[65] Ltr, Maj Brent A. Clemmer to author, 9 May 08, sub: "Shrouded by the Fog of War" Review and Comment, Historians files, CMH.

[66] Interv, Koziar with Capt Brent A. Clemmer, CO, Co C, 2d Bn, 3d Inf, n.d., Historians files, CMH.

[67] AAR, 2d Bn, 3d Inf, 11 Feb 07, p. 8.

On the right, M1126 Strykers from Captain Parsons' Company B, 2d Battalion, 3d Infantry, along with Hillah SWAT and ODA 563, occupy positions southeast of the cult's compound on the second morning of battle. Blowing sand reduced visibility and complicated efforts to evacuate casualties by helicopter.

and unwounded combatants. There were very few in the last category. The battalion surgeon, Lt. Col. Dean C. Pederson, along with Clemmer's medics, began supervising the sorting and treatment of casualties.[68] Although several noncombatants had been killed or wounded by the bombing, the vast majority had taken shelter in the area placed out of bounds by ODA 563 and Colonel Huggins.

The Coalition forces also attended to their own casualties. The dead included the two American pilots, ten soldiers from Colonel Sa'adi's brigade, a dozen Iraqi National Police, and two commandos. Almost a dozen Americans and several times that number of Iraqi security forces had been wounded.[69]

The battalion established a landing zone for medical evacuation, and three Black Hawk helicopters braved decreasing visibility and high winds to lift out sixteen wounded noncombatants. Two of the evacuees died en route, but the remainder survived.[70] The weather continued to deteriorate, however, preventing further such flights. As Clemmer's men assumed the unexpected role of lifesavers, he reflected: "There is not an Army in the world, in my opinion, that can go from taking pins out of grenades and throwing them into trenches . . . to receiving wounded, treating [enemy] wounded and taking care of an enemy they had been killing throughout the night."[71] Company C's senior enlisted soldier, 1st Sgt. Viriato Ferrera, echoed that sentiment: "They needed us . . . I think at that point I realized

---

[68] Ibid.

[69] Santora, "Missteps by Iraqi Forces"; MiTT 0810, "Chronology for Najaf Battle," p. 1; "Special Forces Soldiers Earn Third Highest Combat Medal," *The Fort Campbell Courier*, 10 April 2008; Wooley, "America's Specialized Airpower," p. 13; Interv, Reardon with former Tm Ldr, ODA 563, 26 Feb 08.

[70] AAR, 2d Bn, 3d Inf, 11 Feb 07, p. 8.

[71] Interv, Koziar with Clemmer, n.d.

how unique our Army is and how different we are in regard to that aspect. We will fight them one minute and the next minute we will turn around and become their . . . saviors."[72]

As Company C dealt with the unexpected influx of prisoners, Company B took possession of the trench. It encountered no resistance, largely because most of the enemy fighters had retreated during the night. When the Stryker soldiers climbed the earthen wall concealing the trench from view, they saw dozens of dead cultists, destroyed vehicles mounting antiaircraft guns, RPGs, small arms, and all manner of abandoned military equipment. ODA 563's team leader had to suppress a slight grin when he saw the expression of amazement on the face of the Company B commander.[73]

While one platoon of Company C began combing the village for holdouts, Company B collected weapons and ammunition from the trench system then initiated a systematic search for cultists hiding in the nearby palm groves.[74] The soldiers came upon a parking lot holding the Iraqi Army vehicles seized at the checkpoint along with the cars that comprised the convoy from Diwaniyah. With few exceptions, the vehicles had been destroyed by the AC–130 gunships. The captured Iraqi scout Humvees turned up in the surrounding palm groves. Additional searching revealed the body of Zahra Kadim, the self-proclaimed Mahdi, who had met his fate during the night.[75]

A few cultists continued to fight even after most of their brethren had surrendered. As the Stryker soldiers moved through the village, they killed one determined man trying to place a heavy machine gun into operation.[76] S. Sgt. Darrell R. Griffin Jr., a squad leader in Lieutenant Weber's 3d Platoon, eliminated an armed cultist lying in wait inside a house.[77]

In an effort to assist the American sweep, Colonel Sa'adi's troops and Hillah SWAT personnel also started scouring Zarqa. The MiTT accompanied Colonel Majeed's 2d Battalion into the village. Sergeant Ballard, along with Hughes' second-in-command, Maj. John P. Reed, several Iraqi soldiers, and the team's medic, were approached by a distraught Iraqi child seeking help for some friends. The child led them to a room in a damaged building, where the Americans located a trapdoor hidden under a bed. Lifting the door, Ballard and Reed discovered six men huddled in a secret underground room. The captives included Zahra Kadim's brother, chief financier, and four others highly placed

---

[72] Interv, Koziar with 1st Sgt Viriato Ferrera, 1st Sgt, Co C, 2d Bn, 3d Inf, n.d., Historians files, CMH.

[73] Interv, Reardon with former Tm Ldr, ODA 563, 26 Feb 08.

[74] Interv, William R. Reeder, FLBCTC, with S Sgt Larry Neal, Mtr Sqd Ldr, Co C, 2d Bn, 3d Inf, n.d., Historians files, CMH.

[75] "Iraq Cult Leader Among Najaf Dead"; 2d Bn, 3d Inf, Optimized Fallen Angel Storyboard, 28 Jan 07.

[76] AAR, 2d Bn, 3d Inf, 11 Feb 07, p. 8.

[77] Ltr, 1st Lt Gregory S. Weber, former Plt Ldr, 3d Plt, Co C, 2d Bn, 3d Inf, to author, 20 Mar 08, Historians files, CMH.

Lieutenant Weber's 3d Platoon watches as surrendering cultists (*right*) approach the berm held by Company C, 2d Battalion, 3d Infantry. Before placing prisoners in a temporary holding enclosure, the soldiers screened them for hidden suicide vests.

within the cult. With them was a safe holding millions of dollars, along with documents, passports, videotapes, and cell phones.[78]

Colonel Hughes and Captain Mitcha arranged a smooth handover between the 2d Battalion, 3d Infantry, and the Iraqi security forces. Before dusk on 29 January, the Strykers, along with Hillah SWAT and ODA 563, departed and the Iraqi security forces assumed full responsibility for the compound. At least four hundred captives remained behind makeshift wire enclosures. In addition to making arrangements to feed, house, and care for them, Colonel Sa'adi's brigade oversaw the burial of 256 enemy fighters and 9 noncombatants caught in the crossfire during the battle.[79] Hughes and his advisory team remained with Iraqi security forces at Zarqa for another week as cleanup efforts continued.

The battle, notwithstanding its scale and ferocity, received little attention from U.S. higher headquarters. The corps daily briefing for 28 January mentioned only the loss of an AH–64D, as the focus remained on mapping out the impending surge of American forces into Iraq. The Iraqi government, loathe to admit that violent rifts existed within the Shi'ite community, also downplayed events at Zarqa. One senior Iraqi police official even accused Zahra Kadim of being a Sunni masquerading as a Shi'ite.[80] But the engagement was critical to the success of the Surge, which certainly would have fared differently had the cult's plans to kill senior Shi'ite clerics borne fruit. There is little doubt that such a catastrophic change in the situation would have driven Iraq into much deeper turmoil. An American officer familiar with the events later reflected: "If

---

[78] Interv, Reardon with Ballard, 2 Feb 08.
[79] Ibid.; MiTT 0810, "Chronology for Najaf Battle," p. 1; "Earthly Luxuries for Soldiers of Heaven," *The Australian News Ltd.*, 1 February 2007, copy in Historians files, CMH.
[80] "Iraq: Al-Najaf Mystery."

they'd been able to even just get into Najaf, armed with what they had, with the intent they had and fighting to their dismembered last gasp to kill Sistani . . . Surge or not, things would have been different for sure."[81]

---

[81] Ltr, Lt Col Christopher A. Joslin to author, 7 May 08, sub: U.S. Army Historian Writing About Small Unit Action at Zarqa, Historians files, CMH. Joslin served in Iraq during that period as the commanding officer of the 1st Cavalry Division's 2d Battalion, 227th Aviation Regiment.

CHAPTER EIGHT

HELLFIRE

AND

BRIMSTONE

JON B. MIKOLASHEK

Apache helicopter gunships turn the tables by surprising and destroying insurgents preparing a ground-to-air ambush.

Taji—29 September 2007

On 2 February 2007, a pair of AH–64D Apache Longbow helicopters from the 1st Battalion, 227th Aviation Regiment, were on aerial patrol in Iraq. They were checking out a main supply route dubbed Redlegs, which ran northwest to southeast just west of their home base, Camp Taji. Located about twenty kilometers north of Baghdad in the predominantly Sunni province of Salahuddin, the area was a stronghold of al-Qaeda in Iraq and other insurgent groups. The two helicopters suddenly came under fire from a heavy machine gun concealed near a factory. The Apache flown by CWO4 Keith Yoakum and CWO2 Jason G. Defrenn took numerous hits. Despite severe damage, which included the loss of their 30-mm. chain gun, the two airmen gained altitude for an attack and then nosed down toward the target firing Hydra 2.75-inch rockets. After launching the missiles, the aircraft could not pull out of the dive and crashed, killing both aviators.[1]

Soldiers in the battalion keenly felt the loss of their comrades. Yoakum was one of the most experienced fliers in the unit, and Defrenn was nearing the end of his tour and eager to get back to his pregnant wife. For their valor that day, they would respectively receive the Distinguished Service Cross and the Distinguished Flying Cross.

This shootdown, one of six helicopter losses to enemy fire in Iraq that month, spawned an overhaul of aerial operations designed to minimize the

---

[1] Marc Santora, "2 Killed as U.S. Helicopter Is Shot Down Near Baghdad," *New York Times*, 2 February 2007; Matthew Cox, "Apache Pilot Killed in February To Get DSC," *Army Times*, 12 Nov 07; copies of both in Historians files, U.S. Army Center of Military History (CMH), Washington, D.C.

danger. For transport aircraft, the changes were straightforward: they now flew mostly at night and at higher altitude and varied their routes. The adjustments were immediately effective against an enemy relying mostly on visually aimed heavy machine guns, and the number of ambushes on helicopters dropped quickly throughout Iraq. But gunships could not follow suit. Even when they were not providing fire support to ground troops in contact, most of their tasks required them to search out the enemy, not avoid him. Flying just above heavily traveled convoy routes, villages, and sprawling urban areas placed the pilots under constant stress. Every truck or building could hold an antiaircraft weapon, and even small-arms or rocket-propelled grenades (RPGs) posed significant threats. Pilots not only had to be on constant lookout for insurgents, the low-level flights also forced them to keep their eyes open for man-made obstacles such as power lines and towers, which could be every bit as deadly as hostile fire. The aviators were always on a pivot, their heads turning constantly to scan the ground and the sky. It often took only an instant for a mundane mission to turn into a life-and-death struggle.

Another mission flown by the 1st Battalion, 227th Aviation Regiment, on 31 May 2007, highlighted the continuing danger for attack helicopters. CWO4 Steven E. Kilgore and his copilot/gunner 1st Lt. Brian L. Haas were flying over the contested countryside near Taji when rounds from a heavy machine gun arced up toward their tail rotor. "On my rear, on my rear," shouted Kilgore as he piloted his Apache away from the ambush.[2] They narrowly escaped being shot down, but this was just the start of the engagement. Kilgore and Haas, along with CWO4 William E. Hamm and CWO2 John C. Moughon in the lead Apache, hastily worked out a plan of attack and flew back into enemy fire.[3] Using their experience and the power of the Longbow model, both crews expended a total of 600 30-mm. rounds, 40 Hydra rockets, and 5 Hellfire missiles. The brief battle left fifteen insurgents dead and five gun trucks in ruins.[4]

Those two engagements demonstrated why the Apache outfit, nicknamed the Attack Battalion, had earned a fierce fighting reputation throughout its history. The 1st Battalion, 227th Aviation Regiment's lineal predecessor was among the initial helicopter units in the Army. It had served admirably in Vietnam, and one of its members was the first Army aviator to receive the Medal of Honor in that conflict.[5] The unit deployed to Kuwait during Operation DESERT SHIELD and played a major role in

---

[2] Telecon, Jon Mikolashek, CMH, with CWO4 William E. Ham, Co B, 1st Bn, 227th Avn, 24 Mar 08, Historians files, CMH.

[3] Telecon, Mikolashek with CWO4 Steven E. Kilgore, Co B, 1st Bn, 227th Avn, 24 Mar 08, Historians files, CMH.

[4] Ibid.

[5] During the Vietnam War, the 1st Battalion was designated the 227th Assault Helicopter Battalion.

Two Apache helicopters from the 1st Battalion, 227th Aviation Regiment, return to their base at Camp Taji. Nicknamed the Attack Battalion, the unit provided reconnaissance, route clearance, and fire support during its third tour in Iraq from September 2006 through January 2008.

the 1st Cavalry Division's deception plan that helped throw Iraqi forces into disarray. Following that conflict, the battalion was the first to field the AH–64D Apache Longbow, still the most innovative and advanced attack helicopter. The unit deployed to the Middle East again in February 2003 and participated in Operation IRAQI FREEDOM, returning to Fort Hood with its fighting reputation enhanced.[6] The outfit was back in Iraq again from February 2004 to March 2005.

The battalion arrived in Iraq for the third time in September 2006. Commanded by Lt. Col. Christopher E. Walach, it had 420 soldiers and 26 Apaches (2 more than usual). (The number of additional aircraft would prove prescient, since that many would be lost over the course of the deployment.) The 1st Battalion performed a variety of attack and reconnaissance missions in Iraq; but the most common were route clearance, countermortar operations, missile and rocket interdiction, convoy and air security, and close-in fire support for ground troops.[7] The outfit was one of two helicopter combat units supporting the Multi-National Division–Baghdad, which was led by the headquarters of the 1st Cavalry Division.[8]

---

[6] *1-227th Aviation Reg-History,* http://pao.hood.army.mil/1stCavDiv/units/1acb/1-227/history.htm, copy in Historians files, CMH.

[7] Telecon, Mikolashek with Capt Thomas J. Loux, Co B, 1st Bn, 227th Avn, 9 Apr 08, Historians files, CMH.

[8] Telecon, Mikolashek with Loux, 21 Apr 08.

The battalion's Apache Longbow model is the quintessential attack helicopter. Every inch of the craft maximizes advantages in speed, agility, and firepower. The pilot-in-command, seated behind the copilot/gunner, has a clear picture of the battlefield and flies the aircraft. With two turboshaft engines powering its four rotor blades, the helicopter is highly maneuverable and able to change direction quickly. Survivability features include a boron-armored compartment surrounding the pilots and a canopy composed of transparent panels that are resistant to rounds up to 12.7-mm. caliber.[9] While the defensive capabilities of the AH–64D are important, it is the craft's firepower that makes it such a deadly weapon. In perfect atmospheric conditions, Apaches are armed with up to sixteen AGM–114 Hellfire missiles or seventy-six Hydra 70 2.75-inch rockets or a mix thereof, as well as an M230E1 30-mm. chain gun with twelve hundred rounds.[10] Iraq's hot and dusty summers are not ideal for helicopters, however, providing less lift for their rotor blades and causing the aircraft to burn fuel at a faster rate. In that environment, the Apaches typically carried much less than the full load of ordnance so they could maximize speed, maneuverability, and patrol time.

A mission on 29 September 2007 would tax both the capabilities of the Longbow and the skills of the battalion's veteran pilots. It was a typical assignment for an air weapons team, the designation for a pair of Apaches. In this case, two teams (four helicopters) were involved. Their task was to check in with the 2d Battalion, 8th Cavalry, operating in an area a few miles west of Taji that was notorious for ambushes on the ground and in the air. (*Map 12*) There, the aviators would search along Route Redlegs for insurgents planting improvised explosive devices (IEDs) or setting up mortars or rockets.[11]

The air mission commander for one team was Capt. Thomas J. Loux, a 2004 graduate of West Point from Florida. His job was directing the activities of both Apaches from the front seat of the lead helicopter, call sign Crazyhorse 14, as well as controlling its weapons. The aircraft's pilot-in-command was CWO3 Terry Eldridge. A Native American from Oklahoma and the most experienced aviator on the team, he was the kind of guy, according to Loux, "you want on your side in a bar fight."[12] On their wing was Crazyhorse 15, led by pilot-in-command CWO3 Kyle D. Kittelson, a former noncommissioned officer from Iowa. His copilot/gunner was Chief Warrant Officer Moughon, a young aviator from Georgia and a veteran of the 31 May 2007 engagement.[13]

---

[9] Telecon, Mikolashek with Loux, 2 Apr 08.

[10] Ibid.

[11] Sworn Statement, CWO2 Cole Moughon, Co B, 1st Bn, 227th Avn, 30 Sep 07; Telecon, Mikolashek with CWO3 Kyle D. Kittelson, Co B, 1st Bn, 227th Avn, 24 Mar 08; both in Historians files, CMH.

[12] Telecon, Mikolashek with Loux, 31 Mar 08.

[13] Ibid.

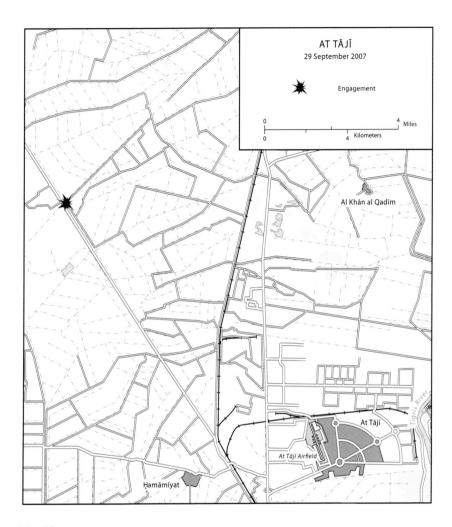

MAP 12

The other team was composed of the air mission commander, Capt. Guyton L. Robinson; his copilot/gunner, Capt. Aaron T. Smead; and their wing, pilot-in-command CWO4 Ernesto J. Hansen and his copilot/gunner, CWO3 Al D. Davison. Captain Loux's team would work the northern half of Redlegs while Robinson's team patrolled the southern end of the supply route.[14] It remained as dangerous as it had been in February 2007; another Apache team had taken fire from a heavy machine gun just a few weeks earlier.[15]

---

[14] Telecon, Mikolashek with Capt Guyton Robinson, Co A, 1st Bn, 227th Avn, 27 Mar 08, Historians files, CMH.
[15] Telecon, Mikolashek with Loux, 31 Mar 08.

Due to the heat that day, Crazyhorse 14 was armed with only 3 Hellfire missiles: 1 F-model, with a shaped-charge warhead designed to kill tanks; 1 N-model, with a thermobaric warhead optimized for use against buildings; and 1 K2A, another antiarmor projectile. Crazyhorse 15 carried 1 N-model and 2 K2A missiles. In addition, each aircraft carried 300 .30-mm. rounds and 26 Hydra rockets: 16 high explosive, 6 fléchette, and 4 illumination. It was not a lot of ammunition, but the mix would be effective against a wide range of targets and in most situations would be enough in the hands of the skilled gunners.[16]

Prior to liftoff, an intelligence briefing warned the aviators that insurgent forces might be gathering in the area they would be patrolling. Captain Loux decided his team would complete the initial task of route clearance and then search for the potential enemy concentration. Taking off at 1520, the Apaches flew over their designated area for an hour before a minor mechanical issue forced Crazyhorse 14 to land at a forward arming and refueling point. The problem with the lead craft involved the tail rotor, but the crew determined that the helicopter could continue on with the mission.[17]

The team had been back in the sky for only ten minutes and had just made a turn to the northeast when Eldridge noticed four white pickup trucks, which soldiers had nicknamed Bongo trucks, stopped at an intersection about two kilometers off. There also were about fifteen people moving in between the vehicles and four nearby buildings.[18] The structures were single-level dwellings made out of white brick and standing by themselves in the flat Iraqi landscape. Suspicious of the activity, both Apaches dropped below one hundred fifty feet—the authorized minimum altitude for aircraft in Iraq and known more casually as the hard deck.

As the team headed toward the scene to investigate, Captain Loux directed fellow front-seater Moughon to use his Apache's advanced target acquisition and designation system to get a better look. Before the equipment could complete the task, Chief Warrant Officer Eldridge spied two heavy machine guns mounted on the pickups. Seconds later, the insurgents confirmed his visual acuity by opening fire. Eldridge coolly informed the air mission commander: "Hey, they're shooting at us."[19] In moments, a barrage of machine-gun rounds and RPGs were streaking into the sky toward the two aircraft. Eldridge was surprised at the ability of the enemy to respond so suddenly and strongly: "As soon as we passed, I kind of veered off to one side, and they started tracking us with the guns from the back of trucks. As

---

[16] Telecons, Mikolashek with Loux, 1 Apr, 12 Jun 08.

[17] Ltr, CWO3 Kyle D. Kittelson, Co B, 1st Bn, 227th Avn, to Jon Mikolashek, 31 Mar 08, Historians files, CMH.

[18] Sworn Statement, Capt Thomas J. Loux, Co B, 1st Bn, 227th Avn, 30 Sep 07, Historians files, CMH.

[19] Apache Longbow Video, "29 September CZ 15 Engagement, Safire Bongo Trucks," copy in Historians files, CMH.

An insurgent (*center*) runs toward one of the four trucks mounting heavy machine guns. In a duel that lasted only a few minutes, the Apaches proved a little quicker than their opponents.

soon as they got where we were inside their range, effectively for their shots, they started shooting so, about the time it takes to swing a turret, in this case a gun on a tripod mount."[20]

Facing 14.5-mm., 12.7-mm., and AK47 fire as well as RPGs, Eldridge responded quickly, dropping his aircraft to below fifty feet. The insurgents tracked him down to the point their rounds began hitting one of the buildings at the intersection. After surviving the opening enemy attack, Crazyhorse 14 swung around for its first firing run. Just seconds after they made the turn, a 7.62-mm. bullet sliced through the canopy of Eldridge's aircraft and narrowly missed his face.[21] In the excitement of the moment, the crew mistakenly triggered the four illumination rockets; but that fusillade at least made the insurgents pause.[22] Switching back to high explosive rockets and cannon fire, the assault caused many of the rebels to scatter into the buildings like "little cockroaches."[23] With memories of their fallen brethren from the February ambush, the two Apaches, in

---

[20] Sfc Rick Emert, "Quick Reaction Helps Pilots Thwart Attack," *Army News*, 10 October 2007, copy in Historians files, CMH.
[21] Sworn Statement, Loux, 30 Sep 07.
[22] Telecon, Mikolashek with Loux, 12 Jun 08.
[23] Emert, "Quick Reaction Helps Pilots Thwart Attack."

communication with each other during the entire fight, decided that the insurgents would not get away to harm more soldiers.[24]

Immediately after the first exchange of fire, Moughon contacted the aviation battalion tactical operations center to inform them of the battle and request another air weapons team.[25] Captain Loux passed the same information via the 2d Battalion, 8th Cavalry's tactical net. Captain Robinson's Apaches, operating to the south over Route Redlegs, responded to the call in three minutes. The two air mission commanders conferred by radio and decided that Robinson's team would remain above two thousand feet to avoid interference with Captain Loux's helicopters.[26] From that vantage point, the reinforcing Apaches could follow the actions of Crazyhorse 14 and 15 while readying themselves to join in if needed.

As the two captains finished their coordination, Crazyhorse 14 turned right and flew back into the enemy to lay down another barrage of cannon fire. Kittelson and Moughon's helicopter broke left and came in from a different direction, adding its 30-mm. chain gun to the fray. Crazyhorse 15 damaged one truck during this attack; but the enemy continued to fight back, and a heavy-caliber round pierced through the canopy right above Moughon's head.[27] As the wing aircraft pulled out of its firing run, the lead Apache came back around again. Crazyhorse 14 set its sights on one of the remaining trucks; within seconds, the Bongo and a nearby building were engulfed by a fireball that killed a number of insurgents.[28]

As the four aviators began gaining the upper hand, they thrashed out the best way to keep the enemy pinned down while minimizing the risk to their aircraft. Communicating by radio, the team developed a plan to keep constant fire on the rebels. As one helicopter finished a firing run, the other would come in for the attack as the first circled around; each time, the Apaches would approach from a different direction. After the first few of these passes, two small black cars accelerated away from the intersection heading north. Shouting into his headset, Kittelson prodded Crazyhorse 14 to "kill them son of a bitches!"[29] Happy to oblige, the lead helicopter chased down the tail sedan and began firing. The crew walked the fire of the chain gun onto the target and sent the sedan flipping over the shoulder of Route Redlegs in flames. The lead vehicle managed to evade immediate destruction by stopping along a canal just to the west of the road. Captain Loux was not about to let anyone escape, however, and

---

[24] Sworn Statement, CWO3 Terry Eldridge, Co B, 1st Bn, 227th Avn, 29 Sep 07, Historians files, CMH.

[25] Sworn Statement, Moughon, 30 Sep 07.

[26] Telecon, Mikolashek with Robinson, 27 Mar 08.

[27] Apache Longbow Video, 29 Sep 07; Sworn Statement, CWO3 Kyle D. Kittelson, Co B, 1st Bn, 227th Avn, 29 Sep 07, Historians files, CMH.

[28] Ibid.

[29] Ltr, Kittelson to Mikolashek, 31 Mar 08.

he soon disabled the vacant automobile and killed the driver as he tried to run away.[30]

Meanwhile, Crazyhorse 15 kept up the attack on the insurgents and the trucks, which now included a blue one parked in the shadows of the compound. Chief Warrant Officer Moughon fired two K2A Hellfire missiles, but weather conditions and the rapid maneuvering of the Apache in the close-quarters engagement caused both to miss. He fared better with the chain gun and rockets, damaging a second truck.[31] The wing helicopter had better luck with its final Hellfire. Moughon launched the N-model and got a solid hit on another Bongo, simultaneously taking out the adjacent building and eliminating several insurgents.[32]

Fresh from the conquest of the fleeing sedans, Crazyhorse 14 returned to the intersection. The Apache took aim at one of the two disabled trucks, but its K2A missile malfunctioned and overshot the target.[33] Eldridge brought the helicopter around for another attempt, but Loux told his pilot to back off, as they were too close to the enemy. While the warrant officer executed that maneuver, the air-mission commander asked Captain Robinson's team to move north and check out the disabled sedans for possible survivors.[34] Then Crazyhorse 14 finished off the truck with an N-model Hellfire. The missile caused a large explosion that killed a few insurgents in a nearby building.[35] By this point, most of the remaining rebels, out-maneuvered and out-gunned, were electing to flee on foot rather than fight. Eldridge took advantage of the lull in enemy firing to move up to a higher and safer altitude while explaining to Loux that they were nearly out of 30-mm. ammunition and should only fire "if we have to."[36]

Ten minutes after making initial contact with the enemy, Captain Loux and Chief Warrant Officer Eldridge caught their breath amidst the adrenalin rush of battle. The team leader commended his pilot for his quick reaction at the beginning of the fight: "Oh my god, good eyes Terry." "I saw them just as they started shooting at me," replied an equally pumped-up Eldridge.[37] The fight wasn't entirely over, though, and the two aviators decided to make one last run at the enemy. Flying down toward the intersection, Crazyhorse 14 destroyed another gun truck with an F-model Hellfire and launched its six fléchette rockets into the buildings.[38] With the two Apaches dangerously low on fuel and with ammunition down to forty 30-mm. shells between them,

[30] Sworn Statement, Loux, 30 Sep 07.
[31] Sworn Statement, Kittelson, 29 Sep 07.
[32] Sworn Statement, Moughon, 30 Sep 07.
[33] Apache Longbow Video, 29 Sep 07.
[34] Ibid.
[35] Ibid.
[36] Apache Longbow Video, 29 Sep 07.
[37] Ibid.
[38] Ibid.

The burned remains of an insurgent pickup truck at the ambush site. The enemy vehicle and its 14.5-mm. antiaircraft gun proved no match for the Apache's Hellfire missile and 30-mm. chain gun.

Captain Loux handed off the battle to Captain Robinson's team, which finished off a previously damaged Bongo with 30-mm. fire.[39]

Flying from the battlefield back to Taji, Loux remarked: "Terry, we just saved a bunch of people today." The veteran chief warrant officer reflected that it hadn't been easy: "Yes we did, but took a lot of fire doing it." Captain Loux chuckled as he expressed a theme common to professional soldiers: "That's our job."[40]

The Apache crews knew they had hurt the enemy, but due to the intensity of the short fight, the aviators were uncertain how many insurgents they had faced and how many they had taken out. A subsequent battle damage assessment determined that Crazyhorse 14 and 15 had destroyed 4 gun trucks and their heavy weapons, 2 sedans, and 4 buildings. Between fifteen to twenty-five insurgents had died. The enemy casualties included a local al-Qaeda military leader killed in one of the fleeing sedans.[41] He had been planning a series of attacks, so the twelve-minute engagement seriously crimped the terrorist group's operations in the area.[42]

---

[39] Telecon, Mikolashek with Robinson, 27 Mar 08.
[40] Apache Longbow Video, 29 Sep 07.
[41] Sworn Statement, Kittelson, 29 Sep 07.
[42] Video Storyboard, 29 Sep 07 Safire Engagement, Zone 93, Historians files, CMH; Ltr, Kittelson to Mikolashek, 31 Mar 08.

Left to Right: Chief Warrant Officer Eldridge, Captain Loux, and Chief Warrant Officers Kittleson and Moughon next to an Apache. The four aviators surprised and defeated insurgents preparing an aerial ambush, making the skies over Iraq a little safer for other American and Iraqi aircraft.

While the fight showcased some of the strengths of the Apache Longbow, it also demonstrated one of the challenges attack helicopter crews face in Iraq. The AH–64D and its weapons were designed for a conventional battle against an armored opponent that would generally involve launching Hellfire missiles at long range (up to eight thousand meters). In an unexpected close-quarters engagement such as that on 29 September 2007, the short distance from the helicopter to the targets (in this case less than twelve hundred meters for all six shots) actually reduced the accuracy of the guided missiles, which had little time to make adjustments in flight. Backing off to increase the distance from the enemy might have improved the effectiveness of the Hellfires, but it would have given the insurgents more opportunity to regroup or escape.[43] The high air temperatures also limited the quantity of ordnance on the aircraft, further restricting the options available.

Despite those difficulties, the Apaches and their crews retained important advantages. In every battle, experience and communications play a vital role. In this engagement, the ability of the aircraft to rapidly and easily coordinate their attacks kept pressure on the enemy and helped ensure the complete

---

[43] After Action Review (AAR), Capt Christopher T. Morton, 3 Oct 07, sub: 29 September Engagement, Historians files, CMH.

destruction of his vehicles and heavy weapons.[44] While Captain Loux and Chief Warrant Officers Kittelson and Moughon were on their first combat deployment, Chief Warrant Officer Eldridge was on his third tour.[45] All four aviators had a vast amount of time in the air and, more important, had all worked together on numerous missions during their first six months in Iraq.[46] Based on this depth of knowledge, skill, and mutual understanding, the two pilots-in-command made a crucial decision that all four crewmen credited with saving their lives. Veteran pilot Eldridge was convinced that the instantaneous reaction to drop below the hard deck at the beginning of the fight not only prevented the insurgents from scoring more hits on the two Apaches but also allowed the American crews to "aggressively engage and destroy the enemy without giving them time to fully react and employ their weapons systems to their fullest extent."[47] In summarizing the battle, Captain Loux placed a slightly different emphasis on the value of teamwork, declaring that the fight "boil[ed] down to four guys who bonded over shared hardships trying to protect each other and in the process doing something good."[48]

---

[44] Sworn Statement, Eldridge, 29 Sep 07.
[45] Telecon, Mikolashek with Loux, 26 Mar 08.
[46] Telecon, Mikolashek with Loux, 31 Mar 08.
[47] Sworn Statement, Eldridge, 29 Sep 07.
[48] Telecon, Mikolashek with Loux, 31 Mar 08.

ABBREVIATIONS

AAR	After Action Review
ADA	Air Defense Artillery
BCT	Brigade Combat Team
CJTF	Combined Joint Task Force
CSI	Combat Studies Institute
EFP	explosively formed penetrator
FIST	fire support team
FOB	forward operating base
GWOT	Global War on Terrorism
HEAT	high-explosive antitank
HMMWV	high mobility multipurpose wheeled vehicle
IED	improvised explosive device
MCLC	mine clearing line charge
MEF	Marine Expeditionary Force
MEU	Marine Expeditionary Unit
MHD	Military History Detachment
MiTT	Military Transition Team
MNC-I	Multi-National Corps–Iraq
MNF-I	Multi-National Force–Iraq
MNF-W	Multi-National Force–West
MPAT	multipurpose antitank
NCO	noncommissioned officer
ODA	Operational Detachment Alpha
ODB	Operational Detachment Bravo
RCT	regimental combat team
RPG	rocket-propelled grenade
SAW	squad automatic weapon
SCIRI	Supreme Council for the Islamic Revolution in Iraq
SEP	system enhancement package
SWAT	Special Weapons and Tactics
TOW	tube-launched, optically tracked, wire guided

Map Symbols

Function		Unit Type
⬭		Armor
⊓		Engineer
⊠		Infantry
⊠ Mar		Marine Corps
⊗		Mechanized Infantry (Bradley Equipped)
⊗		Mechanized Infantry (Stryker Equipped)
MiTT		Military Transition Team
o→		Mortar
SF		Special Forces
SWAT		Special Weapons and Tactics

Unit Size	
••	Section or Detachment
•••	Platoon
I	Battery, Company, or Cavalry Troop
II	Battalion or Cavalry Squadron
III	Regiment

EXAMPLES	
SF | 563	Operational Detatchment Alpha 563
2 | A/82	2d Platoon, Company A, 82d Engineer Battalion
A | 2–12 Cav	Company A, 2d Battalion, 12th Cavalry
2 | 2	2d Battalion (Mech), 2d Infantry
1 | 5 Cav	1st Battalion (Mech), 5th Cavalry
| 1 Mar	1st Marines
TAC | 1–67	Tactical Command Post, 1st Battalion, 67th Armor
| 2/4–8 Ir	Company, 2d Battalion, 4th Brigade, 8th Iraqi Army Division

Note: Units officially designated as cavalry may be composed of armor or mechanized infantry. The map symbol will reflect the actual composition of the unit, with its formal designation as cavalry noted on the right-hand side. In the case of cross-attached units or subordinate components of modular battalions mixing armor and mechanized infantry companies or platoons, the map symbol will reflect the actual composition of the company or platoon, not the designation of the battalion.

INDEX

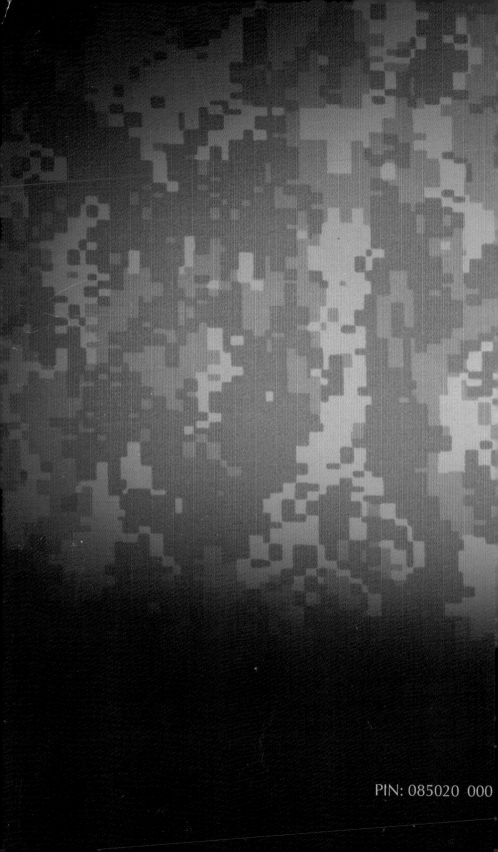

PIN: 085020 000

Troublemaker

**On the day Nelson Mandela was born—
July 18, 1918—his name was not Nelson.
That name would come later.**

At birth, his father gave him the name
Rolihlahla (khol-ee-HLAA-hlaa). Its literal
meaning is "pulling the branch of a tree," but
informally it means "troublemaker." Nobody
claimed that the name was a sign of things
to come—but nobody said it wasn't, either.

Rolihlahla's father, Gadla Henry Mandela,
was a member of the royal house of the Thembu

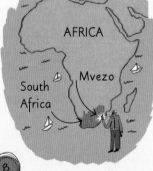

tribe. His job was advising
people and he was well
respected for his opinions.
Baby Rolihlahla lived with
his mother, Nosekeni Fanny,
in Mvezo (oohm-VEH-zoh).

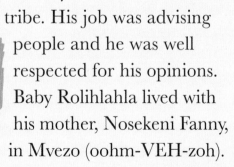

Mvezo was a village on the Mbashe River. It lay deep in the Transkei, a land of gentle hills and shallow valleys 600 miles (965 km) from the big South African city of Johannesburg.

The Mbashe River winds through the Transkei area.

Their home in Mvezo was called a kraal. A kraal is a small farm, with just a few animals and crops, that could support a single family. Rolihlahla's father saw him at the kraal regularly, but for only a few days at a time. Gadla Henry's responsibilities often took him away from home. He had three other wives and many other children to care for. Rolihlahla was the youngest of his four sons, which did not make him very important.

Afrikaans, the language of South Africa today, is mostly Dutch with some differences in vocabulary and grammar.

At the time the native people of South Africa were part of the British Empire. Dutch colonizers had first arrived in South Africa in 1652, and they had not come just to visit. Instead, they had come to settle, and they spent the next 150 years fighting with local tribes until they finally achieved control over the region.

However, their victory was short-lived. In the 1800s, soldiers and pioneers from Great Britain aggressively settled in South Africa. This led to a series of wars that finally ended with a British victory in 1902. Eight years later, South Africa was granted some independence—but it remained in the British Commonwealth, under the firm control of British and Dutch descendants.

---

what are colonizers? People who create a new settlement in a foreign land. Colonizers of South Africa created settlements without caring what the native people thought.

CLASH OF THE COLONIZERS

The Anglo-Boer War was a war of independence fought between the Dutch descendants in South Africa and the British Empire that ruled them. It began in 1899 and ended with a British victory in 1902.

British troops ride into battle during the Anglo-Boer War.

The British and Dutch control over South Africa included control over the land's native people. Where could they live? What education could they receive? Which jobs could they have? These issues were harshly regulated. Certain jobs gave some people power over their fellow black Africans, but no jobs gave black people authority over their white neighbors.

Little Rolihlahla knew none of this, of course. Even so, the outside world soon intruded on his own life. When he was barely a year old, his father got into a heated disagreement with a local white magistrate. The complaint itself was small—something about an ox—but Gadla Henry made an issue of it by defying the magistrate's order that he look into it. Gadla Henry was a member of his tribe's royal family, a descendant of kings. He felt that a mere magistrate should not be able to order him around.

Gadla Henry may have been right in his belief, but he paid dearly for his views.

What is a magistrate?

A government official who administers certain laws in a specific area. The magistrate in Gadla Henry's town was strict.

Black men, even descendants of kings, held power only with the permission of the all-white government. The members of that government did not like seeing their authority challenged. The magistrate dealt harshly with Gadla Henry, taking away much of his land and fortune. This decision sent a clear message to anyone who might share his views.

Among the possessions the magistrate took away was the kraal where Rolihlahla and his mother lived. Under the existing laws, they had no right to argue with this decision.

All they could do was move.

2

A new home

Rolihlahla's family needed a new home, and they didn't have to look far. Gadla Henry still owned some property, including a kraal in Qunu.

It was a nearby village, home to only a few hundred people. It was smaller than Mvezo, but the land was much the same, with grassy fields and hills fed by bubbling streams.

Gadla Henry's kraal in Qunu consisted of three domed mud huts with thatched roofs. One hut was used to sleep in, and the other two were for cooking and storing food. The floors of the huts were made of crushed "ant-heap," which is the hard dirt above an ant colony. Rolihlahla's family used fresh cow poop to keep the floors smooth. There was a hole in the

roofs for cooking smoke to escape through. The only way in or out of each hut was a low doorway.

None of the huts had any wooden furniture. Everyone slept on mats. Outside, there were fields to grow crops and pens for the farm animals. The kraal was not fancy, but it was a comfortable place to live and it allowed Rolihlahla's family to be self-sufficient.

In the nearby fields, Rolihlahla learned to use a slingshot. Like many boys his age, he became skilled enough to shoot birds out of the sky. Later in life, he remembered learning "to gather wild honey and fruits and edible roots, to drink warm, sweet milk straight from the udder of a cow . . . and to catch fish with twine and sharpened bits of wire."

---

what does "self-sufficient" mean?

Being able to survive on your own. Because Rolihlahla's family grew their own food on the kraal, they were self-sufficient.

Besides fishing and gathering food, Rolihlahla played games, too. The most popular was called *thinti*. Rolihlahla also spent time mastering the art of stick fighting. This was a kind of swordplay that featured thrusts and parries, feints and lunges. All the while the participants danced back and forth as nimbly as they could.

Rolihlahla liked the time he spent exploring the land and playing games with his friends, but his parents knew he had a quick mind, worthy of great achievements. His parents could not read or write, but his mother wanted Rolihlahla to do both, so they decided to send him to school.

PLAYING THINTI

Thinti was a game that featured two sticks that were used as targets about 100 ft (30 m) apart. Two teams of boys would each defend their target while trying to throw sticks at the other team's target. Whoever knocked down the opposing team's target would win.

Until he went to school, Rolihlahla had always worn the traditional clothes of his village: a blanket that wrapped over one shoulder and pinned at the waist. At the Methodist school his mother had picked, however, the students dressed in the Western style, which meant wearing a shirt and pants.

A shirt was found for him quickly enough, but pants were more difficult, so Rolihlahla's father cut off a pair of his own trousers. They were roughly the right length, but much too big around the middle. However, with a rope tightened through the belt loops, they stayed firmly in place. Rolihlahla knew the pants did not really fit properly, but they were his father's pants. He was proud to wear them.

DID YOU KNOW?

English names were thought to be better than African ones, partly because the British colonizers found them easier to say.

One of the first things Rolihlahla's teacher, Miss Mdingane, did with the new students was to give them each an English name. At the time, being called by an English name was considered better than being called by an African one. Since the boys were about to receive a British education, the teachers believed each student should have an English name to match. The British didn't believe African culture was important. They thought British culture was superior.

From the moment Miss Mdingane gave him his English name, Rolihlahla would never be known as such to anyone outside his family again.

---

what does "superior" mean?

Better than something. The British thought that their culture was superior to African culture.

His new English name was the only one that would be used in school, and it was the name he would be known by from that day on.

Rolihlahla never learned why Miss Mdingane picked the name for him that she did. It was true that his new first name was the same as the last name of famous British naval hero Admiral Lord Nelson—but Rolihlahla didn't know if that was the reason he got it. All he knew for sure was that from that day on, he was known as Nelson.

Growing up fast

For the next two years, Nelson's life in Qunu was comfortable. He went to school, did chores around the kraal, and played with his friends.

One night, though, Nelson's father arrived home at an unexpected time, and the reason for this soon became clear. Gadla Henry was very sick. He had trouble breathing, and could barely move. A few days later, he died.

Naturally, the death of his father was a significant moment in Nelson's life, but its importance went beyond losing a parent. Shortly afterward, Chief Jongintaba Dalindyebo, whom Gadla Henry had long advised, became Nelson's guardian.

What is a guardian?

A person who is responsible for a child. The chief became Nelson's guardian and looked after him as one of his own.

Nelson's mother, Nosekeni Fanny, told her son that he was to be sent away to the king's home, known as the Great Place, in a village called Mqhekezweni (mu-KEH-zuh-when-ee). Nosekeni Fanny knew that by going away, the opportunities that would open up for Nelson would be far beyond what his mother could provide for him. Although she knew she would miss her son, his mother wanted the best for him.

Nelson adjusted quickly to his new life. He missed his mother, but, as he later wrote,

The king's compound in Mqhekezweni

This photograph of Chief Jongintaba Dalindyebo and his wife was taken in 1930, which was around the time Nelson came to live with them.

he found Mqhekezweni to be "a magical kingdom; everything was delightful . . . When I was not in school, I was a plowboy, a wagon guide, a shepherd. I rode horses and shot birds with slingshots and found boys to joust with."

Nelson did well in school and got along well with Jongintaba's son, Justice, and daughter, Nomafu. He ate what they ate and wore what they wore. Jongintaba and his wife treated Nelson fairly and with care. "Jongintaba was stern, but I never doubted his love," Nelson later said. The chief affectionately called Nelson by the name *Tatomkhulu*, meaning "grandpa," because Nelson so often looked very serious.

Not everything was easy, though. At home in Qunu, everyone simply used their

fingers to eat, but in Mqhekezweni forks and knives were the custom. Nelson was not used to them, and he was embarrassed about looking clumsy at meals. There were days when he ate less than he wanted for fear of looking foolish while fumbling with his utensils.

As time passed, the two anchors of Nelson's life became his education and his time in church. Until that point he had always considered the white European colonists as helpers to the black native people. Now, as a teenager studying history, geography, English, and the Bantu language Xhosa (KAW-suh), he began to see a different picture.

Visitors who came to the Great Place, especially a chief named Joyi, expressed the idea that the African people had been far better off on their own before the white men arrived. Nelson's emerging sense of

Christianity was also
troubled by the
limitations imposed
on black people. He
believed the church was
the ultimate moral guide
for how people should behave
toward one another—but if this
were true, he wondered, how could the church
support the oppression of the black people in
its community?

DID YOU KNOW?

The Zion Christian
Church, founded in 1924
by native Africans, is
now the largest church
in South Africa.

At 16 years old, Nelson had reached the
age at which the tradition of his tribe expected
him to become a man. As a man he would be
able to marry, own property, and participate
in tribal ceremonies. In order to achieve his
new status, Nelson, along with 24 other boys
his age, took part in several rituals to mark this
important occasion.

Nelson felt an understandable pride and
satisfaction at having reached this point in his
young life. His mood was sobered, though, by
the main speaker of the day, Chief Meligqili

(mel-leek-qwee-lee). Even years later, Nelson was to remember the chief's grim words.

"There sit our sons," said Chief Meligqili, "young, healthy, and handsome, the flower of the Xhosa tribe, the pride of our nation." However, Chief Meligqili was not hopeful about their futures. He declared that all black South Africans were "slaves in our own country." Therefore, the harsh truth was that the hopes and dreams of the boys would never be fulfilled. This was because the boys could not receive "the greatest gift of all, which is freedom and independence."

"We have promised them manhood ... a promise that can **never be** fulfilled."

Chief Meligqili,
as quoted in Nelson's
autobiography, *Long
Walk to Freedom*

GETTING AN education

Nelson did not live at a time or in a place where he could expect to choose his own future. That decision was in the hands of Chief Jongintaba.

In the chief's eyes, the first thing Nelson needed was a more complete education. One day, if all went well, he expected that Nelson would become an advisor much like Nelson's father had been before.

Nelson was sent to the Clarkebury Boarding Institute, in the town of Ngcobo. The school buildings were Western in style rather than African.

Nelson was introduced to the headmaster, the Reverend Mr. Harris, in his study. The reverend was warm and friendly toward Nelson, and they shook hands. Nelson was to remember later that it "was the first time I had ever shaken hands with a white man."

In his old school, Nelson was respected because the chief was his guardian— but at Clarkebury, nobody knew who Nelson's guardian was. And nobody cared. At Clarkebury, only Nelson's abilities and achievements would set him apart. Nelson knew that gaining respect from his teachers and fellow students would not be easy, because he had not yet excelled inside the classroom or outside on the playing fields.

In the beginning of his time at Clarkebury, if Nelson stood out at all, it was because he looked like he didn't belong. On the first day

of classes he had
to wear boots for the
first time, and his feet clattered so much on
the polished wooden floors that some of his
classmates laughed at him.

Three years later, in 1937, when Nelson
was 19 years old, he moved on to Healdtown.
Healdtown was a Methodist college in the town
of Fort Beaufort, almost 200 miles (325 km) away.

Nelson at 19
years old

At first, Nelson felt that it
was almost like visiting another
planet. Flush toilets were new
to him. So were pajamas and
toothpaste. (Before coming
to Healdtown and learning
what toothpaste was, Nelson
whitened his teeth by rubbing
ash on them.)

The schedule there was rigorous. Breakfast was early, at 6:40 a.m., and it was nothing more than dry bread and hot sugar water. The morning was filled with four hours of classes. Lunch,

Samp was often mixed with beans.

which was at 12:45 p.m., usually featured sour milk and beans, and dried corn kernels, called samp. Classes continued for another four hours, followed by a break for exercise and dinner. An evening of homework ended with lights out at 9:30 p.m.

At Healdtown, Nelson participated in school sports for the first time. He took up cross-country running and boxing, both of which took discipline and helped him fit in with other students. At first he was not especially good at either, but through practice—and by gaining a few more pounds of muscle—he soon improved.

As for his classroom education, Nelson was not just gaining academic knowledge.

He was also gaining a better understanding of the limitations a black man faced in the white man's world. This growing awareness continued to build as he moved on to the University College of Fort Hare, in the town of Alice, in 1939. There, as at his other schools, he remembered being taught that he should respect the political authorities and be thankful for the educational opportunities given to him by the church and by the government.

As his thinking grew more sophisticated, though, it was difficult for Nelson to make all these ideas fit nicely together. On the one hand, he was being taught to use logic to solve problems and work out situations. On the other hand, he was also being told to accept certain social and political boundaries that were ingrained into society. And these, he was well aware, were not really logical at all.

Being clear about his ideas helped Nelson to develop a new sense of independence. In his second year at Fort Hare he was elected to the Student Representative Council. When the university administration refused to grant the council some of the authority the council believed it should have, Nelson resigned in protest. He had the power to do that—but the university had power, too. The principal chose to send him home early for what he called insubordination.

What is insubordination? Insubordination means to disobey an order from a higher authority. The headmaster judged that Nelson was insubordinate when he resigned from the school council.

Chief Jongintaba was surprised and displeased to see Nelson come home before his term at Fort Hare was over. He made it clear to Nelson that he, the chief, was in charge of Nelson's life. The boy should simply do as he was told. To make this point even clearer, the chief soon informed Nelson that he had chosen a wife for him to marry.

Now it was Nelson's turn to be surprised. He didn't know if arranging a marriage was the chief's way of reminding him who was the boss in their relationship or whether he genuinely thought this young woman was the perfect partner for Nelson. Either way, he knew better

ARRANGED MARRIAGE

It was common in many societies (and still is in some cultures today) for parents or guardians to arrange the marriages of their children. The reasons behind the matchmaking were often quite practical. Money was a common factor, because the fortunes of two families would be joined together by the union. Or it might be that the two pairs of parents simply liked the idea of their families becoming related through marriage.

than to argue because, as his guardian, the
chief had the traditional right to arrange such
a marriage. Yet that didn't mean Nelson would
meekly accept his decision. Nelson was stubborn,
just as his father had been, but he knew he could
not refuse the arranged marriage and continue to
live under the chief's roof. His only alternative
would be to run away.

And so, in 1941, at the age of 22, he did.

Fighting FOR A cause

When Nelson decided to run away, there was no question about where he would go. His destination was Johannesburg.

In Johannesburg, the largest city in South Africa, Nelson believed he might be able to improve his social status and achieve his goals. He was also very excited to see a place he had heard so much about. In his mind the city had almost a mythical status.

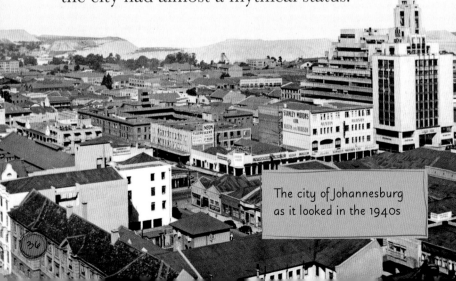

The city of Johannesburg as it looked in the 1940s

Johannesburg was not simply a larger version of a town. He had been told stories of "buildings so tall you could not see the tops, of crowds of people speaking languages you had never heard of . . ." What should he do once he got to Johannesburg? Nelson wasn't sure. He hadn't done much planning in advance, so it took him some time to settle in. He worked as a night watchman in a mine and as a real estate agent while he finished his college degree with courses he completed through the mail.

For all the time that he was growing up, Nelson had always imagined himself returning home to Qunu at some point to take up a career. In 1943, he enrolled in law school because it seemed like the logical next step,

"**Johannesburg** had always been **depicted** as a city of **dreams**, a place where one could **transform oneself** from a **poor peasant** to a **wealthy sophisticate** ..."

Nelson Mandela,
Long Walk to Freedom

but he did not really apply himself to his courses. And, in the end, he did not complete the requirements for graduation.

Nelson had only been in Johannesburg a short time when he started to focus more on political activism. He wanted to change things in the government. The central problem facing black people in South Africa was the crushing oppression they met at every turn. Black people were kept down and not allowed the same opportunities or freedoms that were allowed to others. After the British created the Union of South Africa in 1910, new laws were designed and enforced to keep black people from pursuing any number of careers.

FORGIVE AND FORGET

Toward the end of 1941, Nelson's guardian, Chief Jongintaba, visited Johannesburg and met with Nelson, forgiving him for running away. Jongintaba died only a few months later.

It didn't matter how smart they were or how hard they worked. They were trapped in a web of regulations to keep progress out of reach. Nelson clearly saw the widespread injustice in this system, and he was determined to do something about it and help his people.

To make sure his efforts were as effective as possible, he joined the African National Congress (ANC). The ANC was an organization trying to improve the conditions for black South Africans. Its protests, though, were largely very

NEW LAWS

In 1911, the Mines and Works Act was passed. It meant that black South Africans worked in low-paying jobs. The more skilled, higher-paying jobs, such as surveying, were reserved for whites. Two years later, the Natives Land Act severely limited where black people could own land. Even when they were allowed to own it, this land had little value. It was always set deep in the countryside away from the cities. Could black people hope for change to come through the political process? Not really. The Native Representation Act of 1936 meant that only elite (high-class) black people could vote, the majority couldn't, and they could only vote for white candidates.

The ANC had its roots in the South African Native National Congress. Some of its members are shown here in 1914.

polite efforts. Petitions would be circulated and signed by black people. These petitions were then submitted to the white authorities, who would either ignore them or bury them in administrative red tape.

The aim of Nelson and his friends was to transform the ANC from a small group

what does "red tape" mean? Red tape is lots of unnecessary paperwork demanded by governments or big businesses. The South African authorities used red tape as a way of avoiding dealing with the petitions.

of intellectual activists into a much larger organization. It would have a mass membership of black people from all over the country. Educated or not, these people had never been given the chance to speak up. They had suffered largely in silence. Maybe now their voices would be heard.

As a first step, Nelson and some others created the African National Congress Youth League in 1944. They intended to change things politically, to make life better for black people. They wanted more rights relating to voting and land ownership. They called for free education for all children regardless of their skin color. Nelson was passionate about these issues, but he still had a personal life. One of his friends in the ANC, Walter Sisulu, had a cousin called

Walter Sisulu

Here's Nelson.

This is Evelyn.

Nelson and Evelyn, as bridesmaid, were guests at
Walter Sisulu's wedding.

Evelyn who was a nurse. She and Nelson soon
started dating, and a few months later they were
married. For now the pieces of Nelson's life had
fallen into place. Yet even though those pieces
seemed to fit together well, it was not clear how
long they would continue to do so.

Revolutionary thoughts

Nelson had opposed many South African laws because they kept black people from freely improving their lives.

These prohibitions, bad as they were, soon became much worse. In 1948 the new all-white Afrikaner National Party took control of the government. Soon after that, South Africa made into law the policy of apartheid.

Apartheid formally separated black people from white people in many ways. It kept people apart politically, socially, and economically on the basis of their race. Black people would now have to live in separate areas from whites. Marriages between them were banned. Black South Africans were also separated from one another by their tribal backgrounds.

Chapter 6

44

PROTESTS AGAINST APARTHEID

At first, there was little response from other countries to South Africa's new policy of apartheid. However, some people did form groups to protest. Unfortunately, although these protests received some attention, the laws remained in force.

People protesting against racial discrimination in London, England

This was a political strategy, or plan. If tribes were kept apart, they were unlikely to ever come together to threaten the existing authority.

The government did not even pretend that these changes were at all for the benefit or the good of black people. It was cold and ruthless in its mission to put black people in their place and keep them there. No change, no new regulation, that would achieve this was too outrageous to propose.

Although the white people of South Africa were comfortable with apartheid because of their sense of superiority, there was another

LAND REFORMS

A few years later, in the 1950s, further steps were taken to strengthen white control. Black people were often forcibly removed from the parts of the countryside where they had lived for generations. The land they left behind was then sold to white farmers at artificially low prices. As white people became increasingly wealthier than black people, whites gained even more control of the country.

reason they wanted
these new laws in place.
That reason was fear.
For all of the power they
held over black South
Africans, white people
were still a minority when it
came to actual numbers. This
knowledge made them nervous. To overcome
this fear, they tried to build up as much support
from the legal system as they could get.

As things turned out, the new policies
triggered huge outrage. The black activists
living in South Africa reacted to apartheid
with renewed energy.

In 1949, the ANC pushed hard to become
a much bigger organization. No longer would
its members be content to politely raise their
hands when objecting to government policies.
Previously, the ANC had tried to keep their
protests within legal bounds—an approach that
had clearly not brought them much success.
Their new strategy would call for more action.

TREASON TRIAL

DECE[...]
19[...]

[...]ie
[...]SED

Nelson Mandela and the other activists were gathered up in raids around the country and arrested for their allegedly treasonous activities. Eventually all of the accused were set free.

48

They would focus on passive resistance. This meant that their protests would not use violence. There were risks in taking even non-violent actions, but Nelson and his colleagues were willing to accept those risks.

In the next few years, Nelson was repeatedly arrested for joining in protests around the country. In 1952, he was one of the leaders of the ANC's Campaign for the Defiance of Unjust Laws. Nelson was committed to protesting against apartheid whatever the price he might personally have to pay. He worked with the ANC and other organizations to write the Freedom Charter, which set out rules for a fairer society. This led, in 1956–1961, to Nelson and 155 activists being unsuccessfully prosecuted for treason.

In 1952, Nelson founded a law firm with Oliver Tambo, a friend from his former school days. Their aim was not to

Oliver Tambo

make money, although some payment would have certainly been welcome since neither of them had independent sources of income. Their main purpose was to provide free or low cost legal representation to black people in need.

All of this activity, however, came at a price for his family. Nelson's fight against injustice for black South Africans consumed him. Nelson remembered later that it was during this period when his wife, Evelyn, told him that their "elder son, Thembi, then five,

DID YOU KNOW?

Thembi's formal name was Thembekile, which means "faithful" in Zulu.

had asked her, 'Where does Daddy live?' I had been returning home late at night, long after he had gone to sleep, and departing early in the morning before he woke."

Evelyn harbored resentments of her own. Certainly, she had married Nelson for love, but her dreams differed from his. Evelyn had expected that his life would be a normal one devoted to his family and a regular job. Nelson wrote that she could not live with him being devoted to something apart from herself and her family. The harder Nelson worked, the more their relationship suffered. They managed to stay together for a few more years, but were finally divorced in 1958.

Chapter 7

Raising the stakes

Nelson had been committed to non-violent protest. His hope was that the government would see the error of its prejudiced ways.

However, there was a problem. This hope was based on the idea that the government would actually *want* to be shown the error of its prejudiced ways. The South African government wasn't actually interested in seeing this at all. They knew their laws were prejudiced against black South Africans. They knew that these laws would oppress, or keep down, black people and keep them serving the needs of white people. The truth was, they liked things that way.

what does "prejudice" mean? Prejudice is having unfair feelings against certain people. The government was prejudiced against black South Africans.

Nelson and his comrades began to feel that non-violent actions were not the answer. In 1960, a peaceful protest ended in the police shooting dead many protesters. It became known as the Sharpeville Massacre. This terrible event helped confirm to Nelson and his fellow activists that more violent steps were now necessary.

The activists knew that using violence would be dangerous, and they were afraid for their own

SHARPEVILLE MASSACRE

On March 21, 1960, a crowd of several thousand protesters went to the local police station at Sharpeville in the Transvaal. Although the crowd was unarmed, police officers opened fire. They continued to shoot even as the crowd fled in fear. Sixty-nine people were killed and more than 400 were wounded, including women and children. Even under the laws of apartheid, the massacre created a crisis for the government.

Black protesters being fired on by police

safety. However, as Nelson later wrote, "The brave man is not he who does not feel afraid, but he who conquers that fear."

It was just a few years earlier that Nelson had met Nomzamo Winnie Madikizela. She was the first black female social worker ever trained in South Africa and an active member of the ANC. As Nelson later wrote, "I cannot say for certain if there is such a thing as love at first sight, but I do know that the moment I first glimpsed Winnie Nomzamo, I knew that I wanted to have her as my wife."

Unlike Nelson's first wife, Evelyn, Winnie was well aware of Nelson's priorities. His law practice was not going well, but he was unwilling to sacrifice any of the time he was devoting to the ANC. He told Winnie that they would very likely have to live on her small salary as a social worker. Winnie understood and was prepared to do this.

Eventually, after years of peaceful protests, and no changes by the government, Nelson

Nelson married Winnie on June 14, 1958. They later had two children together.

saw violent protest as the only way to get the white minority to listen. In 1961, new tactics began, including planting bombs in places like electrical plants or transportation facilities. Nelson did not pretend that these actions were not violent. However, targets were chosen to avoid loss of life as much as possible.

During this time, warrants were issued for Nelson's arrest. His many friends and supporters helped keep him hidden. He also escaped capture by sometimes traveling in disguise. At one point he drove around the country giving speeches while pretending to be a chauffeur.

However, Nelson's luck finally ran out. He was captured in August 1962 and accused of

False travel documents used by Nelson in 1962

various crimes against the state. At his trial
he did not really defend himself. (He actually
agreed that he was guilty of the charges.)
Instead, he concentrated on promoting the
ANC cause. His actions were reluctant ones,
he insisted. Desperate times, he argued, called
for desperate actions.

The court did not agree. Nelson was
sentenced to five years in prison. However,
the next year he was found to be connected to
other illegal activities against the government.
The charges were serious. Once more he
was accused of sabotage. A second trial took
place between October 1963 and June 1964.

Outside the court, a large crowd gathered to protest. Toward the end of the trial, Nelson made an impassioned speech. His words rang out, not only in the courtroom, but also later throughout the country and around the world.

"During my lifetime," he stated, "I have dedicated myself to this struggle of the African people. I have fought against white domination, and I have fought against black domination. I have cherished the ideal of a democratic and free society in which all persons live together in harmony and with equal opportunities. It is an ideal which I

what does "sabotage" mean?

To destroy or damage a plan or property. The revolutionaries sabotaged power plants to stop them from working.

hope to live for and to achieve. But if need be, it is an ideal for which I am prepared to die."

When the verdict was announced, Nelson and the others were found guilty. They were sentenced to life imprisonment. It was a scary moment. If the sentences were carried out, only death would set them free.

Chapter 8

Life behind bars

Robben Island lies little more than 4 miles (6.5 km) off the lower west coast of South Africa.

The island had long been used as a place for people who were classed as "undesirables"—people who were not wanted. It had once been a colony for people who suffered from the disease of leprosy. Usually, though, Robben Island served as a jail for political prisoners and convicted criminals. And that was its purpose when Nelson was sent there in 1964.

Nelson and six fellow prisoners faced a difficult journey to the island. They were taken away in the middle of the night, under heavy police guard. They soon arrived at a small military airport and boarded

ROBBENEILAND

WE SERVE
WITH PRIDE

ONS DIEN MET TROTS

This is how the entrance to the Robben Island prison looks today. It is no longer used to keep prisoners, and is now a UNESCO World Heritage site that is open to visitors.

an old plane. The prisoners were frightened, some had never flown before.

Upon arriving on the island, Nelson and the other prisoners were met by armed guards. Nelson remembered the chill winter wind blowing through their thin prison uniforms.

Nelson was initially classified as the lowest grade of prisoner—Class D. This meant that he was allowed one visit and one letter every six months. At first Nelson was housed with several other prisoners, but in later years he lived alone in a small, damp concrete cell. When Nelson lay down, he could feel one wall at his feet while the other end grazed the top of his head. The cell had no mattress or bed, only a flat straw mat to sleep on. As for the food, Nelson later recorded his opinion. He recalled that the authorities liked to say that prisoners received a balanced diet. Nelson agreed that it was balanced—a balance between tasteless and being uneatable.

Every morning, Nelson, along with the other prisoners, waited while a load of stones

This was Nelson Mandela's prison cell on Robben Island.

was dumped on the ground outside. Each one was about as big as a volleyball. The prisoners' job was to crush the stones into gravel using a hammer.

Nine months later, Nelson began working at a limestone quarry. There he extracted limestone from layers of rock

DID YOU KNOW?

At first, Nelson was forbidden to wear sunglasses, and the glare from the limestone permanently damaged his eyesight.

with a pick and shovel. The commander in charge assured the prisoners that this kind of heavy labor would last for six months at most. That turned out to be a lie. The prisoners worked at the quarry for much longer than six months—they worked there for 13 years.

Physical hardships were not the only worries. A prisoner's mental health was always vulnerable. No matter how strong-willed the prisoners were, the prison environment was designed to break them. If the men had been isolated, or kept alone, they might not have been able to survive. Fortunately the authorities kept the prisoners together, and being together, they could draw on mutual support.

Even though he was in prison, Nelson continued to work hard to support people.

"We supported each other and gained strength from each other. Whatever we knew, whatever we learned, we shared ..."

From Nelson's autobiography, *Long Walk to Freedom*

He offered guidance and leadership to many of his fellow inmates, representing them in grievances with prison authorities. Gradually, his living conditions improved. In the 1970s, he was allowed more visitors and greater freedom to correspond by mail.

Meanwhile, the force of apartheid continued to oppress black South Africans. On June 16,

High-school students in Soweto, South Africa, protesting for a better education in 1976

1976, between 10,000 and 20,000 children marched in protest in the township of Soweto. The crowd was peaceful and unarmed, but the police became alarmed and eventually began shooting at them. Twenty-three people died in that first response. More protests followed, leading to further deaths.

With Nelson and other leaders in prison, and the ANC barred from the country and in exile, other people took the lead. In the late 1960s another group in South Africa, the Black People's Convention, arose to challenge the institution of apartheid. One of its leaders was Steve Biko, who was threatened several times by the authorities. Finally arrested in 1977, he was severely beaten while in custody. He died from this attack. His death inspired people to continue to protest even more strongly against apartheid.

Such incidents brought the problems in South Africa to people's attention all around the world. Boycotts of South African companies were organized. This meant that people withdrew from

STEVE BIKO

Steve Biko was born in 1946. He was a member of the Xhosa people in the Eastern Cape, a province of South Africa. While growing up, Steve planned to study law, but he changed his mind and decided to study medicine at the University of Natal. However, law again became his focus when he struggled against unjust laws in the fight against apartheid.

trading with South Africa. Many
foreign leaders protested against the
prejudicial system that had been in place for
decades. In 1980, the United Nations Security
Council called for Nelson's release. The request
was ignored.

Through it all, Nelson's spirits remained
strong. "I never seriously considered the possibility
that I would not emerge from prison one day," he
wrote later. "I never thought that a life sentence
truly meant life and that I would die behind bars.
Perhaps I was denying this prospect because it was
too unpleasant to contemplate."

Chapter 9

Freedom

Although some changes to apartheid took place in the 1980s, the government under President P. W. Botha continued to oppress black people.

Botha, known as "The Great Crocodile," had the reputation of being a stubborn man. In a major speech given in 1985, Botha refused to change the apartheid system. He

was not going to be the one to change a policy and way of life that had been in place for so many years. He also refused to release Nelson Mandela from prison, despite requests from many international figures and organizations.

P. W. Botha

Both these decisions sparked strong reactions from the international community. Many countries were now punishing South Africa for its policies by refusing to invest in South African companies. Many international corporations withdrew support as well. The rest of the world was waking up and paying attention to what was happening in South Africa.

Only when a new president, F. W. de Klerk, was elected in 1989, however, did dramatic changes occur. Originally viewed as simply the latest in a long line of apartheid-supporting leaders, de Klerk surprised many onlookers with a more understanding outlook. De Klerk was well aware that the tensions between black and white South Africans were growing. The country might soon erupt into a racial civil war. If that happened, South Africa would be torn apart.

To lessen those tensions, the de Klerk government began allowing anti-apartheid groups to meet. Most importantly, he ordered the release of prisoners who had been convicted for their anti-apartheid activities. Among them was Nelson Mandela.

During the 27 years Nelson had spent in prison, the world had changed in many ways. Important civil rights acts had been passed in the United States. People had landed on the moon. An American president had been forced to resign in disgrace. The Soviet Union had fallen apart. Nations that had belonged to the Soviet Union had again become independent countries.

Also, while in prison, Nelson had suffered two terrible losses. In 1968, his mother died. Just a year later, his eldest son,

In Soweto, an overjoyed boy holds up a newspaper announcing Nelson's release from prison. It made headline news around the world.

Thembi, died in a car accident. Nelson was not allowed to attend the funerals.

Nelson's release in February 1990 ushered in a new era in South African life. He had already met with President de Klerk during the last months of his imprisonment, which helped make sure that de Klerk made good on his promise to dismantle some apartheid restrictions.

One of the first places Nelson visited as a free man was Soweto, the scene of so much violence and unhappiness. There, 120,000 people gathered to hear him speak. Nelson spoke plainly. Injustice, he insisted, was no excuse for unacceptable behavior.

As he emerged from prison, with Winnie by his side, Nelson raised his fist in the traditional ANC salute. The act was met with a great roar from the waiting crowd.

Nelson said that he had heard of criminals pretending to be political activists, preying on innocent people and setting alight vehicles. These criminals had no place in the struggle against apartheid. Violence was not the answer—they must move forward peacefully.

Within a few months Nelson was hard at work within the ANC to build on the changes that President de Klerk had started to set up. He also traveled abroad, meeting with many foreign leaders including Pope John Paul II, Prime Minister Margaret Thatcher of the United Kingdom, and Presidents George H. W. Bush of the United States, Fidel Castro of Cuba, and François Mitterrand of France.

WINNIE MANDELA

When Winnie Madikizela married Nelson, she was viewed as a supportive partner who shared his political views. She appeared loyal during his many years in prison. However, stories reached Nelson that Winnie had been unfaithful. He also heard that she was involved with a violent street gang in her fight against apartheid. In 1995, Nelson dismissed Winnie from her role in his government. Their marriage finally broke down in 1992, and they divorced in 1996.

Several conferences that sought to move things forward were then held within South Africa, but it was unclear at first what the outcome might be. Some South Africans wanted things to continue the way they had before. Others wanted South Africa broken up into more than one country as a way to ensure that black people would have their proper rights.

Several uncertain years passed before the government took on a new shape, one that Nelson and the ANC had worked to create and could support. After more than three centuries of rule, the white minority was admitting defeat and turning over power to the black majority. In April 1994 new elections were held, and the ANC was swept in to power. Members of the new National Assembly then formally elected Nelson as the country's first black president. It was a truly historic moment, but as Nelson himself said, it did not represent the end of his quest. "We have not taken the final step of our journey," he said, "but the first step on a longer and even more difficult road."

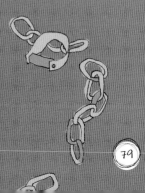

"... to be free is not merely to cast off one's chains, but to live in a way that respects and enhances the freedom of others."

Nelson Mandela, from his autobiography, *Long Walk to Freedom*

Revolutionary ideals

The new president of South Africa was 77 years old when he took office. The years Nelson had spent in prison had taken a physical toll.

Nelson had suffered from both tuberculosis and cancer before assuming the presidency. Still, he felt full of new energy at the idea of finally getting rid of apartheid, which had plagued his country for so long. Nelson made a powerful speech when he was sworn in as president: "The time for the healing of wounds has come. The moment to bridge the chasms that divided us has come. The time to build is upon us. We have, at last, achieved our political emancipation." Nelson meant by this that his people had achieved political freedom.

In a way, Nelson's goal was simple. He wanted to make sure that black people and white people were treated equally. However, achieving this goal would not be simple at all. It was daunting. Nelson did not want to swap one kind of oppression for another, and he didn't want to use force to bluntly and perhaps violently achieve the changes he wanted. He knew certain changes required patience and a delicate touch. "In nation building," he wrote, "you sometimes need a bulldozer, and sometimes a feather duster."

He was also not seeking revenge. The past was filled with outrages and injustices, but he couldn't change the past—although if there were injustices that could be addressed and corrected he certainly wanted to do so. He knew that instituting, or making into law, a new round of punishments would only make people feel bitter on both sides.

What President Mandela hoped and worked for was a peaceful transition, or change, to a new South African reality. He didn't want to punish white people for their past behavior. At the same time he made it clear that this behavior would no longer be tolerated.

Nelson stands to attention as the South African national anthem is played during his presidential inauguration at the Union Building in Pretoria, South Africa, on May 10, 1994.

A supporter waves an ANC flag during Nelson Mandela's presidential inauguration.

DID YOU KNOW?

Basic services, such as electricity and running water, were still unavailable to millions of black South Africans at the time.

Nelson kept a careful balance between compromise and change. He wanted to ensure that basic human needs of housing and health care were met for everyone, black and white alike. The policies governing land ownership, for example, which had excluded black people for so long, needed a complete overhaul.

All these changes represented a huge upheaval. Nelson, however, was determined to make these changes while keeping racial harmony between the people. One of Nelson's largest concerns, or worries, was South Africa's economic health. The country would be in big trouble if the white population became so afraid or disenchanted that they chose to leave South Africa, taking their skills and resources with them.

What is disenchanted?

Disenchanted means to no longer be in favor of something. Nelson was worried that the white people in South Africa might become disenchanted with the new regime.

"At a time when some of the **most vibrant economies** in the world have been **buffeted by storms**, we have performed relatively well."

Nelson Mandela, from his New Year's message as president, December 31, 1997

In 1996, two years after becoming president, Nelson signed into law a new constitution. It was a historic moment. Freedom of expression would now be available for anyone and everyone regardless of their political leanings. This meant that people were free to speak out about their beliefs. These changes reflected Nelson's idea that a government could not only survive, but actually improve, from listening to criticism that might come its way.

Sometimes Nelson found that a symbol of progress could be as powerful and influential as any new law. In 1995 South Africa hosted the

CONSTITUTION

A constitution is a set of laws that governs an organization or country. The new South African constitution ensured the government was ruled by the majority, in which all people of all colors and religions were eligible to vote. Those opposing the government would no longer be able to be arrested and imprisoned simply for their beliefs.

Nelson meeting the South African national rugby team, Springboks, at the Rugby World Cup in May 1995.

Rugby World Cup. This was a very important step forward for South Africa. Under the rules of apartheid, black people had not been able to play for the national team, the Springboks. Apartheid might now have been abolished, but bad feeling toward the Springboks remained. This was because most people in the team were still white. The Springboks went on to win the cup. Nelson publicly showed his support for the Springboks and he encouraged all black citizens to follow his example.

Nelson's interest extended far beyond the South African borders. Whether he wanted it or not, Nelson had become a symbol of Africa as a whole. He used that position to further more improvements. In a speech helping to launch the "Kick Polio Out of Africa" campaign (which used a soccer ball as its symbol), he said, "Africa is renowned for its beauty, its rich natural heritage, and huge resources—but equally, the image of its suffering children haunts the conscience of our continent and the world."

"KICK POLIO OUT OF AFRICA"

Polio is a disease that often leads to loss of movement. It continued to affect people in Africa, especially children, long after it had been removed from most other parts of the world. The campaign against polio encouraged the use of vaccination as a way of getting rid of the disease.

President Nelson Mandela chats with Deputy President Thabo Mbeki as he attends his last cabinet meeting, on June 9, 1999.

Nelson Mandela's whole term as president was dominated by moving on from the oppressive regime of the past, which had kept black people down for so long. Now having reached his eighties, Nelson recognized that it was time to step back from daily political responsibilities. He had long maintained that he would serve only one term—and as so many people already knew about Nelson, he was a man of his word.

Chapter **11**

Shifting gears

When Nelson retired from political life in 2004, he was certainly not expecting to disappear from sight.

He had become much more than a high-ranking government figure in South Africa. Nelson was now an international celebrity, and he hoped to use his fame and influence to further worthy causes. Among the organizations he helped to establish was the Nelson Mandela Foundation. Its mission was to help make a just and free society that treated people with fairness, wherever they came from.

Nelson Mandela and singer and activist Bob Geldof speaking at the launch of the Make Poverty History campaign rally in London, England, in 2005.

MAKE POVERTY HISTORY

There was still much Nelson hoped to achieve. He was committed to fighting for human rights around the world. He also fought to raise awareness of the AIDS epidemic. The cumulative effects of AIDS had been devastating. More than 30 million people had been infected around the world. Nelson's son Makhatho died of AIDS in 2005, at the age of 55. Nelson described AIDS as "one of the greatest threats humankind has faced."

WHAT IS AIDS?

AIDS is an infection that attacks the human body's immune system (which helps the body keep free from infection). It is caused by the virus HIV. From the 1980s, AIDS had spread rapidly all over the world. Its effects had been particularly deadly in Africa. Nelson dedicated himself to promoting the cause of making lifesaving drugs more widely available.

Nelson Mandela with AIDS activist Zackie Achmat

Nelson celebrated his 90th birthday surrounded by his grandchildren on July 18, 2008.

Nelson also wanted to spend more time with his family. He could not replace the time he had lost with his children and grandchildren because of prison and his career, but he could at least see them more often now that the daily responsibilities of political life had been removed.

His personal life had also taken another turn. After his divorce from Winnie, he had come to know Graça Machel, a former education minister in Mozambique. Her husband, Samora Machel, the president of Mozambique, had died in a plane crash in 1986.

Graça was 27 years younger than Nelson, and at first they simply became good friends. While Graça continued her humanitarian work on behalf of refugees, her friendship with Nelson deepened as they spent more and more time together. They were finally married in 1998, just before Mandela's term as president ended.

GRAÇA MACHEL

Graça Machel was born in 1945 and grew up in the southern African country of Mozambique. She attended the University of Lisbon in Portugal, where she first took an interest in issues of independence. When Mozambique declared its independence from Portugal in 1975, she became its first Minister for Education and Culture.

Queen Sofía of Spain talks with Nelson Mandela at a pre-wedding royal dinner in Madrid in 2004.

Nelson Mandela sits with US president George W. Bush in the White House's Oval Office in May 2005.

British prime minister Gordon Brown greets Nelson Mandela at Downing Street, London, in August 2007.

Although he lacked the energy of earlier years, Nelson still traveled widely and hosted leaders who came to visit him. When speaking at the birthday celebration of his friend Walter Sisulu in 2002, he said, "What counts in life is not the mere fact that we have lived."

Nelson continued to face a number of health issues. He had survived several bouts with cancer by the time he decided to formally retire from public life in 2004. He then returned to his home in the village of Qunu where he had lived as a boy so many years before.

"It is **what** difference we have **made** to the lives of others that will determine the **significance of** the life we lead."

From a speech by Nelson during the 90th birthday celebrations of his friend Walter Sisulu in 2002

But he was not done yet. On his birthday, on July 18, in 2007, Nelson and Graça announced the creation of a new organization, the Elders. Its members were retired political and religious leaders, who viewed themselves as independent world leaders working together for peace and human rights. Membership of the Elders included Kofi Annan, former United Nations Secretary General; Jimmy Carter, former United States President; and Li Zhaoxing, former Foreign Minister of the People's Republic of China. The group's small size reflected Nelson's preference for one-on-one meetings over large organized gatherings. In the years since, they have worked to promote women's equality and dealt with humanitarian crises such as famine.

Nelson's reputation as a worldwide champion of democracy and social justice was further underscored in 2009. On his birthday that year, the United Nations declared July 18 to be forever known as Nelson Mandela International Day in honor of his contributions to peace and human rights. In keeping with Nelson's spirit, the day was not meant to be a holiday, but a day devoted to the idea of making the world a better place for everyone who lives in it.

A year later, in 2010, Nelson made his final public appearance at the end of the soccer World Cup tournament in South Africa. Three years after that, at the age of 95 on December 5, 2013, Nelson died.

South African fans show their support for Nelson at the opening ceremony ahead of the 2010 FIFA World Cup in South Africa.

Nelson and his wife, Graça, wave to the crowd before the 2010 World Cup final between the Netherlands and Spain on July 11.

Chapter 2

Remembered

Nelson's death itself was not a surprise to his family. They had gathered at his bedside knowing the end was near.

Nelson Mandela had lived through the end of World War I, the entirety of World War II, the invention of frozen foods, television, and cell phones. Explorers in his youth were still circling the globe in ships—now astronauts orbited the Earth from space.

Perhaps most of all, Nelson had witnessed the peaceful growth of incredible political and social change in South Africa. The country was hardly perfect. It had some of the same shortcomings as other countries, such as the inequality between rich and poor. But South Africa had fundamentally transformed from the rigid, racially based society of the early 1900s, and Nelson had led the charge for that change for more than 70 years.

Upon the news of Nelson's death, Jacob Zuma, the president of South Africa, released a statement. He declared that whether in South Africa or somewhere else in the world, people should continue to

Jacob Zuma

follow Nelson's vision of a way of life in which everyone treated one another with respect and fairness. "Let us reaffirm his vision of a society in which none is exploited, oppressed, or dispossessed by another."

CHANGES IN SOUTH AFRICA

By the time of Nelson's death, South Africa was a vibrant part of the international community. This was only possible because of the changes that had come to South Africa. Black people now had the same political rights as white people, which had enormous social, economic, and cultural consequences.

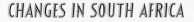

"When a man has done what he considers to be his duty to his country and his people, he can rest in peace."

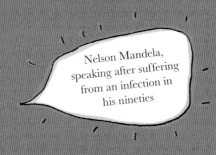

Nelson Mandela, speaking after suffering from an infection in his nineties

Tributes quickly poured in from all over the world. "Nelson Mandela's shining example and his political legacy of non-violence and the condemnation of all forms of racism will continue to inspire people around the world for many years to come," said German chancellor Angela Merkel. Israeli prime minister Benjamin Netanyahu noted, "He was the father of his people, a man of vision, a freedom fighter who rejected violence." American television talk show host Oprah Winfrey remembered, "Being in his presence was like sitting with grace and majesty at the same time."

Today in South Africa, Nelson Mandela is often called the "Father of the Nation." Throughout his life he was certainly happy to accept a compliment, but he would have been the first to declare that he was far from perfect. He made mistakes like everyone else— but to the world, perhaps his flaws had faded into the background while his better qualities had stepped to the front.

A sea of flowers lies at the road's edge as crowds gather to pay their respects at Nelson Mandela's Johannesburg home. This was only a few days after the former leader's death was announced. Although Mandela had been ill for some time, his death still sparked an outpouring of grief and dismay.

The British leader Winston Churchill, upon hearing one of his opponents described as a modest man, immediately replied that the man had a lot to be modest about. Nelson's supporters and opponents alike described him as a stubborn man. However, considering the oppression and difficulties he had confronted in his lifetime, truly he had much to be stubborn about, too.

Certainly, Nelson could never have survived so many obstacles without a fierce stubbornness to help him through the hard times. His long life had been marked with hurdles: The early death of his father, his interrupted education, his time as a hunted activist, and,

The largest statue of Nelson Mandela in the world is 26 ft (8 m) high. It stands on Naval Hill in Bloemfontein, the city of roses, in South Africa.

most of all, his 27 years in prison, would have broken a lesser man.

Yet this same stubbornness, fed by his faith in the righteousness of his ideals, had not led to anger or resentment. No one would have faulted Nelson for seeking revenge against those who had unjustly harmed him. But Nelson stubbornly resisted taking that path as well. Given what he had endured, he was also the most forgiving of men.

DID YOU KNOW?

Nelson was often called "Madiba" by close friends and family. It was a tribal name bestowed as a sign of great respect.

MADIBA SHIRT

The Madiba shirt, made popular by Nelson, is made of silk and usually has a bold and colorful print. The shirt was named after Nelson's nickname. He wore them often, to social gatherings and more formal business or political meetings. People still wear the Madiba shirt today.

He wrote, "No one is born hating another person because of the colour of his skin, or his background, or his religion. People must learn to hate, and if they can learn to hate, they can be taught to love, for love comes more naturally to the human heart than its opposite."

Nelson Mandela believed that people, whatever their faults, are capable of doing better. Nelson, and the people that he guided, brought freedom and fairness to South Africa and set an example for peace that has inspired others all over the world.

109

Nelson's
family tree

First wife

Evelyn Ntoko Mase
1922–2004

Son

Madiba
Thembekile
Mandela
1945–1969

Makaziwe
Mandela
1948–1948
(aged nine months)

Daughter

Son

Magkatho
Lewanika
Mandela
1950–2005

Pumla
Makaziwe
Mandela
1954–

Daughter

110

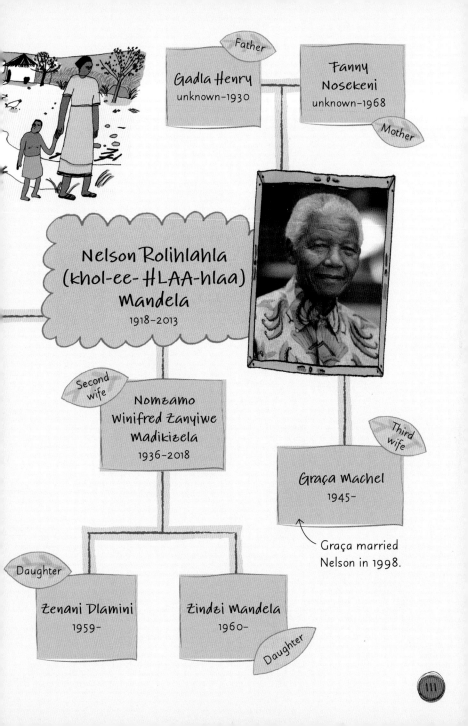

Father

Gadla Henry
unknown–1930

Fanny
Nosekeni
unknown–1968

Mother

Nelson Rolihlahla
(khol-ee-HLAA-hlaa)
Mandela
1918–2013

Second wife

Nomzamo
Winifred Zanyiwe
Madikizela
1936–2018

Third wife

Graça Machel
1945–

Graça married
Nelson in 1998.

Daughter

Zenani Dlamini
1959–

Zindzi Mandela
1960–

Daughter

Timeline

Nelson Mandela is born in Mvezo, South Africa, on July 18.

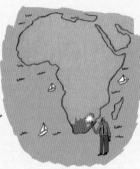

The all-white Afrikaner National Party makes apartheid law in South Africa. Nelson will spend much of his life fighting against this racist policy.

1918

1930

1944

1948

Nelson and others found the African National Congress Youth League. They plan to push for equality for black people.

Nelson goes to live with Chief Jongintaba Dalindyebo at the Great Place, in Mqhekezweni (mu-KEH-zuh-when-ee).

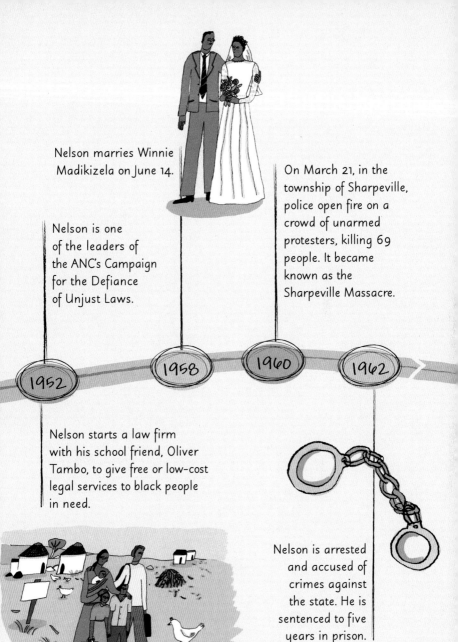

Nelson marries Winnie Madikizela on June 14.

Nelson is one of the leaders of the ANC's Campaign for the Defiance of Unjust Laws.

On March 21, in the township of Sharpeville, police open fire on a crowd of unarmed protesters, killing 69 people. It became known as the Sharpeville Massacre.

1952

1958

1960

1962

Nelson starts a law firm with his school friend, Oliver Tambo, to give free or low-cost legal services to black people in need.

Nelson is arrested and accused of crimes against the state. He is sentenced to five years in prison.

113

Nelson is tried for more crimes against the government. He is sentenced to life imprisonment and is sent to Robben Island.

Nelson turns 70 in prison. A concert in the UK celebrates his birthday, and 200 million people around the world tune in to watch it on television.

1963–1964

1976

1988

1990

On June 16, police shoot at an unarmed crowd of children marching in protest in the township of Soweto. Twenty-three people die.

After 27 years, Nelson is released from prison.

Nelson, jointly with South African president F. W. de Klerk, is awarded the Nobel Peace Prize.

New, free elections are held in South Africa. The ANC wins, and Nelson is elected president.

On July 18, the United Nations declares Nelson's birthday to be Nelson Mandela International Day in honor of his contributions to peace and human rights.

1993   1994   2004   2009   2013

After many health issues, Nelson formally retires from public life.

Nelson's autobiography, *Long Walk to Freedom*, is published.

On December 5, at 95 years old, Nelson dies.

Quiz

 In what year did Dutch colonizers come to South Africa?

 When Nelson borrowed his father's pants to wear to school, what did he use for a belt to hold them up?

 What is the name of Nelson's tribe?

 Who was the first white man Nelson shook hands with?

 What political group did Nelson join in Johannesburg?

 Were white people a majority or a minority in South Africa?

 What did Nelson's second wife, Winnie, do for a living when he met her?

Do you remember what you've read?
How many of these questions about
Nelson's life can you answer?

 What is the name of the prison where Nelson served most of his sentence?

 How many years did Nelson spend in prison?

 How old was Nelson when he took office as president of South Africa?

 At what event did Nelson make his last public appearance?

 What name did Nelson's close friends and family call him?

Answers on page 128

Who's who?

Achmat, Zackie
(1962–) South African
AIDS and gay rights activist

Annan, Kofi
(1938–2018) United Nations
secretary-general from 1997
to 2006

Biko, Steve
(1946–1977) Black People's
Convention leader

Botha, P. W.
(1916–2006) prime minister
(1978–1984) and then
president (1984–1989) of
South Africa

Brown, Gordon
(1951–) British prime
minister from 2007 to 2010

Bush, George H. W.
(1924–2018) president of
the United States from 1989
to 1993

Bush, George W.
(1946–) president of the
United States from 2001
to 2009

Castro, Fidel
(1926–2016) Cuban
revolutionary and president
of Cuba until 2008

Dalindyebo, Jongintaba
(1865–1923) chief who
became Nelson's guardian
after his father's death

de Klerk, F. W.
(1936–) president of
South Africa (1989–1994)

Geldof, Bob
(1951–) Irish singer and
political activist

Harris, Reverend Mr.
(unknown) headmaster of
Clarkebury Boarding
Institute

John Paul II
(1920–2005) Pope and head
of the Catholic Church
from 1978 to 2005

**Joyi, Zwelibhangile
(swoh-lib-haan-geel)**
(unknown) chief who visited
the Great Place

Machel, Graça
(1945–) first education minister in free Mozambique, and Nelson's third wife

Mandela, Gadla Henry
(unknown–1930) Nelson's father

Mandela, Nomzamo Winnie Madikizela
(1936–2018) social worker, political activist, and Nelson's second wife

Mandela, Nosekeni Fanny
(unknown–1968) Nelson's mother

Mbeki, Thabo
(1942–) president of South Africa from 1999 to 2008

Mdingane, Miss
(unknown) Nelson's first teacher

Meligqili (mel-leek-qwee-lee)
(unknown) chief who spoke at Nelson's manhood ceremony

Mitterrand, François
(1916–1996) president of France from 1981 to 1995

Nelson, Admiral Lord
(1758–1805) British naval hero

Ntoko Mase, Evelyn
(1922–2004) Nelson's first wife

Sisulu, Walter
(1912–2003) Nelson's friend in the African National Congress, cousin of his first wife

Sofía, Queen
(1938–) queen of Spain

Tambo, Oliver
(1917–1993) Nelson's school friend with whom he started a law firm in 1952

Thatcher, Margaret
(1925–2013) British prime minister from 1979 to 1990

Zuma, Jacob
(1942–) president of South Africa from 2009 to 2018

leprosy
disease in which the body
wastes away

logic
organized and reasoned
method of thinking about
something

magistrate
government official who
administers certain laws
in a specific area

mythical
imaginary, or from a
made-up story

oppress
keep down a certain group
of people or a person

parry
defend against a blow by
pushing it to the side

peasant
poor farm worker

plowboy
boy who leads a plow

polio
disease that often leads
to loss of movement

political activism
trying to change things
in the government

political prisoner
someone in jail because
of their political beliefs

prejudice
unfair feeling against
certain people or a person

prohibitions
rules that stop people from
doing certain things

red tape
lots of unnecessary
paperwork demanded
by governments or
big business

ruthless
without pity, cruel

sabotage
destroy or damage a plan
or property

self-sufficient
able to survive on your own

shepherd
person who cares for sheep

significant
important

slingshot
weapon for shooting small stones, made of a V-shaped stick with a handle, and a rubber band

sophisticate
person who knows a lot about world art, culture, and literature

status
social or political position that a person has compared with others

stern
serious in a severe way

strategy
plan

superior
better than something

thatched
made of dried plant material

townships
neighborhoods in South Africa that were racially segregated during apartheid; only black people lived in townships

transition
change from one state to another

treason
trying to overthrow your country's government

twine
type of string made of two or more strings twisted together

undesirable
person who is not wanted

Index

Madiba shirt 107
magistrates 12–13
Make Poverty History
 campaign 90
Mandela, Evelyn 43,
 50–51, 54
Mandela, Gadla Henry
 8–9, 12–14, 20, 107
Mandela, Makhatho
 91
Mandela, Nosekeni Fanny
 8, 21, 72
Mandela, Thembi 50–51,
 73
Mandela, Winnie 54–55,
 74–75, 77, 92
marriages 34–35, 44, 77,
 92–93
Mbashe River 9
Mbeki, Thabo 89
Mdingane, Miss 18–19
Meligqili, Chief 25–27
Merkel, Angela 103
Methodist schools 17,
 30
Mines and Works Act (1911)
 40
Mitterrand, François
 76
Mozambique 93
Mqhekezweni 20–24
mud huts 14–15
Mvezo 8–9, 14

Nn

names 8, 18–19, 107
National Assembly
 78
Native Representation Act
 (1936) 40
Natives Land Act (1913) 40
Nelson, Admiral Lord 19
Nelson Mandela Foundation
 90
Nelson Mandela
 International Day 98
Netanyahu, Benjamin
 103
Ngcobo 28
non-violent protests 49,
 52–53, 103

Pp

pants 17
polio 88
prejudice 52
president of South Africa
 78, 80–84, 89
prisons 57, 59–66, 69,
 72–73
protests 49, 52–56, 66–67,
 103

Qq

quarries 63–64
Qunu 14, 20, 23–24,
 37, 95

Acknowledgments

DK would like to thank Rebekah Wallin for proofreading; Hilary Bird for the index; and Seeta Parmar for additional editorial work.

The publisher would like to thank the following for their kind permission to reproduce their photographs:
(Key: a-above; b-below/bottom; c-center; f-far; l-left; r-right; t-top)
9 Alamy Stock Photo: Gallo Images (tr). 11 Alamy Stock Photo: De Luan (c). 21 Getty Images: Matthew Willman / Gallo Images (b). 22 Unity Archives - Moravian Archives Herrnhut. 30 Alamy Stock Photo: GL Archive (bl). 31 iStockphoto.com: Hipokrat (tr). 36 Getty Images: Popperfoto (b). 41 akg-images: Africa Media Online (t). 42 Getty Images: Universal History Archive / UIG (bl). 43 Alamy Stock Photo: Archive PL (c). 45 Getty Images: Hulton-Deutsch Collection / Corbis (c). 48 Rex by Shutterstock: Sipa. 49 Alamy Stock Photo: Peter Jordan (br). 53 akg-images: Africa Media Online (br). 55 Rex by Shutterstock: Sipa. 57 Alamy Stock Photo: Blaine Harrington III (t). 61 Alamy Stock Photo: Robertharding. 63 Getty Images: Dave Hogan (t). 66-67 Getty Images: Bongani Mnguni / City Press / Gallo Images (b). 68 Rex by Shutterstock: (bl). 70 Alamy Stock Photo: Peter Jordan (bl). 72 Getty Images: Trevor Samson / AFP (bl). 74-75 Getty Images: David Turnley / Corbis / VCG. 77 Getty Images: Bernard Bisson / Sygma (tr). 83 Getty Images: Walter Dhladhla / AFP (t); Hanner Frankenfeld / AFP (b). 87 Getty Images: Gary Benard / AFP (t). 89 Getty Images: Odd Andersen / AFP (t). 90 Getty Images: Photofusion / UIG (b). 91 Getty Images: Anna Zieminski / AFP (br).

92 Getty Images: Themba Hadebe / AFP (t). 93 Getty Images: Per-Anders Pettersson (br). 94 Getty Images: Alberto Martin / AFP (tc); Mannie Garcia (cr); Cate Gillon (bc). 99 Getty Images: Pierre-Philippe Marcou / AFP (b); Cameron Spencer (t). 101 Getty Images: Unkel / ullstein bild (tr). 104-105 Getty Images: Erhan Sevenler / Anadolu Agency. 106 Dreamstime.com: Grobler Du Preez. 109 Getty Images: Louise Gubb / Corbis SABA. 111 Getty Images: Chris Jackson (cr)

Cover images: *Front:* Alamy Stock Photo: Interfoto b; *Spine:* Alamy Stock Photo: Interfoto ca

All other images © Dorling Kindersley
For further information see: www.dkimages.com

ANSWERS TO THE QUIZ ON PAGES 116–117

1. 1652; 2. A rope; 3. The Xhosa; 4. Reverend Mr. Harris, Clarkebury Boarding Institute Headmaster; 5. The African National Congress (ANC); 6. A minority (always have been); 7. She was a social worker; 8. Robben Island; 9. 27; 10. 77; 11. The soccer World Cup finals in South Africa in 2010; 12. Madiba